the revelation answer book

mark hitchcock

HARVEST PROPHECY
An Imprint of Harvest House Publishers

Published in association with William K. Jensen Literary Agency, 119 Bampton Court, Eugene, Oregon 97404.

Cover design by Studio Gearbox

Cover images © alexmstudio, Olga Vasileva, IgorZh, Melkor3D, joshimerbin, Lizavetta, Vadim Sadovski / Shutterstock

Interior design by Janelle Coury

For bulk, special sales, or ministry purchases, please call 1-800-547-8979.
Email: CustomerService@hhpbooks.com

The Revelation Answer Book

Some content was previously published in *101 Answers to Questions About the Book of Revelation*

Published by Harvest House Publishers
Eugene, Oregon 97408
www.harvesthousepublishers.com

ISBN 978-0-7369-9174-2 (pbk)
ISBN 978-0-7369-9175-9 (eBook)

The Library of Congress has cataloged the previous edition as follows:
Hitchcock, Mark, 1959-
101 answers to questions about the book of Revelation / Mark Hitchcock.
p. cm.
ISBN 978-0-7369-4975-0 (pbk.)
ISBN 978-0-7369-4976-7 (eBook)
1. Bible. N.T. Revelation—Criticism, interpretation, etc.—Miscellanea. I. Title.
BS2825.52.H575 2012
228'.06—dc23
2012010773

Printed in the United States of America

25 26 27 28 29 30 31 32 33 / BP / 10 9 8 7 6 5 4

To Jonathan Murphy

*Thank you for your faithful friendship, fellowship,
and love for our Lord and my family.
You and your family are a blessing beyond description
to us and so many others.*

Contents

Preface 15

Part One: The Interpretation of Revelation

Why study the book of Revelation? Why is it important? 19

What are the five main views of Revelation? 20

What are some of the keys to interpreting Revelation, especially all the symbols? 26

Are the numbers and time periods in Revelation literal? 34

What is the outline of the book? 37

Part Two: The Background of Revelation

Who was the human author of Revelation? 41

When was Revelation written? 42

Who were the recipients of Revelation? 50

What is Revelation about? 52

What are some of the key words in Revelation? 53

Was Patmos a penal colony in the first century? 54

Part Three: The Revelation of Jesus Christ (Revelation 1)

What does the title "the Revelation of Jesus Christ" mean? 59

What are the names and titles for Jesus in Revelation? 60

What do "soon" and "near" mean in 1:1 and 1:3? 61
Who are the "seven Spirits of God"? 65
What does it mean that Jesus is the firstborn of the dead (1:5)?. 67
How can every eye see Jesus when He returns to Earth (1:7)? 68
What does "Almighty" mean (1:8)? 70
What does it mean that John was "in the Spirit" (1:10)? . . 70
What is "the Lord's day" (1:10)? 71
Who are the "angels" of the seven churches? Are they angelic beings or humans? 72

Part Four: The Churches (Revelation 2–3)

Why did Jesus address these seven churches? 79
Do the seven churches represent seven stages of church history? 80
What does it mean that the people in the church at Ephesus left their first love? 84
Who were the Nicolaitans? 86
What does it mean to be an "overcomer"? 88
What is the synagogue of Satan (2:9; 3:9)?. 89
What are the "ten days" of tribulation (2:10)? 91
What is Satan's throne (2:13)? 92
What is the "hidden manna" (2:17)? 93
What is the "white stone, and a new name written on the stone" (2:17)? 94
Who is Jezebel (2:20)? 95
What is the morning star (2:28)? 96

Can the names of believers be erased from the book of life (3:5)? 97

What is the key of David (3:7)? 98

What is the open door (3:7)? 99

Does Revelation 3:10 support the pretribulation rapture view? 99

Who are the "earth dwellers" in Revelation? 101

What does it mean to be a "pillar in the temple of My God" and have "the name of the city of My God" (3:12)? 103

What does it mean that Jesus is "the Amen" (3:14)? 104

What does it mean that Jesus is "the Beginning of the Creation of God" in 3:14? 104

What is meant by "hot," "cold," and "lukewarm" in 3:15-16? 106

Is Revelation 3:20 a gospel invitation? 109

Part Five: The Consummation (Revelation 4–22)

Section One: The Scene in Heaven (4–5)

Is Revelation 4:1 a reference to the rapture? 117

Will believers see God in heaven? 119

Who are the 24 elders? 122

Who are the four creatures like a lion, calf, man, and eagle (4:7)? 124

What is the seven-sealed scroll in Revelation 5? 125

Section Two: The Tribulation (6–18)

Why do the scenes in Revelation alternate back and forth between heaven and Earth? 131

Who is the rider on the white horse in 6:1-2? 133

What does "do not damage the oil and the wine" mean (6:6)? 137
What are the "wild beasts" in 6:8 that kill one-fourth of the earth? 140
What's the relationship between the seven seals, seven trumpets, and seven bowls? 145
Why do some people believe the rapture occurs between the sixth and seventh seals? 147
Who are the 144,000 in 7:1-8? 150
Why is the tribe of Dan omitted from the list of the 12 tribes of Israel in Revelation 7? 153
Who is the great multitude in 7:9-17? 154
Why is there silence in heaven for about 30 minutes (8:1)? 155
Are the trumpet judgments symbolic or literal? 156
Are the trumpet judgments the result of human actions or divine judgment? 158
What is "Wormwood" (8:11)? 159
Are the trumpets in the first or second half of the tribulation? 160
Who is the "star from heaven" who opens the bottomless pit (9:1)? 161
What are the "locusts" in 9:1-12? 162
Who is Apollyon? 167
Who are the four angels bound at the River Euphrates? 168
What is the army of 200 million in 9:16? 169
Who is the strong angel in chapter 10? Is this a reference to Jesus? 172

What is the "little book" in 10:2? 173
What are the "seven peals of thunder" in 10:3-4? 174
What does it mean for John to eat the book (10:9-10)? 175
What is the temple in Revelation 11:1-2? 175
Who are the two witnesses? 177
What will the two witnesses do? 182
Do the two witnesses minister during the first or second half of the tribulation? 183
Is the seventh trumpet in 11:15 the same as the "last trumpet" in 1 Corinthians 15:52? 184
Is the ark of the covenant in heaven? 185
Who is the woman clothed with the sun in Revelation 12? 187
Who are the dragon and the "third of the stars of heaven" in Revelation 12? 188
What are the "two wings of the great eagle" given to the woman (12:14)? 189
Is the beast of Revelation 13:1-10 an empire or an individual? 190
Is the beast past or future? Could he be Nero? 190
Will the beast be assassinated and come back to life? 192
Will the Antichrist be a Jew or a Gentile? 194
What will the beast in Revelation 13:1-10 do? 196
Who is the second beast or "beast coming up out of the earth" in Revelation 13:11-18? 196
Will the second beast be a Jew or a Gentile? 198
What is the mark of the beast (666)? 199

Is the scene in 14:1-5 in heaven or on Earth? 200

What is the "eternal gospel" in 14:6? 202

Will hell really last for eternity (14:10-11)? 203

Will blood literally flow as high as the horses' bridles at Armageddon (14:19-20)? 206

Are the judgments in Revelation 14:14-16 and 14:17-20 the same? 207

What is the song of Moses in 15:1-3? 208

When will the bowl judgments be poured out? 209

What does *Armageddon* mean? Is it a real place (16:12)? . . 210

What will happen during Armageddon? 210

Who are the kings of the East (16:12)? 211

Why will the kings of the earth gather at Armageddon? 212

What is Babylon in Revelation 17–18? 213

What do the seven heads (seven kings) in 17:9 represent? 220

Section Three: The Second Coming of Christ (19)

Can people in heaven see what's happening on Earth? 229

What and when are the marriage and marriage supper of the Lamb? 231

When Jesus comes, will He really ride on a white horse? . 233

Who are the armies in heaven who will return with Jesus? 234

Will the armies of heaven join in the fight against Jesus' enemies? 235

Is the rapture the same event as the second coming? 236

Section Four: The Millennium, Final Revolt, and Great White Throne (20)

What is the millennium? 241

What are the different views of the millennium? 241

Which view of the millennium best represents scriptural teaching? 244

What is meant by "came to life" and "the first resurrection" in 20:4-6? 249

Where will believers be during the millennium, and what will they do? 250

Who is "Gog and Magog" in 20:8? 252

Why will God release Satan at the end of the 1,000 years? 253

What is the Great White Throne Judgment in 20:11-15? 255

Section Five: The New Heaven, New Earth, and New Jerusalem (21–22)

Will this present heaven and Earth be destroyed or just renovated? 259

What's the relationship between the new heaven and new earth and the New Jerusalem? 261

What is the size and shape of the New Jerusalem? 262

What is meant by "the kings of the earth will bring their glory" into the heavenly city (21:24-26)? 263

Will people in heaven need to be healed (22:2)? 265

Are the gold, gems, and measurements of heaven literal or symbolic? 266

Why is John told not to seal up the words of the book of Revelation (22:10)? 267
What does it mean that those who do wrong are still to do wrong (22:11)? 267
What does the warning about adding to or taking away from Revelation mean (22:18-20)? 268
How can I be sure I'm going to heaven? 270

Recommended Further Reading on Revelation 273
Notes 275

We are living in the strangest days that man has ever known. The world has passed through terrible times before, but never has the whole earth been so bound together in its wild plunging through one catastrophe after another as today. There have been wars down through the ages, but never wars that have touched so many nations as the conflicts through which we have passed in this generation. There have been political crises, but not on a scale that touched all of the continents.

Civilization has brought so many new means of communication that the matters that affect one nation affect all. Events that take place in Europe and Asia become news that vitally concerns the farmer in the Mississippi Valley. Thoughtful Bible students agree almost universally that we are living near the end of the age, and that at any moment the outline of prophetic events preserved for us in Scripture will begin its course of fulfillment. The world will then rush rapidly through all of the scenes of history that God has written in advance.

The book of Revelation is the book for the present hour.[1]

—Donald Grey Barnhouse

Generally speaking, there are two extreme attitudes toward Revelation. Some say the book cannot be understood, and therefore should not be studied, taught or preached. Differences of interpretation, they point out, have divided Christians, and therefore the book should not be interpreted. Others consider themselves so sure of every detail of the book that they set dates and propose highly fanciful interpretations. To them Revelation seems the only book in the Bible worth studying...Let our approach be neither theoretical and detached but always personal and involved...God can motivate believers today by the understanding of those things which He has revealed through John in Revelation.[2]

—Charles C. Ryrie

Preface

Where are we today? How much longer do we have? What on Earth is happening? Where are we on God's prophetic calendar? Whatever one's background or beliefs, these are the questions on the minds of people everywhere today.

The book of Revelation is the capstone of God's Word to man. It tells us where this world is headed. It answers the great questions we all have about the future. Yet for many it remains a closed book. Sadly, its panorama of prophecy is a sealed mystery for most Christians.

There are many excellent commentaries and studies on Revelation, but many people find them too intimidating, too in-depth, or too irrelevant.

Given what is happening in the world today, it has never been more important for people to understand Revelation. Yet at the same time, many don't seem to know where to begin. I thought it would be helpful to put together a book that answers the key questions about Revelation in an accessible, user-friendly format. When this idea was presented to the folks at Harvest House, they enthusiastically agreed that this format would offer a fresh, unique contribution alongside the many fine commentaries that are available on Revelation.

At Faith Bible Church in Edmond, Oklahoma, where I serve as pastor, we took a full year to complete a verse-by-verse study of Revelation. As research professor at Dallas Theological Seminary in the Department of Bible Exposition, I've had the privilege on many occasions to teach through Revelation. Even after all this study, I don't claim to have all the answers about the book of Revelation (not even close). But I do believe I've become familiar with the kinds of questions people are asking. I've compiled 125 of these questions in this book, and my hope is that this resource will help you understand Revelation better, and that it will also deepen your love for God's Word and our Lord, who is the subject of Revelation.

In this book I have two goals: (1) to answer key questions about Revelation in a clear, concise manner, and (2) to motivate you to live as God would want you to live in light of what is coming in the days ahead.

PART ONE

The Interpretation of Revelation

Why study the book of Revelation? Why is it important?

Revelation is an important book to study if for no other reason than it is the capstone of God's self-revelation to man. Revelation is the book of consummation. It tells us the ending of the story that began in Genesis 1. The greatest value of Revelation is what it teaches us about the future. It discloses that this world is headed for a devastating seven-year period of divine judgment; the rise of a final world ruler; a global government, economy, and worship; the great war of Armageddon; the second coming of Christ; the 1,000-year reign of Christ on the earth; the final judgment; and the new heaven and new earth. Revelation tells us where this world is headed, and where we are headed.

Revelation is also important because it reveals and reaffirms many of the great doctrines of Scripture. Revelation is theologically thick. It displays the sovereignty and holiness of God. It teaches us that God is in control, that He has a plan that He is bringing to fulfillment. It reveals that God alone can foretell the future and that He does so with 100 percent accuracy.

The Christology (doctrine of Christ) is glorious in Revelation. Jesus is the Lamb (28 times) who was slain, yet is alive forevermore. He is God (Revelation 1:17; see also Isaiah 44:6). He is worshipped as God (Revelation 5:13). He is the focus of all history and prophecy (19:10). Salvation comes through Christ alone by faith alone in His death on the cross (1:5). Only His blood can wash away our sins (5:9; 7:14). He is the Lion of Judah who is coming again as King of kings and Lord of lords (19:16).

Revelation unveils the total depravity of man, who deserves

judgment, and shows man's desperate need for the grace of God. Nowhere in Scripture do we see a more awful picture of man's depravity, rebellion, and blasphemy. The book of Revelation provides a divine view of history. We see that no human empire can endure. Man's day will come to a tragic end.

In the 404 verses in Revelation, there are about 278 allusions to the Old Testament. Revelation is saturated with the Old Testament. John believes the Old Testament Scripture is the Word of God, and he claims that his own message is divinely inspired and authoritative (1:2).

Revelation has a great deal to say about angels and demons. In fact, it talks about angels more than any other book of the Bible. Angels are active throughout the chapters, especially in bringing God's wrath to the earth. The reality and evil of Satan and his demonic host is also evident. Satan accuses and persecutes God's people, hates the Jews and tries to destroy them, empowers the Antichrist and the false prophet, and finally, is doomed to the lake of fire.

One final reason to study Revelation is that it's the only book of the Bible that contains a special blessing for those who read it and keep the things written in it (Revelation 1:3). For this reason, Revelation has been aptly called "the Blessing Book." I pray that the Lord's rich hand of blessing will rest upon you as we study this book together and strive to understand and apply its truths to our lives.

What are the five main views of Revelation?

The vivid imagery and striking symbolism in Revelation have led to very different views on how it should be interpreted and what time period it describes. Broadly speaking, there are five main ways that people approach the book of Revelation related to how and when its prophecies are fulfilled: past, present, future, timeless, and a mixture of the previous four.

1. Preterist View (Past)

This view holds that Revelation is primarily a prophecy of events surrounding the destruction of Jerusalem in AD 70. There are two main branches of preterism: partial (moderate) and full (extreme or radical). R.C. Sproul, a partial preterist, defines the preterist approach: "An eschatological viewpoint that places many or all eschatological events in the past, especially during the destruction of Jerusalem in AD 70."[3]

Preterists believe that Christ returned in AD 70 during the destruction of Jerusalem by the Romans. Sproul says, "Preterists argue not only that the kingdom is a present reality, but also that in a real historical event the *parousia* [Christ's coming] has already occurred."[4] They believe that Nero was the beast of Revelation 13; that the seal, trumpet, and bowl judgments were judgments on unfaithful Israel; that Babylon in Revelation 17–18 was Jerusalem; and that Revelation 19 describes the coming of Jesus in AD 70 to destroy Jerusalem.

The primary distinction between partial and full preterists is that partial preterists, while maintaining that most of Revelation was fulfilled in the past, still believe in a future second coming of Christ. Full preterits believe that all prophecies—including those pertaining to the second coming and the resurrection of believers—are past events. They view the resurrection as spiritual. According to this view, we are beyond the millennium and are presently in the new heaven and new earth. Full preterists don't know if there is an end to history. By rejecting orthodox biblical truths about the second coming of Christ, the bodily resurrection, and the final judgment, full preterists are outside the pale of orthodox Christianity.

When preterists defend their viewpoint, they lean heavily on the "timing" statements in Revelation, such as "soon" (1:1) and "at hand" (1:3). They argue that these words demand the fulfillment of the prophecies in Revelation soon after the book was written. They date the writing of Revelation as having taken place around AD 65.

While there are many problems with preterism, two stand out as particularly indefensible. First, when proponents of this view try to relate and limit the global, catastrophic events described in Revelation to the period leading up to the fall of Jerusalem, they are unable to stay consistently literal in their interpretation of the scriptural text. As they work their way through Revelation, they frequently shift back and forth between spiritualizing and allegorizing the text or taking it literally. When the text of God's Word doesn't fit what actually took place in AD 70, they abandon literal interpretation.

Second, as will be discussed in Part 2 of this book, there is strong evidence that Revelation was written in AD 95 by John; therefore, it cannot be a prophecy about events that occurred 25 years earlier in Jerusalem. If it's true that Revelation was written in AD 95, then that serves as a death blow to the preterist view.

2. Historicist View (Present)

This view, which began with Joachim of Fiore in the twelfth century, interprets Revelation as a panorama or overview of the entire church age. This view was very common among the Reformers at the time of the Protestant Reformation. It was held by John Wycliffe, John Knox, William Tyndale, Martin Luther, John Calvin, Sir Isaac Newton, George Whitefield, Charles Spurgeon, and Matthew Henry. However, very few hold this view today. The key problem with historicism is that there is little agreement on what the symbols in Revelation refer to and thus what the book means.

3. Idealist View (Timeless)

Idealism, also known sometimes as the spiritual approach, does "not look for individual or specific fulfillments of the prophecies of

Revelation in the natural sense," but believes "only that spiritual lessons and principles (which may find recurrent expression in history) are depicted symbolically in the visions."[5] For idealists, the symbols in Revelation picture the ever-present struggle between good and evil and teach ideal, timeless principles to inspire believers as they endure the setbacks and suffering of life.

> According to this view, the great themes of the triumph of good over evil, of Christ over Satan, of the vindication of the martyrs and the sovereignty of God are played out throughout Revelation without necessary reference to single historical events. The battles in Revelation may be seen as referring to spiritual warfare, to the persecution of Christians, or to natural warfare in general throughout history. The beast from the sea may be identified as the satanically inspired political opposition to the church in any age, and the beast from the land as the opposition of pagan or corrupt religion to Christianity. The Harlot represents either the compromised church or the seduction of the world in general. Each broken seal or sounded trumpet depicts some reality (famine, war, natural disaster) which happens in history on a recurring basis as part of the sovereign outworking of God's purpose in history.[6]

Idealism grew out of the allegorical method of interpreting Scripture, upheld by Origen and Clement, and gained traction through the amillennial view held by Augustine. This is probably the predominant view today among scholars.

The main appeal of idealism seems to be the desire of its proponents to relate the message of the book to readers in every period of history. However, this aspiration is offset by idealism's inability to give concrete meaning to the symbols of the book. This is a serious shortcoming. The book of Revelation is filled with symbols, yet these symbols refer to things that are literal. They have literal referents (see, for example, the explanation that appears in Revelation 1:20). The idealist view has no interpretive anchor that helps hold Revelation together. This view is extremely reader-centered and not tied to the original meaning of the text. Meaning becomes a moving target. Moreover, if the purpose of Revelation is to teach timeless principles by the use of symbols, then what timeless principles are we to draw from this book, and are they really relevant? Idealism is not a reliable guide to the meaning of Revelation.

4. Futurist View (Future)

Futurists interpret Revelation 4–22 as describing real people and events yet to appear on the world scene. Many of the luminaries in the early church adopted a futurist view: Justin Martyr, Irenaeus, Hippolytus, and Victorinus. Some contemporary futurists are John Walvoord, Billy Graham, John MacArthur, Charles Ryrie, David Jeremiah, Tim LaHaye, J. Dwight Pentecost, and Thomas Ice.

One main objection to the futurist view is that "it removes Revelation from its original setting so that the book has little meaning for the original audience."[7] After all, some would argue, how can Revelation have been relevant to the original readers if the events described in it wouldn't take place until more than 2,000 years in the future?

There are two answers to this objection. First, one could make the same argument about hundreds of Old Testament prophecies. For instance, Isaiah's prophecies about the coming Messiah, such as the virgin birth in 7:14, were written 700 years before His birth. Micah's prophecy about the birthplace of the Messiah in Bethlehem (in Micah 5:2) was also written about 700 years before His coming. Many of Daniel's predictions weren't fulfilled for centuries, and some of Daniel's prophecies, written more than 2,500 years ago, have still not been fulfilled today.

All these Old Testament prophecies were relevant at the time they were given because the readers did not know when they would be fulfilled. Likewise, the believers in Asia Minor who first received the book of Revelation didn't know these events wouldn't be fulfilled for over 2,000 years. They believed the prophecies could very well take place in their lifetime. And each subsequent generation that has read and studied Revelation has lived with the hope that the prophecies within it could be fulfilled in their generation. Not knowing when these events will come to pass makes them relevant for every generation.

Second, knowing how history will end, whether it is in our lifetime or not, gives great comfort and hope. Revelation teaches us that God is sovereign, that He rules from His throne in heaven, that He has a plan, and that His kingdom will ultimately come to Earth. These great truths apply to people of every generation for as long as we await the consummation of the ages.

I believe the futurist approach is far superior to the other views. It is the only view that consistently follows the principles of interpreting Scripture literally. Moreover, it makes sense that the final book of God's Word would focus on the future and tell us how everything finally comes out in the end, just as Genesis told us how everything began. Bible teacher Ed Hindson summarizes the futurist approach in this way:

> The Apocalypse reveals the future. It is God's road map to help us understand where human history is going. The fact that it points to the time of the end is clear throughout the entire book. It serves as the final consummation of biblical revelation. It takes us from the first century to the last century. From persecution to triumph. From the struggling church to the bride of Christ. From Patmos to paradise.[8]

5. Eclectic View (Mixture)

This is a newer approach to Revelation that attempts to combine the four other views to maximize their strengths and minimize their weaknesses.[9] Some of the more prominent eclectics are Greg Beale, G.R. Beasley-Murray, and Craig Keener. Proponents of this view seek to understand the message to the original audience and take special note of the historical-cultural context of Revelation. They also acknowledge that some of the events will be fulfilled in the final consummation. While claiming to be eclectic, it seems to me that most who adopt this approach still lean primarily toward idealism.

The strength of this view is its desire to avoid the weaknesses of some of the other positions and present a balanced approach. Yet I believe its idealistic leanings leave it open to the same subjective, inconsistent patterns of interpretation that plague the idealistic view.

When all factors are taken into account, I believe the futurist view provides the best explanation for a clear and consistent understanding of Revelation. This is the approach adopted throughout this book.

What are some of the keys to interpreting Revelation, especially all the symbols?

The book of Revelation may be the most neglected book in the Bible. There are undoubtedly many reasons for this, but a chief one is that there are people who either claim or assume that no one can really understand what it means. They view Revelation the same way that Winston Churchill once described the Soviet Union: as "a riddle wrapped up in a mystery inside an enigma." With all the mystifying symbols and striking images that appear throughout the book, many people despair of ever understanding the book. Even many pastors never preach on Revelation. Or if they do, they preach only from the first three chapters.

This neglect of the capstone of God's revelation to man is tragic. As we observed earlier, Revelation gives us the end of the story just as Genesis gives us the beginning. To not take the time to understand Revelation would be like reading a mesmerizing novel but not finishing it to see how the story ends.

There are three practical keys to unlocking the meaning of this great book—keys that can help every reader understand it better. The first key is to recognize that the Lord *meant* for us to understand Revelation. To say that it can't be understood by believers denies the truth behind the title of the book—"The Revelation of Jesus Christ." The word "revelation" is a translation of the Greek word *apokalupsis*, which means "to uncover, to unveil, or to take the lid off something." In other words, the purpose of this book is not to hide the truth from us or make it confusing, but for Jesus Christ to uncover or take the lid off the future so we can know about the end times.

Remember, the Lord promises a special blessing on those who study and apply the message of Revelation to their lives: "God blesses the one who reads this prophecy to the church, and he blesses all who listen to it and obey what it says" (1:3). The fact God chose to mention this blessing seems to anticipate that the subject of Bible prophecy—especially in connection with the book of Revelation—would be ignored and neglected by many.

This final book of the Bible contains seven blessings or beatitudes throughout its pages (1:3; 14:13; 16:15; 19:9; 20:6; 22:7; 22:14). The blessing in 1:3 is the first and most comprehensive one. It is a blessing that anyone reading Revelation can experience. And notice that it is threefold:

The one who reads	In the early church, not everyone had a copy of the Scriptures, so someone would read them aloud to the people. Today, this blessing extends to all who read this grand climax to God's prophetic program.
The one who listens	Just to hear the book of Revelation read (and other prophecies of the Bible) is a great blessing in troubled times like today.
The one who obeys	It is not only important to read and hear Bible prophecy but also to observe, pay attention to, and obey what is written. After reading and listening to what Revelation is teaching us, we should pay attention and watch for the events that signal the coming of the end times.

The fact that those who hear the words of this book are to keep, practice, and obey what it says presupposes that they must be able to understand what it means.

The second key to unlocking the meaning of Revelation is to realize that most of what is in the book is not new information. There's an old saying that Revelation is the Grand Central Station of the Bible because it's where all the trains of thought throughout the whole Bible come in. While it is certainly true that Revelation looks ahead and reveals the future, it also looks back and brings together all the threads running through the first 65 books of the Bible. Revelation has a total of 404 verses, and 278 of them allude back to the Old Testament. Revelation has no direct quotations from the Old Testament, but includes a total of 550 allusions or references (which appear in 278 verses) back to the Old

Testament. So a significant portion of Revelation brings together content from the Old Testament into a comprehensive sequence of events. Arnold Fruchtenbaum observes:

> The majority of things found in the first twenty chapters of Revelation are found elsewhere in the Old Testament. Only the last two chapters deal with things totally new. If this is true, what is the importance of the book of Revelation? The Old Testament prophecies are scattered throughout the books of Moses and the various prophets and Writings. It would have been impossible to develop these prophecies into any chronological sequence of events. The value of the book of Revelation is not that it provides a lot of new information, but rather that it takes the scattered Old Testament prophecies and puts them in chronological order so that the sequence of events may be determined. This book provides a framework for the understanding of the order and the sequence of events found in the Old Testament prophecies. This is the reason for so many references to the Old Testament. However, the material found in the last two chapters is totally new material which describes the Eternal Order. The Old Testament prophets never foresaw anything beyond the Messianic Kingdom. Indeed, the Kingdom was the high point of Old Testament prophecy and no prophet ever saw anything beyond that. But the Eternal Order is the high point of New Testament prophecy, and Revelation 21 and 22 provide new information, as they describe the Eternal Order.[10]

The third key to understanding Revelation is to correctly interpret the symbols in the book. When we come to Revelation, we often feel like Alice in Wonderland, who ran down a rabbit hole and stumbled into a world of fantasy, make-believe, and enigma—a world of talking caterpillars, rabbits, etc. People often feel like they have fallen into another world when they step into the book of Revelation, for it includes a broad assortment of symbols, such as horns, beasts, stars, and varied colored horses to graphically communicate its meaning.

This has led some people to end up adopting one of two extremes in interpretation. Some say that the presence of so many symbols means that the book cannot be understood at all. They say that we are able to discern that the book talks about a cosmic struggle between good and evil, but that none of the specific details can be understood. The other extreme is unchecked speculation and sensationalism that manipulates all the symbols so they represent certain people or events of our time—in other words, the reader makes the text mean whatever he wants. Those who follow this method can best be described by the old saying, "Amazing things in the Bible I see, especially those put there by you and by me."

The proper method of interpreting the symbols in Revelation involves two steps. The first is to remember that when symbols are employed, they refer to something that is literal. Symbols are not just symbols of nothing. They aren't meaningless. They aren't just symbols of symbols. They refer to something that is literal. Paul Benware notes,

> Symbols are valuable tools of communication. Symbols communicate truth concisely, and they communicate it graphically. In Revelation 11 the apostle John could have spent a great deal of time describing the spiritual and moral conditions of Jerusalem. Instead, he called the city "Sodom and Egypt." Quickly and vividly he communicated a volume of truth that remains graphically fixed in our minds. Symbols and figures of speech, then, represent something literal. It is the task of the interpreter to investigate this figurative language to discover what literal truth is there.[11]

There's a clear example of this at the very outset of Revelation as Jesus stands in the middle of seven golden lampstands holding seven stars in His right hand (1:13, 16). At the end of the chapter, Jesus identifies the seven lampstands as the seven churches of Asia and the seven stars as seven angels (1:20). Jesus Himself is providing us with a key to unlock the meaning of symbols in Revelation—that is, when we see a symbol in prophecy, we are to look for the literal referent, or the literal person, place, or event that the symbol represents.

Step two of properly interpreting a symbol in Revelation is to recognize that all the symbols in the book are explained either in Revelation itself or in other parts of the Bible. We cannot make them mean whatever we want them to mean. No interpreter has the freedom to make a symbol mean whatever he wants. Scripture sets the parameters for our interpretation of symbols. The infallible guide to the meaning of these symbols is God's Word. As Fruchtenbaum says,

> While recognizing the existence of symbols, there will be no resorting to guesswork. Rather, this study will proceed on the premise that all symbols in the Book of Revelation are explained elsewhere: either in a different part of the Book of Revelation or in some other part of the Bible. There are symbols, but the Bible itself will explain what these symbols mean either by direct statement or through a comparison of the usage of the symbol elsewhere in the Scriptures. The meaning of the symbols will not be determined by speculation.[12]

The first place we should look when we encounter a symbol is the immediate context to see if there's a built-in interpretation. Often, we don't have to look any further for the meaning of a symbol than the immediate context. The example I just gave of Jesus in Revelation 1 is an apt illustration of this. Jesus tells the reader the meaning of the seven lampstands and the seven stars in the same chapter (1:20). This kind of built-in interpretation occurs often in Revelation. Frequently, the meaning of a symbol is given by John in the immediate context, sometimes even in the same verse. Here are a few examples.[13]

Symbol	Meaning
the seven stars (1:16)	seven angels (1:20)
the seven lampstands (1:13)	seven churches (1:20)
the morning star (2:28)	Christ (22:16)
the seven lamps of fire (4:5)	the sevenfold Spirit of God (4:5)
the seven eyes (5:6)	the sevenfold Spirit of God (5:6)
the incense (5:8)	the prayers of God's people (5:8)
the fallen star (9:1)	the angel of the abyss (9:11)
the great city, Sodom and Egypt (11:8)	Jerusalem (11:8)
the stars in the sky (12:4)	fallen angels (12:9)
the woman and the child (12:1-2)	Israel and Christ (12:5-6)
the large, red great dragon (12:3)	Satan (12:9)
the ancient serpent (12:9)	Satan (12:9)
the times, time, and half a time (12:14)	1,260 days (12:6)
the beast out of the sea (13:1-10)	future world ruler and his empire (13:1-10)
the beast out of the earth (13:11-17)	the false prophet (19:20)

Symbol	Meaning
the great prostitute (17:1)	the great city, Babylon (17:18)
the waters on which the woman sits (17:1)	the peoples of the world (17:15)
the ten horns (17:12)	ten kings associated with the beast (13:1; 17:3, 7-8, 11-13, 16-17)
the fine linen (19:8)	the righteous deeds of the saints (19:8)
the rider on the white horse (19:16)	Jesus Christ, the King of kings (19:11-16, 19)
the bride (21:9)	the Lamb's wife (21:9)
the bride (21:9)	the holy city, New Jerusalem (21:9-10)

So, the first step to discerning the meaning of a symbol is to look at the immediate context for clues as to its meaning.

If there is no clear interpretation in the immediate context, widen the search to the broader context of the book of Revelation. And if it's not found there, then look to the rest of Scripture. Many of the symbols used in prophetic passages are used elsewhere in Scripture and have an established meaning. J.B. Smith summarizes: "Therefore the conclusion may be drawn that symbols occurring in the book are either explained in the text or may be understood from their use in previous Scriptures. The inference follows that *whatever is not thus explained is to be taken as literal.*"[14]

Symbols, therefore, are not meaningless. Neither are they an open invitation to let our imagination run wild. They do not give the interpreter free rein to make the symbol mean whatever he wants it to mean. In most cases the immediate context or the use of that same symbol by other biblical writers will establish the boundaries for proper interpretation.

The bottom line is this: Don't be afraid of or intimidated by Revelation. God wants you to understand and apply the truth of this book to your life. Follow these three keys with thought and care, and ask the Lord to open your heart and mind to the precious truths about our coming King!

Are the numbers and time periods in Revelation literal?

The book of Revelation is filled with numbers. "There are 174 cardinal numbers in the book of Revelation. In addition there are 19 numbers which are fractions (e.g., ⅓) or cardinal numbers with fractions (e.g., 3½). Finally, there are 61 ordinal numbers which make a total of 254 numbers in the book."[15] The presence of so many numbers has led to all kinds of speculation. The central issue is this: How are we to understand these numbers? Are they all literal? Are they all symbolic? Or are they a mixture of the two?

To answer this question, it's best to begin with Revelation itself. In Revelation 1, Jesus is pictured standing in the midst of seven lampstands with seven stars in His right hand. Then in the final verse of the chapter, He provides the divine interpretation of these symbols. He says that the seven lampstands are "seven churches" (Ephesus, Smyrna, Pergamum, Thyatira, Sardis, Philadelphia, and Laodicea), and the seven stars are the "seven angels [messengers] of the seven churches." Clearly, for Jesus, the number seven—in both cases—is literal. We can safely assume that Jesus knew how to interpret the numbers in Revelation. He established this understanding of the numbers in Revelation right from the beginning.

When it comes to the interpretation of numbers in Revelation, John Walvoord summarizes the issue well:

> Numbers are very prominent in the book: 2, 3, 3½, 4, 5, 6, 7, 10, 12, 24, 42, 144, 666, 1,000, 1,260, 1,600, 7,000,

> 12,000, 144,000, 100,000,000, and 200,000,000. These numbers may be understood literally, but even when understood in this way, they often carry with them a symbolic meaning. Hence the number seven, used fifty-four times, more than any other number in the book, refers to seven historical churches in the opening chapter. Yet by the very use of this number (which speaks of completion or perfection) the concept is conveyed that these were representative churches which in some sense were complete in their description of the normal needs of the church. There were not only seven churches but seven lampstands, seven stars, seven spirits of God, seven seals on the scroll, seven angels with seven trumpets, seven bowls containing seven last plagues, seven thunders, seven thousand killed in the earthquake of chapter 12, a dragon with seven heads and seven crowns, the beast of chapter 13 with seven heads, seven mountains of chapter 17, and the seven kings.
>
> Next in importance to the number seven and in the order of their frequency are the numbers twelve, ten, and four. Some of this stems from the fact that there are twelve tribes of Israel. Twelve thousand were sealed from each of the twelve tribes. The elders of chapter 4 are twice twelve or twenty-four. The New Jerusalem is declared to be 12,000 furlongs wide and long, and its wall twelve times twelve, or 144 cubits in height. Clearly, the use of these numbers is not accidental. Though the symbolism is not always obvious, the general rule should be followed to interpret numbers literally unless there is clear evidence to the contrary. The numbers nevertheless convey more than their bare numerical significance.[16]

Steve Sullivan agrees for the most part with the literal interpretation of numbers.

> The mentioning of 42 months (11:2; 13:5) as 1260 days (11:3; 12:6) is the conventional use of time. In addition, one could add ½ an hour (8:1), 10 days (2:10), and 5 months (9:5, 10). Round numbers are rarely used in Revelation. It is reasonable to see round numbers in the fractions 1/10 (11:13), 1/4 (6:8), and 1/3 (8:7, 8, 9, 10, 11, 12; 9:15, 18; 12:4). It is possible that the 7000 men killed in the earthquake (11:13), 200,000,000 armies and 1600 stadia could be round numbers…A quick look at a concordance will indicate when a number is used with the word "year" it refers to a literal year. Everywhere there is a number with a time indicator in Revelation, such as days, months and years, one finds nothing in the text which would compel the reader to understand this to be anything other than a conventional use of numbers.[17]

This issue is of special significance in texts such as Revelation 20:1-6, where 1,000 years is mentioned six times in seven verses. While it's possible, of course, that some numbers in Revelation could be rounded off, when the word "year" appears with a number, it seems we can take the number literally. This is helpful in resolving the debate over whether the millennium is a literal 1,000 years in length.

When interpreting numbers in Revelation, as with other areas of interpretation, it is important to establish some basic rules. If some numbers are taken literally and others are not, what are the criteria for making the decision? The decision cannot be up to the whims of each individual interpreter of the text, or Revelation would be largely rendered meaningless.

For consistency's sake, it is best to take the numbers at face value unless there is some clear indication to the contrary, or taking the number literally makes no sense. Because Jesus opens the first chapter with two literal uses of the number seven, this approach should guide us through the rest of the book.

What is the outline of the book?

Many different outlines have been proposed for Revelation, and the best one is the divinely inspired threefold outline stated in Revelation 1:19: "Therefore write the things which you have seen, and the things which are, and the things which will take place after these things."

Here's a basic outline based on Revelation 1:19.

Outline of Revelation

The Christ
I. "The things which you have seen" (chapter 1)
The Glorified Christ

The Churches
II. "The things which are" (chapters 2–3)
The Letters to the Seven Churches
Ephesus (2:1-7)
Smyrna (2:8-11)
Pergamum (2:12-17)
Thyatira (2:18-29)
Sardis (3:1-6)
Philadelphia (3:7-13)
Laodicea (3:14-22)

The Consummation
III. "The things which will take place after these things" (chapters 4–22)
Worship in Heaven (4–5)
The Tribulation (6–18)
The Second Coming of Christ (19)
The Millennium (20)
The Eternal State (21–22)

PART TWO

The Background of Revelation

Who was the human author of Revelation?

The human author of Revelation identifies himself four times: "His bond-servant John...John...I, John, your brother...I, John" (1:1, 4, 9; 22:8). Several candidates have been suggested as to which John wrote this book: (1) John the apostle, (2) the elder John, (3) John Mark, (4) John the Baptist, and (5) another John.[18] It's not the purpose of this book to give all the arguments for and against each of these views, so I will focus on the view that, based on careful study, I believe is correct—the apostle John.[19]

There are some who reject the apostle John as the human author of Revelation. The primary reasons they give are the differences that appear in the language, writing style, and grammar of Revelation and the Gospel of John and the fact that the author never declares his status as an apostle, calling himself "servant," "brother," and "prophet."

While it is true there are some variations, they are not as significant as some claim, and they can easily be accounted for by considering the character and purpose of these two writings. For example, in Revelation, John was recording visions he received, and he was relating these visions to the Old Testament Scriptures. As Bible commentator Grant Osborne notes, "Such powerful experiences as the ecstatic visions would naturally affect one's writing style."[20] Also, the dissimilarities of John's Gospel and Revelation are often exaggerated without noting the even greater similarities. For instance, there is striking similarity in many of the terms used, especially those referring to Jesus as the Word, the Lamb of God, and the Son of Man.[21]

One key support for Johannine authorship of Revelation is found in the early church, which universally believed John the apostle was the author. In the second century AD, Justin Martyr identified the apostle John as the author (*Dialogue with Trypho* 81.4). This became the accepted view in the early church (Irenaeus, Tertullian, Clement of Alexandria, Hippolytus, and Origen all held this view). So those who were closest in time to the writing of Revelation believed that the apostle John was the author. Few books in the New Testament enjoy stronger, earlier apostolic attestation than Revelation.

The first mention of someone else as the author of Revelation was by Dionysius of Alexandria, who served as an overseer in the church of Alexandria in the last half of the third century (about AD 247–264). As Robert Thomas observes, "The fact remains that the external evidence for authorship by John the apostle is earlier, clearer, more definite, and more positive for Revelation than for the traditional authorship of any other New Testament book. Testimony of the earliest Fathers is unanimous in favor of the apostolic authorship and authority of the book."[22] Thus, I believe their testimony that the apostle John was the human author of Revelation.

When was Revelation written?

Two main dates for the composition of Revelation have been held by the majority of scholars: the early or Neronic date, or during the reign of the emperor Nero (circa AD 65), and the late or Domitianic date, or during the reign of Domitian (circa AD 95). The date of composition for Revelation has become a major issue in recent years due to the rise of preterism, which teaches that the book of Revelation prophesied about the fall of Jerusalem, and not about events that are still future for us today. What should we believe—that Revelation speaks of events that have already taken place in the past, or that it still remains to be fulfilled in the future?

The linchpin of the preterist view is an early date (AD 64–67) for the writing of the book of Revelation. Obviously, if Revelation was written *after* AD 70, when Jerusalem fell to Rome, then it could not be prophesying this event. Preterists openly recognize the critical importance of the early date of Revelation to their own position. In a review of fellow preterist David Chilton's commentary on Revelation, entitled *The Days of Vengeance*, Kenneth Gentry observes, "If it could be demonstrated that Revelation were written 25 years after the Fall of Jerusalem, Chilton's entire labor would go up in smoke."[23] Another preterist, R.C. Sproul, observes, "If the book was written after AD 70, then its contents manifestly do not refer to events surrounding the fall of Jerusalem—unless the book is a wholesale fraud, having been composed after the predicted events had already occurred."[24]

Unlike the preterist view, the futurist approach does not depend on any specific date for the writing of the book. Even if the early date is true, the futurist view of Revelation could still be correct, and the preterist view could be incorrect. As has often been pointed out, a theological position is only as strong as its weakest link. The date of Revelation is the weakest link—the Achilles' heel—for the preterist view.

Since Revelation does not give the date when it was written, we are left to look for clues as to the most likely date for its composition. And when it comes to determining the date of a book of the Bible, there are two main kinds of evidence: external and internal. *External evidence* examines material outside the Bible to gain insight into the book's date. *Internal evidence* considers evidence within the text of the book itself for clues that point to the time of writing.

Both lines of evidence point strongly in the direction of the late or Domitianic date (AD 95) as the correct view. Here, we have only a brief amount of space to survey the external and internal evidence. If you would like more material about this, you can read my PhD dissertation done at Dallas Theological Seminary, which is available at pre-trib.org.

The External Evidence

The most important ancient witness concerning the date of Revelation is Irenaeus. He is Exhibit A for the late date. The importance of his testimony cannot be overemphasized because his credibility as a witness is outstanding. Irenaeus spent his youth in Smyrna, the location of one of the seven churches to which Revelation was addressed, and claims to have been a pupil of Polycarp, bishop of Smyrna, who in turn was a student of the apostle John. Therefore, a more knowledgeable, reliable witness could hardly be imagined.[25]

Irenaeus' compelling statement concerning the date of the writing of Revelation is preserved in Latin by Irenaeus and in Greek by Eusebius. The Latin version of Irenaeus is found in his comments on Revelation 13:18 in his work *Against Heresies,* which was probably written about AD 180. He wrote, "For if it were necessary that the name of him [Antichrist] should be distinctly revealed in this present time, it would have been told by him who saw the apocalyptic vision. For it was seen no long time ago, but almost in our generation, toward the end of Domitian's reign."[26] Irenaeus referred to the "apocalyptic vision" of John, and placed it "toward the end of Domitian's reign." Because Domitian's reign ended in AD 96, on the basis of Irenaeus's testimony, Revelation could credibly be said to have been written about AD 95–96. Irenaeus' statement about the writing of the book "toward the end of Domitian's reign" is clear, and his credibility as a witness is unimpeachable.

After Irenaeus, there's a long, consistent line of support for the AD 95 date of Revelation, whereas the first witness for the AD 65 date doesn't appear for almost 500 years. I believe that's very significant. To save time, let's put the two categories for the external evidence side by side. Only the witnesses that are clear and unambiguous for each date are presented.

Witnesses for the Domitianic Date	Witnesses for the Neronic Date
Hegesippus (AD 150)	
Irenaeus (AD 180)	
Victorinus (c. 300)	
Eusebius (c. 300)	
Jerome (c. 400)	
Sulpicius Severus (c. 400)	
The Acts of John (c. 650)	
Primasius (c. 540)	Syriac Version of NT (550)
Orosius (c. 600)	
Andreas (c. 600)	
Venerable Bede (700)	
	Arethas (c. 900)
	Theophylact (d. 1107)

The first clear, accepted, unambiguous witness to the Neronic date is a one-line subscription in the Syriac translation of the New Testament that was written in AD 550. Then come two other witnesses to the early date, Arethas (c. 900) and Theophylact (d. 1107). These witnesses were 800 or more years removed from the writing of the book of Revelation.

The late date, on the other hand, has an unbroken line of support from some of the greatest, most reliable names in church history, beginning with Ireneaus in AD 180. Moreover, Clement of Alexandria, Tertullian, and Origen all supported the late date; however, they are not included in the chart because they don't specifically say that John was banished by Domitian. The external evidence for the AD 95 date is overwhelming.

The Internal Evidence

As we look within Revelation itself for clues about when it was written, we see that there are two key lines of internal evidence that favor the Domitianic date.

The Condition of the Seven Churches

One of the key internal arguments for the late date of Revelation is the condition of the seven churches of Asia Minor in Revelation 2–3. They all show the symptoms of being second-generation churches, and six of them have serious problems. The period of Paul's great mission is now well in the past. There are several important clues that support the late date of Revelation from three of the churches addressed in Revelation 2–3.

Church of Ephesus

If John wrote Revelation in AD 64–67, then the letter to the church of Ephesus in Revelation 2:1-7 would have been written at around the same time as Paul's two letters to Timothy, who was the pastor of the church in Ephesus when Paul wrote to him. So if Revelation was written in 64–67, then John's words to the church in Revelation 2:1-7 would have been very closely followed by Paul's two letters to Timothy. That raises a serious problem: Why did John mention the Ephesians' loss of first love for the Lord, or the presence of the Nicolaitans in their midst, but not Paul? And why didn't Paul mention these problems in the book of Ephesians, which was probably written in AD 62? Jesus' statement to the church of Ephesus in Revelation 2:2 that it had guarded itself well against error does not fit what we know of this church in Nero's day (Acts 20:29-30; 1 Timothy 1:3-7; 2 Timothy 2:17-18).

Those who support the early date for Revelation often respond to this point by noting that error can erupt very quickly in a church. As an example, they sometimes cite the churches of Galatia, which Paul rebuked for so quickly deserting the gospel (Galatians 1:6). But there is a great difference between the condition and maturity of the Galatian churches after Paul's brief visit there on his first missionary journey and the church at Ephesus, where Paul taught for three years, where Apollos taught, where Prisca and Aquila ministered, and where Timothy pastored for several years.

Moreover, Revelation 2:1-7 makes no mention of the great missionary work of Paul in Asia Minor. On his third missionary journey, Paul made Ephesus his headquarters for three years and had a profound ministry there. If John had written Revelation in AD 64–67, then the omission of any mention of Paul in the letters to the seven churches of Asia Minor is inexplicable. However, if John wrote 30 years later, to the *second* generation of churchgoers, then the omission is easily understood.

Church of Smyrna

Apparently the church at Smyrna did not even exist during the time of Paul's ministry. Polycarp was the bishop at Smyrna, and in his letter to the Philippians, written about AD 110, Polycarp said that the Smyrnaeans did not know the Lord during the time Paul was ministering (11.3):

> I have not observed or heard of any such thing among you, in whose midst the blessed Paul labored, and who were his letters of recommendation in the beginning. For he boasts about you in all the churches—those alone, that is, which at that time had come to know the Lord, for we had not yet come to know him.

Polycarp was saying that Paul praised the Philippian believers in all the churches, but that during Paul's ministry in the AD 50s and 60s, the church at Smyrna did not even exist.

Church of Laodicea

The church at Laodicea is the only one of the seven churches (and Sardis may be another) that does not receive any commendation in the New Testament. In his letter to the Colossians, probably written in AD 60–62, Paul mentioned the church there three times (2:2; 4:13, 16). At no point did he say anything negative. By contrast, John's words about the church at Laodicea were very negative (Revelation 3:14-22). If John had written Revelation in AD 64–67 as preterists claim, that would have been immediately after Paul's comments in Colossians. But it would surely have taken more than two to seven years for the church at Laodicea to depart so completely from its earlier acceptable status that absolutely nothing good could be said about it. Laodicea is also described in Revelation as flourishing economically. Jesus quotes the church as saying, "I am rich, and have become wealthy, and have need of nothing" (3:17). Yet it's interesting to note that the city suffered great devastation from an earthquake in AD 60. After the earthquake, the Laodiceans refused all aid and assistance from Rome, preferring to rebuild their ruined city from their own resources.

Tacitus, the Roman historian, in his *Annals* 14.27, describes this independent spirit. "In the same year, Laodicea, one of the famous Asiatic cities, was laid in ruins by an earthquake, but recovered by its own resources, without assistance from ourselves." The extent of the damage to Laodicea and the length of time it took to reconstruct the city are powerful evidence in support of the late date for Revelation.

Most of the main ruins that survive today in Laodicea are of buildings constructed after the earthquake. They were rebuilt at the expense of individual citizens and were not finished until about the year AD 90. In fact, the completion of the stadium can be precisely dated to the latter part of AD 79, and the inscriptions on several other buildings indicate that they too can be dated to this same period. New gates and fortifications seem to have culminated the rebuilding of Laodicea. It is likely that the great triple gate (Syrian Gate) and towers were not finished until AD 88–90.

This means the rebuilding of Laodicea took an entire generation. With the earthquake taking place in AD 60, it is highly problematic for proponents of the early date of Revelation to assume that Laodicea was rich, wealthy, and in need of nothing in AD 64–67. During those years the city was still in the early stages of a rebuilding program that would last another 25 years. However, if Revelation was written in AD 95, the description of Laodicea as a wealthy city in need of nothing would be very plausible, for by this time the city was completely rebuilt and prosperous, and its inhabitants were basking in the pride of their great accomplishment.

The Banishment of John to Patmos

The second key point of internal evidence for the late date of Revelation is found in Revelation 1:9. There, we read that when John received the contents of Revelation, he was exiled on the island of Patmos. Church history consistently testifies that both Peter and Paul were executed in Rome near the end of Nero's reign. Those who hold to the early date for the writing of Revelation maintain that during this same time the apostle John was banished to Patmos by Nero. But why would Nero execute Peter and Paul, yet merely banish John? This seems inconsistent. The fact John was given a different punishment argues for the fact he was persecuted under a different ruler. Moreover, there is no evidence that Nero banished Christians.

Domitian, who was Nero's successor, also persecuted Christians, and banishment was one of his favorite modes of punishment. Therefore, John's exile to Patmos is much more likely to have taken place under Domitian rather than Nero.

Summarizing the Evidence

In Revelation 2–3, the churches of Asia Minor show all the symptoms of a considerable passage of time since their founding. The period of Paul's great missionary journeys seems to lie in the past. John is the recognized human superintendent of the churches, and he fails to mention Paul in any of the letters in Revelation 2–3. Likewise, Paul makes no mention of John in any of his three letters to Ephesus written in the early to mid-60s (Ephesians, 1 and 2 Timothy). Every key date indicator in Revelation 2–3 points to a late date for the writing of Revelation. As a result of his intensive study of the local imagery of the seven churches, New Testament scholar Colin Hemer concludes, "I started with a provisional acceptance of the orthodox Domitianic dating, and have been confirmed in that view by further study...We accordingly affirm the Domitianic date of the letters in light of the kind of evidence considered, while recognizing that many of these indications are uncertain. Cumulatively they align themselves with the case widely accepted on other grounds that the Revelation was written about AD 95."[27]

Taking into account all the relevant evidence, both external and internal, the strongest view is that the apostle John wrote the book of Revelation in the year AD 95 while exiled by the Roman emperor Domitian to the island of Patmos.

Who were the recipients of Revelation?

The original recipients or audience for the apocalypse were seven local assemblies of believers located in the western part of Asia Minor, or what today is Turkey. These assemblies were the churches in Ephesus, Smyrna, Pergamum, Thyatira, Sardis, Philadelphia, and Laodicea. According to church tradition, the apostle

John relocated to this area from Israel in the late AD 60s as the Jewish War was approaching. John settled and made Ephesus his headquarters, the key city of the area with its population of about 250,000. From there, John became an apostolic shepherd and overseer of the churches in Asia. These were some of the churches that would have flourished under John's influence.

The majority of the believers in these churches were probably Gentiles, but there were certainly many Jewish believers as well. John wrote to encourage these believers, in light of the future, to live faithfully in the present as they faced growing apathy from the inside and gathering aggression from the outside.

The 5 W's of Revelation[28]

WHO?	The apostle John—the author of the Gospel of John and 1, 2, and 3 John
WHAT?	The written record of the prophecies, visions, and messages John saw and heard
WHERE?	The island of Patmos, about 40 miles off the coast of Ephesus, where John was banished for his witness for Christ
WHEN?	About AD 95
WHY?	To encourage God's people to live faithfully in the present in light of the future

What is Revelation about?

In the study of any biblical book, it's important to understand the overall purpose of the book. Why was it written? What is it about? What purpose did the author have in mind when he set pen to parchment? From that we can develop a purpose statement—one that is specific enough to capture the essence of the book, yet broad enough to encompass the entire book.

Here is the one-sentence purpose statement I've written for the book:

> Against the dark background of external and internal pressure on the church, Revelation was written to reveal the final outcome of human history to God's people to encourage them and exhort them to faithfulness because even though evil seems to prevail, God is in control of all the events of human history and Christ will return someday in power and great glory to punish the wicked and establish His kingdom.

To state it more concisely, Revelation is an account of how Jesus Christ will someday become King by means of judgment. It is about the establishment of God's kingdom on this Earth, and then on into eternity. In Revelation 5, we read about Jesus taking a scroll from the Father's hand. This scroll, which bears seven seals, speaks of the inheritance that Christ has been given by the Father (see Psalm 2:7-9). When the scroll is finally opened, the kingdom of God, the inheritance of Christ, is fully realized on Earth.

The knowledge of the coming of God's rule to this Earth encourages God's people to persevere even in times of trouble and distress. The kingdom of Christ is coming, but before it does, there will be a period of jarring judgment on this Earth. Jesus will establish His kingdom by means of judgment on a wicked world. Revelation is a book filled with judgment from chapter 6 onward. But the judgment is not meaningless or mindless. It has a divine purpose. God will judge the world in preparation for the coming kingdom of Christ on Earth. All of history is driving inexorably toward the messianic kingdom; that's what Revelation is about.

What are some of the key words in Revelation?

Every book in the Bible contains some key words that occur frequently and reveal the emphasis in the book. Here are ten key words that define the focus of Revelation:

1. *And*

   This might seem like a strange word to include in a key-word list because it's such a common term, but "and" (*kai* in the original Greek text) occurs more than 1,200 times in Revelation. Nearly every verse in Revelation begins with the word *kai* in the original Greek text of the New Testament. It is sometimes translated as "but," "even," "both," "also," "then," "yet," or "indeed," yet it is most often translated simply as "and." The rapid-fire repetition of this word rushes the book along at a breathtaking rate. As you go through Revelation, you read "and...and...and...and..." Using "and" in this way is a powerful literary technique. As Ed Hindson notes,

   > One cannot read this book and mentally stand still. The reader will sense, consciously or unconsciously, that he or she is moving through a series of events that appear like instantaneous flashes on a video screen. These glimpses of the future are intended to keep us moving toward the final consummation of human history. The closing chapters actually fast-forward us into eternity itself![29]

2. *Throne* (46 times)
3. *Power and authority* (40 times)
4. *King* (37 times)
5. *Lamb* (30 times total, 28 times it's used of Jesus)
6. *Seven* (54 times)
7. *Overcome, victorious, conquer* (17 times)
8. *Like, similar to* (22 times)

   This word is used with much of the imagery in Revelation to point out the similarity between two things. It usually involves a symbolic correlation, where one thing represents another.

9. *Worship* (24 times)

   Revelation is a book of worship lifted up to the Lord.

10. *Prophecy, prophet, prophesy* (17 times in its various forms)

    Revelation is a book filled with prophecies.

Was Patmos a penal colony in the first century?

According to Revelation 1:9, John was on the island of Patmos when he received the book of Revelation. Patmos is a small, rocky island, about ten miles long and six miles wide, which is about 40 miles off the coast of Asia Minor (modern Turkey) from Ephesus. John says he was on the island "because of the word of God and the testimony of Jesus" (1:9). Some think this means that John was there to share the Word and Jesus. But it's more likely John was referring to the fact he was banished there by the Roman emperor Domitian as punishment for preaching the Word and Jesus. That seems to be affirmed by the first part of verse 9, where John refers to himself as "your brother and fellow partaker in the tribulation and kingdom and perseverance which are in Jesus."

It's common to read that Patmos was a small island inhabited by a penal colony in the first century, and that John was forced to work in the mines there while in his 90s. I've heard some preachers compare Patmos to Alcatraz, an island prison near San Francisco where dangerous criminals were sequestered from society. While this makes for dramatic preaching, it's not accurate. There is no evidence that, in John's day, Patmos had a penal colony or was commonly used for banishment. The erroneous notion that Patmos was inhabited by a penal colony is often cited from the Roman historian Pliny (*Pliny Hist. Nat.* 4.12.69). This citation from Pliny has been quoted in Bible commentaries. However, Pliny never refers to Patmos as having a penal colony or being a place of banishment.

We know from history that there was a military garrison and administrative building on the island, possibly a hippodrome (horse-racing track), a temple to Artemis, and probably a temple to Apollo. John was probably sent there because it was the closest place Domitian could use to remove his influence from Asia Minor. Osborne summarizes the situation well: "Life there was not too harsh, as indicated by its decent-size population and two gymnasia as well as a temple of Artemis. Thus John would have lived a fairly normal life as an exile on that island. He was likely there only a short time and was allowed to go to Ephesus in a general amnesty for exiles by the emperor Nerva in AD 96 after Domitian died."[30]

PART THREE

The Revelation of Jesus Christ

(Revelation 1)

What does the title "the Revelation of Jesus Christ" mean?

Unlike most books of the Bible, Revelation states its own title in the very opening verse: "The Revelation [Greek, *apokalupsis*] of Jesus Christ." While the title is clearly presented, it's common to hear it incorrectly stated in two different ways. First, there are people—and even some preachers—who refer to this book as "Revelations" (plural). But notice that in 1:1 "Revelation" is singular. Second, even in Bible commentaries, this book is called "The Revelation of St. John." But that is not the title of the book. John specifically states it is "The Revelation of Jesus Christ." Just as we are not permitted to change the title an author has selected for an already-published book, we have no right to alter the divine self-title of the Revelation of Jesus Christ.

The title "Revelation of Jesus Christ" is subject to two different interpretations. The title can mean "a revelation *about* Christ" (the one who is revealed), or "a revelation *given by* Christ" (the one who gives the revelation). Either meaning is permitted by the original Greek text. Certainly, this book powerfully reveals Christ, and a great deal of the book is about Him. No one would argue about that. However, I believe it is best to take the expression "of Christ" as meaning a revelation *from* or *given by* Christ. I favor this view for two key reasons. First, Christ is pictured throughout the book as a revealer. He admonishes and comforts the seven churches, opens the scroll, and reveals its contents. Second, Revelation 1:1 specifically states that Jesus gave the message to the angels and John just as the Father had revealed it to Him.[31] Right after stating the title "The Revelation of Jesus Christ," Jesus is immediately pictured as the revealer of the contents of this book. Therefore, this seems to be the primary meaning of the words "of Christ."

The transmission or chain of communication for Revelation is clearly stated in 1:1 as well: "The revelation of Jesus Christ, which God gave Him to show to His bond-servants, the things which must soon take place; and He sent and communicated it by His angel *to His bond-servant John*" (emphasis added).

What we see here is that the Father originally gave the revelation to the Son, and the Son transmitted it to John sometimes directly from Himself and sometimes using an angel as the go-between. Then John, in turn, shared the message with the churches. The main point in this chain of communication is that the information in this book originated with God Himself. Revelation is the capstone of God's Word, and like the previous 65 books of the Bible, it is the very word of God (2 Timothy 3:16-17; 2 Peter 2:20-21). There was a four-stage process involved in transmitting the Revelation to the churches.

The Chain of Communication

God the Father → Jesus → angels → John → God's other servants

What are the names and titles for Jesus in Revelation?

Revelation is about Jesus Christ from beginning to end—it is "the testimony of Jesus" (Revelation 19:10). The final revelation from God contains numerous names and titles for our Lord. The main ones are listed in the accompanying chart.

Names and Titles of Christ in Revelation	
1. Jesus Christ (1:1) 2. faithful witness (1:5) 3. firstborn of the dead (1:5) 4. ruler of the kings of the earth (1:5) 5. the Alpha and the Omega (1:8) 6. He who is, was, and is to come (1:8) 7. the Almighty (1:8) 8. son of man (1:13) 9. the living One (1:18) 10. the One who holds the seven stars (2:1) 11. the One who walks among the lampstands (2:1) 12. the One who has the two-edged sword (2:12) 13. the Son of God (2:18) 14. He who has eyes like fire (2:18) 15. He who has the seven Spirits of God (3:1)	16. He who is holy and true (3:7) 17. He who has the key of David (3:7) 18. the Amen (3:14) 19. faithful and true Witness (3:14) 20. Beginning of the creation of God (3:14) 21. Lion of the tribe of Judah (5:5) 22. Root of David (5:5) 23. the Lamb (28 times) 24. Lord, holy and true (6:10) 25. Lord (11:8) 26. male child (12:5) 27. King of the nations (15:3) 28. Word of God (19:13) 29. King of kings and Lord of lords (19:16) 30. Bright morning star (22:16)

What do "soon" and "near" mean in 1:1 and 1:3?

Revelation opens by stressing the urgency of the message. John refers to the events in the books as that, "which must soon take place...for the time is near" (1:1, 3). The Greek term for "soon" is *en tachei* (1:1), and the word for "near" is *engus* (1:3). Preterists, who believe that the prophecies of Revelation were fulfilled in the events surrounding the destruction of Jerusalem in AD 70, contend that "soon" and "near" refer to the events of AD 70, because they occurred just a few years after John wrote Revelation in about AD 65. However, as demonstrated earlier, Revelation was written in AD 95 and not AD 65, so the prophecies in Revelation cannot be interpreted as pointing to the events of AD 70. That being the case, how should the terms "soon" and "near" be understood? There are three main views.

First, some maintain that "soon" in Revelation denotes the manner or qualitative nature of Christ's coming, not its timing, and should therefore be translated "quickly" or "suddenly."[32] In other words, the events will occur "suddenly," "quickly," or without delay once the appointed time arrives, and they will rapidly run their course once they commence.[33] However, there are two points that favor assigning a temporal or timing meaning to "soon" in Revelation 1:1. First, from the lexical standpoint, the standard reference work *A Greek-English Lexicon of the New Testament and other Early Christian Literature* (also known as BDAG) cites a temporal meaning ("soon, in a short time") for *en tachei* in Revelation 1:1 and 22:6.[34] Second, the temporal meaning is reinforced in the immediate context by the appearance of the words "for the time is near" only two verses later in Revelation 1:3.[35] According to BDAG, *engus* in Revelation 1:3 denotes "being close in point of time, *near*."[36] Since e*ngus* in Revelation 1:3 carries a temporal meaning, it seems more contextually consistent to translate "soon" (*en tachei*) in Revelation 1:1 temporally as well.[37]

Another common understanding of the timing statements in Revelation is that the author is presenting time according to God's timetable, not man's.[38] In other words, "soon" and "near" mean "soon" and "near" from God's view of time. Support for this view is drawn from 2 Peter 3:8, which says, "Do not let this one fact escape your notice, beloved, that with the Lord one day is like a thousand years, and a thousand years like one day." Proponents of this view note that God is not limited in His consideration of time the way man is.[39] While this view could be part of the meaning that was intended, it does not seem to be a satisfactory explanation by itself of the terms used in Revelation. It seems doubtful that a reader would naturally make a connection between these timing terms and a passage like 2 Peter 3:8.

The third view, and the one that I believe makes the most sense, is that the timing terms in Revelation 1:1, 3 assume the prophetic viewpoint of the author and do not necessarily mean that the events had to occur within a few years of the time Revelation was written. The New Testament authors consistently describe this present age, or the time between Christ's two comings, as the "last days" or "latter days."[40] This attitude is expressed in 1 John 2:18, where the present age is designated as the "last hour."[41] This means that the "last days" and even the "last hour" have been ongoing for more than 1,900 years. The phrase in 1 John 2:18 is especially significant because it was written by John—who also wrote Revelation—and provides further insight into the apostle John's prophetic viewpoint.

The phrases "last days" and "last hour" both carry an eschatological dimension. Every generation of believers has lived in times that strongly cry out the sense of impending and overhanging destiny,[42] and that is true about today's generation as well. The last of these last days is always imminent or impending. Because no man knows God's schedule for the future, the time of fulfillment is always "at hand." These events are near in the sense that they are the *next* events on God's prophetic calendar. There is a nearness, next-ness, or at-hand-ness of the time.[43] As Bible commentator Robert Thomas notes, "The purpose of *en tachei* is to teach the imminence of the events foretold, not to set a time limit in which they must occur."[44] The imminency of these events, emphasized in Revelation from its commencement to its close, calls each generation to possess an attitude of expectancy and readiness.[45]

In the Olivet Discourse, a sermon that appears in Matthew 24–25, Jesus repeatedly urges believers toward imminent expectancy and emphasizes the necessity of readiness (Matthew 24:36,

42, 44; 25:10-13). Vern Poythress concludes, "Neither Old Testament prophecy nor New Testament prophecy is preoccupied with lengths of time as measured by the clock. They focus more on the character of the times. Jesus' exhortations to watch (Mark 13:32-37) do not depend on whether the Second Coming is five days away or five millennia away, but on the responsibility of the disciples after he, the master, 'leaves his house.'"[46]

Greek scholar Robert Mounce also favors the imminency view of the timing statements in Revelation:

> The most satisfying solution is to take the expression "must soon take place" in a straightforward sense, remembering that in the prophetic outlook the end is always imminent. Time as chronological sequence is of secondary concern in prophecy. This perspective is common to the entire NT [New Testament]. Jesus taught that God would vindicate his elect without delay (Luke 18:8), and Paul wrote to the Romans that God would "soon" crush Satan under their feet (Rom 16:20).[47]

First Peter 4:7, which says, "The end of all things is near; therefore, be of sound judgment and sober spirit for the purpose of prayer," is another New Testament text that uses the language of imminence to draw the reader into a sense of expectation, motivation, and responsibility. Alan Johnson states, "In eschatology and apocalyptic literature, the future is always viewed as imminent without the necessity of intervening time (cf. Luke 18:8)... Therefore, 'soonness' means imminency in eschatological terms. The church in every age has always lived with the expectancy of the consummation of all things in its day. Imminency describes an event possible any day, impossible no day."[48] Bible teacher Charles Swindoll also supports this view:

> When Revelation says Christ will come "soon" (*en tachei*) (1:1) or that his return is "near" (*engus*) (1:3),

> these terms express Christ's coming as impending, not immediate. They reflect the suddenness of Christ's coming, not a short lapse of time before His coming. If Scripture meant to indicate that Christ's coming would be in a short amount of time after His ascension, it would likely have used *oligos,* used by John in Rev. 12:12 and 17:10 to indicate a short span of time. The terms *engus* and *en tachei* support the doctrine of imminence—that Christ could come at any moment.[49]

When the time texts of Revelation are understood in light of the prophetic viewpoint of the author, the nature of the entire church age in the New Testament as the "last hour," and the imminency of the end times, it becomes clear that these texts don't necessarily refer to something immediate, but rather, something imminent. Christ's coming is *impending,* not *immediate.* "Jesus Christ can come at any moment...We are always living on the edge of eternity. And we are to be living on 'ready.'"[50] Every generation who reads the Bible is to live as if these events could come to pass at any time.

Who are the "seven Spirits of God"?

One of the potentially confusing descriptions in Revelation is the reference to the "seven Spirits" or "seven Spirits of God," which are mentioned four times (1:4; 3:1; 4:5; 5:6). Does this mean there are seven Holy Spirits?

There are two main orthodox views concerning the identity of the seven Spirits. First, some believe this refers to seven angelic beings who stand before God's throne in heaven. This view is possible because angels are sometimes called spirits. The problem with this view is that Revelation 1:4 says, "Grace to you and peace, from Him who is and who was and who is to come, and from the seven Spirits who are before His throne." Angels cannot be the source of this blessing that comes from God Himself. Whoever the seven Spirits of God are, they must be equal with God.

For this reason, it's best to interpret "the seven Spirits" as a reference to the Holy Spirit. But this raises another obvious question: Why refer to the Holy Spirit in this way? It's interesting that the Holy Spirit is referred to four times in this way, but is often referred to only as the Spirit (1:10; 4:2; 17:3; 21:10). The phrases "seven Spirits" and "seven Spirits of God" are used by John "only when the perspective is that of heaven."[51] This is John's heavenly way of referring to the Holy Spirit. But again, why this particular title?

Some believe the Holy Spirit is described this way because He operates in the seven churches (Revelation 1:11). That is possible, but the seven Spirits of God are sent out into the whole world in Revelation 5:6, not just to the seven churches, so this view seems inadequate to account for all the uses of this title. The best interpretation is to take this as a reference back to two Old Testament passages. The first one is Isaiah 11:2-5:

> The Spirit of the Lord will rest on Him, the spirit of wisdom and understanding, the spirit of counsel and strength, the spirit of knowledge and the fear of the Lord. And He will delight in the fear of the Lord, and He will not judge by what His eyes see, nor make a decision by what His ears hear; but with righteousness He will judge the poor, and decide with fairness for the afflicted of the earth; and He will strike the earth with the rod of His mouth, and with the breath of His lips He will slay the wicked. Also righteousness will be the belt about His loins, and faithfulness the belt about His waist.

Some object to the use of Isaiah 11:2-5 because there are only six activities of the Spirit listed, not seven. However, the Septuagint, which is the earliest Greek translation of the Old Testament, adds a seventh virtue—godliness—to the six.[52] Seven is the number of completion or perfection, so the mention of the seven Spirits can be understood as a reference to the character and ministry of the Spirit in His fullness and plenitude.

The second Old Testament allusion is to Zechariah 4:2-6:

> He said to me, "What do you see?" And I said, "I see, and behold, a lampstand all of gold with its bowl on the top of it, and its seven lamps on it with seven spouts belonging to each of the lamps which are on the top of it; also two olive trees by it, one on the right side of the bowl and the other on its left side." Then I said to the angel who was speaking with me saying, "What are these, my lord?" So the angel who was speaking with me answered and said to me, "Do you not know what these are?" And I said, "No, my lord." Then he said to me, "This is the word of the LORD to Zerubbabel saying, 'Not by might nor by power, but by My Spirit,'" says the LORD of hosts.

John seems to beautifully blend these two passages as a symbolic method of referring to the one Holy Spirit.[53]

What does it mean that Jesus is the firstborn of the dead (1:5)?

The word "firstborn" is *prototokos* in Greek. It's the same title used for Jesus in Colossians 1:18. It means that Jesus' resurrection is the first of its kind. Several people in the Old and New Testaments were brought back to life, but they all died again. We might say they were resuscitated. Before the empty tomb, no one returned from the grave with a glorified body, never to die again. Jesus is the firstfruits of the resurrection (1 Corinthians 15:23).

This means that the victory of Jesus over death through His resurrection guarantees resurrection life for His followers. This would have been especially meaningful to John's original readers, as they faced the threat and possibility of death for following Christ. This comforts us today, too, when a friend or loved one dies. Because of Jesus, we, too, will be raised if we know Him. We don't really buy a burial plot; we simply rent it for a while. When the trumpet sounds, all who have died in Christ will be raised to life in an immortal, imperishable, incorruptible body fit for heaven.

How can every eye see Jesus when He returns to Earth (1:7)?

Scripture is clear that when Jesus returns to Earth in power and great glory at His second advent, every person on Earth will see Him: "Behold, He is coming with the clouds, and every eye will see Him, even those who pierced Him; and all the tribes of the earth will mourn over Him. So it is to be. Amen" (Revelation 1:7). Some believe this verse includes even those who are dead at the time of Christ's coming. Tim LaHaye observes,

> This does not mean only those who are on earth at that time. It means *every* eye. Jesus Himself said to Caiaphas, the high priest, 'I say to all of you: in the future you will see the Son of Man sitting at the right hand of the Mighty One and coming on the clouds of heaven' (Matthew 26:64). Caiaphas is now dead and, unless he repented with those on the day of Pentecost, is in Hades. Thus we see that even those in Hades will see Him.[54]

For those who are alive when Jesus returns, the question remains: How can every eye see Him when He comes, since it will be day on one side of the earth and night on the other side? Many people will be on the opposite side of the earth when Jesus returns. So how can everyone see Him at the same time? There are two answers to this question that make sense.

First, it could be that Jesus will reflect His glory or even the image of His coming around the earth. His radiance could circumscribe the earth so that all will see Him.

Second, some suggest that the second coming will be gradual, transpiring over a period of time, possibly as long as 24 hours, which will allow every eye to see Him. John Walvoord said,

> Taken as a whole, the second coming of Christ is a majestic event, not instantaneous like the rapture, but extending over many hours. This perhaps explains why everyone can see it, because in the course of a day, the earth will rotate and the entire world will be able to see the approach of Christ accompanied by the hosts of heaven, which will descend to the earth in the area of the Mount of Olives (Zechariah 14:4).[55]

The second coming of Christ could last for 24 hours or even longer as His victory train marches slowly and majestically from heaven to Earth. This could be hinted at in Matthew 24:30, which says, "Then the sign of the Son of Man will appear in the sky, and then all the tribes of the earth will mourn, and they will see the Son of Man coming on the clouds of the sky with power and great glory." The "sign of the Son of Man" is probably the coming of Christ as it first appears and people on Earth begin to get their first glimpse of His approaching glory.

While we can't be certain about the exact details of *how* Christ's return will happen, we can be sure it *will* happen, and that when it does, every eye will see Him.

What does "Almighty" mean (1:8)?

Nine times in Revelation, God is referred to as the "Almighty" (1:8; 4:8; 11:17; 15:3; 16:7, 14; 19:6, 15; 21:22). He is referred to by this title only one other time in the New Testament (2 Corinthians 6:18). The reference in Revelation 1:8 may be a reference to Jesus. Some red-letter translations record these words in red, indicating that they are the words of Jesus (NASB, ESV, NKJV). If this is correct, it's a clear statement of the full deity of Christ.

The word "Almighty" is translated from the Greek term *pantokrator*, which consists of two Greek words—*pantos* ("all" or "everything") and *krator* ("to hold"). Putting this together, it means that Jesus Christ has everything in His hands, or He has His hands on everything. There is no greater truth to know and believe than that Jesus has His hands on everything. He has His hands on every planet, star, king, kingdom, church, and person, including you and me.

What does it mean that John was "in the Spirit" (1:10)?

In Revelation 1:9, John informed his readers of his geographical relocation—he had been banished to Patmos. In 1:10, he told them about another change he had undergone—a spiritual relocation. The apostle described himself as being "in the Spirit" when he recorded the visions in Revelation (see also 4:2). What does this expression mean?

This phrase probably indicates that John was caught up in the Spirit's control in a trance-like state as God transported him into the future to see and record the visions of the end of days. As Bible commentator Robert Thomas says, "In this kind of condition the natural senses, mind, and spirit are not operative in relation to and responsive to the natural world. God brings a man's spirit into direct contact with the invisible spiritual world and with the things in God's own mind, yet always accommodated to finite human perception."[56] John was "transported to a plane of experience and perception beyond that of the human senses. In that state, God supernaturally revealed things to him."[57] What John saw, heard, and recorded was the result of supernatural revelation.

What is "the Lord's day" (1:10)?

In Revelation 1:10, John said, "I was in the Spirit on the Lord's day." The phrase "the Lord's day" has been understood in two main ways. Some take this to refer to the end-time "Day of the Lord"—that is, John was saying that he had been transported in a spiritual state to the future Day of the Lord. While there are many who agree John was indeed transported in a spiritual state to the future, there are some who don't think that's what this specific passage is saying. Note that John said "the Lord's Day," not "the Day of the Lord."

The second view, which is preferred, is that John is referring to the first day of the week or what we know today as Sunday. Against this view, it's often argued that this designation for Sunday is never found anywhere else in Scripture. In the New Testament, Sunday, the day of Christian worship, is consistently referred to as "the first day of the week" (Matthew 28:1; Mark 16:2; Luke 24:1; John 20:1, 19; Acts 20:7) or "the first day of every week" (1 Corinthians 16:2). However, we need to keep in mind that Revelation was the final book of the New Testament. It's very possible that at the time John wrote it, the phrase "the Lord's day" had come into usage after the rest of the New Testament books were completed.

This terminology for Sunday is also found in the early Christian document known as *The Didache* or *The Teaching of the Twelve Apostles.* "On the Lord's own day gather together and break bread and give thanks, having first confessed your sins so that your sacrifice may be pure" (*Didache* 14:1). Most scholars date *The Didache* between AD 60–80, making it one of the earliest extrabiblical writings with bearing on the New Testament.[58] Referring to Sunday as the Lord's day became customary by the end of the second century because it was the day when the Lord was raised from the dead.[59] That is what I believe John was saying in Revelation 1:10.

Who are the "angels" of the seven churches? Are they angelic beings or humans?

In Revelation 1:20, Jesus identifies the seven stars in His right hand as "the angels of the seven churches." Then in Revelation 2–3, each of the letters to the seven churches are addressed to the "angel of the church" in each location. Apparently, after writing down the messages and visions revealed to him by Christ, John dispatched the messages intended for each of the seven churches by means of an angel. There are two main views regarding the identity of these seven angels: (1) they are angelic, heavenly beings, or (2) they are human messengers, possibly the leader of each church.

Some hold that they are angelic beings (unfallen angels). This view is attractive because the Greek word *angelos* carries this meaning consistently throughout Revelation and the rest of the New Testament. The word *angelos* occurs 175 times in the New Testament and 67 times in Revelation. Also, stars symbolize angels elsewhere in the Bible (Job 38:7; Isaiah 14:12ff). However, those who hold the angels-as-angels view of Revelation 2–3 are not agreed upon regarding the function of the angels in relation to the churches. Some maintain the angels serve as guardian angels over the churches, exercising oversight, guidance, and protection. Ray Stedman supports this view:

> In other parts of the New Testament this word in the original language does mean "messenger" rather than "angel"—but it does *not* have that meaning anywhere else in Revelation. Everywhere this word appears outside of chapters 2 and 3, it definitely refers to an *angel*—a heavenly being…Remember that in Hebrews angels are called "ministering spirits, sent forth to serve the heirs of salvation"—that is, Christians like you and me. It seems likely, therefore, that in those invisible but utterly real dimensions of spirit, there are angels assigned to each church to help the leaders and congregation know what is on God's heart. I am convinced that the "angel" or "messenger" addressed in Revelation 2 and 3 is *not* a human leader or pastor. I believe these seven letters are addressed to the *angels* of the seven churches—heavenly beings responsible for guiding the human leaders of each church.[60]

Robert Dean supports the angels-as-angels view, but holds that because angels in Revelation serve as the instruments of God's judgment, the angels in Revelation 2–3 are legal witnesses or observers to Christ's evaluation of each church.

> It is proposed in light of the attested role of angels as legal witnesses throughout Scripture and especially in Revelation that their being addressed in the letters can be explained. Just as Israel's writing prophets called upon angels to witness Israel's covenant violations, John is told to call upon angelic observers of the seven churches in the evaluation reports. The churches were expected to soberly reflect upon the realization that their performance was being reported to the same kind

> of supernatural beings that would eventually execute the coming judgments of God upon heaven and earth.[61]

While the angels-as-angels view is plausible, there are some serious difficulties with it. First, holding this view mixes up the transmission process the Lord outlined in Revelation 1:1. Remember that the order of transmission is from God the Father to Jesus, to an angel, to John, to God's people. If the angels in Revelation 2–3 are angelic beings, then the message is from the Father to Jesus to John to the angel to the churches. This changes the order originally stated in Revelation 1:1. Commenting on the angels-as-angels view, Robert Thomas says, "The complexity of the communication process is one thing that raises problems with it. It presumes that Christ is sending a message to heavenly beings through John, an earthly agent, so that it may reach earthly churches through angelic representatives."[62]

Second, the angel to each church seems to be included in the message. In most of the letters, any bad behavior taking place in the church is condemned, and angelic beings cannot be charged with wrongdoing and be called upon to repent. Thomas notes, "An even more decisive consideration against the view of guardian angels lies in the sinful conduct of which these angels are accused. Most of the rebukes of chapters 2–3 are second person singular, messages that look first at the individual messengers and presumably through them to the churches they represent. Unfallen angels do not sin, neither are they in need of repentance, as these messengers along with their churches were (e.g., 2:4-5, 14, 20; 3:1, 2, 3, 15, 17, 19)."[63]

In the original Greek text, the word translated "angel" simply means messenger, and I believe that in the context of Revelation 2–3 it is best to see these "angels" as human messengers or couriers (probably leaders) from each of the seven churches who had come to visit John on Patmos and returned to their respective churches with a copy of Revelation. "The messenger would have made the letter known to the congregation when he read it publicly. It seems unlikely that God would have sent the letter to a spirit being. The word translated 'angel' usually refers to a heavenly messenger in the New Testament, but it describes human messengers as well (cf. Matthew 11:10; Mark 1:2; Luke 7:24, 27; 9:52)."[64] The fact that the messengers of Revelation 2–3 seem to represent and bear responsibility for the actions of each respective church also supports the idea that they are the human leaders of the churches.

PART FOUR

The Churches

(Revelation 2–3)

Why did Jesus address these seven churches?

In the New Testament, there are about 30 different local churches mentioned. Why did Jesus choose to address these seven specifically in Revelation 2–3? Practically speaking, these were seven of the churches John supervised from his headquarters in Ephesus. As the last living apostle, John seems to have exercised considerable influence in Asia Minor in the AD 70s–90s after the death of the apostle Paul. It was natural for Jesus to address churches in Asia Minor that were familiar with John, who had been banished off the coast of Ephesus on the island of Patmos. Yet this still doesn't fully answer why John addressed these particular churches. These seven clearly aren't the most important churches in the New Testament. Only two of them are mentioned elsewhere in the New Testament: Ephesus and Laodicea (the city of Thyatira is mentioned elsewhere, but not the church itself). Jesus could have written to the churches in Hierapolis or Colossae, which were also in the same area, but He didn't.

I believe these seven churches were selected because they possessed spiritual conditions that were the most representative of what Jesus wanted to address as a whole. The Lord knew that His letters to these particular churches and the issues they faced would resonate with God's people throughout the church age. In every age, church leaders and members have read these letters and found themselves and their churches, their successes, their failures, their triumphs, their challenges, and their comfort in them. Also, the cities where these seven churches were located "were centers of seven postal districts, which made them well-suited to publicize the message further, once they received it."[65]

Another related question is, Why did Jesus address the seven churches in this specific sequence? Ephesus is undoubtedly first because it was the key church of the seven, and it was the closest geographically to Patmos. From there the order of the churches follows the normal postal route of that day. "The seven cities chosen as recipients of the apocalypse were situated on a great circular road that tied together the most populous, wealthy, and influential part of the Asian province, the west-central part."[66] Evidently the seven messengers to the churches carried a copy of Revelation with them. As they reached each destination, the messenger who was a part of that church would stay behind, and the others would travel on to the next location. This was done until a copy of Revelation had been delivered to each of the churches. As Thomas explains, "A messenger from each city would present the scroll to his own church who would read and probably make a copy of it before the remaining messenger(s) moved on with the original to the next city."[67]

Do the seven churches represent seven stages of church history?

Revelation begins with three chapters that deal with the present church age. The focus in these chapters is on the *lordship of Christ* (chapter 1) and the *letters of Christ* (chapters 2–3). The seven churches of Asia Minor appear as lampstands arranged in a circle. This imagery suggests that one of the key purposes of the church in this current age is to shine light into the darkness of this world. Jesus Christ is pictured standing in the middle of the lampstands as Lord of the church and walking among the lampstands as the One who sees and knows everything that is happening in and to the churches (1:12-13; 2:1). Christ is portrayed as being at the center of the churches, as He should be.

Each of Christ's letters followed this basic pattern, with a few exceptions:

1. The Commission
2. The Character
3. The Commendation (letter to Laodicea lacked this)
4. The Condemnation (letters to Smyrna and Philadelphia lacked this)
5. The Correction
6. The Call
7. The Challenge

The seven churches are significant for two main reasons. First, they had a *practical* meaning for the seven original, historical churches to which they were addressed. The original message applied first to them. Churches are a lot like people in that no two are exactly alike. There are all kinds of churches—they come in different shapes and sizes, and each has its own unique set of strengths and weaknesses. Each resides in a different location and has its own blend of people within their congregations. The same was true about churches in the first century, which is why Jesus' message to each one was different. Each letter was directed to the needs or problems that existed in each congregation.

Second, the seven churches have a *perennial* meaning, in that they are representative of all the different kinds of churches that will be present during the entire church age. There are seven churches mentioned because biblically, seven is the number of completeness or totality. These seven represent the totality of the basic kinds of churches that will always be present on Earth during the church age. The following is a simple list and description of these various kinds of churches. As you survey this list, you might ask yourself, Which of these churches represents the church I attend? And, What would Jesus say to my church? "Without a doubt, Revelation 2–3 gives us the greatest insights into what Christ values in His church and what He considers vile. These seven churches provide models to which we can compare our churches and answer the question, 'What does Christ think about our church?'"[68]

Ephesus	The Lost Love Church
Smyrna	The Suffering Church
Pergamum	The Compromising Church
Thyatira	The Tolerant Church
Sardis	The Dead Church
Philadelphia	The Faithful Church
Laodicea	The Self-sufficient Church

Here's a helpful alliterated description of the churches.[69]

Ephesus	The Loveless Church
Smyrna	The Loyal Church
Pergamum	The Lax Church
Thyatira	The Liberal Church
Sardis	The Lifeless Church
Philadelphia	The Laboring Church
Laodicea	The Lukewarm Church

Many students of Bible prophecy believe that these seven churches, in addition to their *practical* and *perennial* meanings, also represent seven successive periods of church history—that they have a *prophetic* meaning as well. Those who hold this view maintain that "they also reveal the history of the church from the time John wrote to the Rapture in seven successive periods."[70]

Thomas Constable holds this view and says, "These letters have also proved prophetic of the history of Christianity following their writing. Most Christians in the first century may not have seen this, but one can hardly deny it now. It has become increasingly obvious as church history has unfolded. Chapters 2 and 3 are therefore prophetic as are the rest of the chapters of Revelation."[71] The seven eras of church history are usually broken down as shown in the accompanying chart.

The Prophetic History of the Church in Revelation 2–3

2:1-7	Ephesus—Apostolic Era	ca. AD 33–64
2:8-11	Smyrna—Period of Persecution	ca. AD 64–313
2:12-17	Pergamum—Era of Official Patronage	ca. AD 313–606
2:18-29	Thyatira—Middle Ages	ca. AD 606–1520
3:1-6	Sardis—Protestant Reformation	ca. AD 1520–1750
3:7-13	Philadelphia—Missionary Era	ca. AD 1750–1900
3:14-22	Laodicea—Modern Period	ca. AD 1900–?

Although this prophetic view of the churches in Revelation 2–3 is popular in many circles, I believe that it is a forced interpretation of the biblical text. There is nothing explicit in the text of Revelation 2–3 or anywhere else in Revelation to indicate that these seven churches are intended to represent seven stages of church history.[72] What hint or sign is there in the text to alert the reader that seven periods of church history are in view? The seven churches Jesus addressed were seven real churches that all existed at the same time.

Another problem with this view is that the parallels are applicable only to Western Christianity. For instance, churches today in the Middle East, Southeast Asia, or Haiti would hardly be described as wealthy, self-confident Laodicean churches. Many of them are poor and persecuted. The appraisal of William Lee at this point is helpful: "That such teaching is applicable for reproof and for encouragement throughout all future time, is firmly to be maintained; but that definite periods of the Church are here predicted, or that these Epistles refer severally to successive aspects of the Divine Kingdom, may well be doubted."[73]

What does it mean that the people in the church at Ephesus left their first love?

The church at Ephesus was a flagship church in the first century. Paul, Apollos, Timothy, and the apostle John had all served and pastored there. At least eight New Testament books were written to the network of churches in Ephesus: John, Ephesians, 1 Timothy, 2 Timothy, 1 John, 2 John, 3 John, and Revelation.

As with all the letters to the seven churches, Jesus begins with commendation. He starts with the positive. He applauds this church for its dedication, discernment, and determination. The people were tireless in their service, orthodox in their doctrine, and determined in the face of discouragement. This was a five-star church with a rich heritage. But in Revelation 2:4, Jesus suddenly turns from commendation to concern, from approval to accusation, from positive to negative.

The church had one glaring deficiency—the people had "left [their] first love." The main question is, Does this refer to love for one another or love for Christ? I believe this refers primarily to their love for Christ. Revelation 2 picks up where the book of Ephesians left off about 30 years earlier. Ephesians ends with these words: "Grace be with all those who love our Lord Jesus Christ with incorruptible love" (Ephesians 6:24). The Ephesian church had failed to heed these words.

Notice that in Revelation 2, Jesus doesn't say, "You don't love Me." He says, "You don't love Me like you did at first." They no longer loved Christ the way they did at first. Their hands and their heads were in it, but not their hearts. Functional love had replaced first love. The furnace was still there, but the fire had gone out. When that happens, grace is no longer amazing. Hearing Christ's voice in the Word is no longer exciting.

This tells us that nothing substitutes for love. Neither service, nor dedication, nor orthodoxy. It also tells us that we can serve and sacrifice without really loving Christ. We can serve and wear ourselves out in ministry just out of duty—like filling out a checklist. We can hold to the right doctrine without any love or affection. Even theological orthodoxy isn't enough on its own. It's not a substitute for love for Christ. As I once heard someone say, "You can be straight as a gun barrel theologically, but as cold as a gun barrel spiritually." This loss of first love probably happened imperceptibly, like erosion, over time. I like to call this "Ephesian Erosion."

I've had the opportunity to travel to the ruins of ancient Ephesus several times. The shores of the Aegean Sea, which used to lie right next to the city of Ephesus, are now five miles away. The harbor in Ephesus filled up with silt over time via the Cayster River. The harbor slowly, steadily, silently filled up over the years. What was happening in the harbor of their city was also happening in their hearts. As Wayne Stiles says,

> Grain after grain of busyness, year after year of neglected devotion to Jesus, had finally reduced a church of such

> doctrinal strength to devotional attrition. The Ephesian Christians had lost their first love by allowing the silt of spiritual indifference to accumulate over the years. It can happen to anyone, Even to you and me...As believers we never outgrow the basics. We either build on them or abandon them. We can wake up after a number of years and discover that our lack of passion for Jesus had gradually silted Him five miles away from our hearts. We then find ourselves living in the ruins of once-vibrant spiritual lives.[74]

Jesus gives the remedy for the loss of first love in Revelation 2:5.

- Remember—Go back to the beginning and remember how God forgave you.
- Repent / Return—Turn around, do an about-face, and repent of your inner drift.
- Repeat—Do the things you used to do. Draw close to the Lord by talking to Him in prayer, reading and obeying His Word, giving and serving generously, and fellowshipping with His people.

May the Lord deliver us from Ephesian Erosion.

Who were the Nicolaitans?

Two times in Revelation, reference is made to a dangerous group within the church known as the "Nicolaitans" (2:6, 15). While much concerning this group remains shrouded in mystery, there are two main views concerning their nature and practices.

The first is that the Nicolaitans were the forerunners of the clerical hierarchy that later mushroomed in the church. This view is derived primarily from the etymology of the word "Nicolaitan," which is made up of two Greek words: *nikos* ("to conquer or overcome, victory") and *laos* ("the people"). Some believe that the Nicolaitans fostered a stark division between the clergy and the laity in the church. They are said to have been the precursors "of the clerical hierarchy superimposed upon the laity and robbing them of spiritual freedom."[75] The primary problem with this view is that it stretches what one could expect the original readers to infer from the term "Nicolaitan" without some further clarification in the text.

The second main view, and the one I hold, is that the Nicolaitans were a heretical sect that followed Nicolaus of Antioch, one of the seven original apostles' assistants mentioned in Acts 6:5. According to church history, Nicolaus later apostatized. Robert Thomas supports this view:

> The explanation that takes the Nicolaitans to be composed of followers of Nicolaus of Antioch has strong support in the early church. Added to Irenaeus are the testimonies of Tertullian Hippolytus, Dorotheus of Tyre, Jerome, Augustine, Eusebius and others. They all say this was a sect of licentious antinomian Gnostics who lapsed into their antinomian license because of an over-strained asceticism. Hippolytus adds that Nicolaus was the forerunner of Hymenaeus and Philetus who are condemned in 2 Tim. 2:17. Eusebius adds that after the group was censured by John in the Apocalypse, the sect disappeared in a very short time.[76]

No one can be dogmatic about this issue due to our limited knowledge of this group, but their connection to the practices of Balaam (2:14-15) and Jezebel (2:20-23) shed light on the nature of their error:

> While we know next to nothing about their doctrine, we can be more certain of their practices. The key is the practices linked with Balaam (2:14-15) and Jezebel

> (2:20-23). The two sins found in both are idolatry and immorality. Therefore it is likely that the twin problems were syncretism (trying to accommodate the pagans by participating in practices like emperor worship)...and an antinomian type of libertinism (showing freedom from the law by doing what one wishes).[77]

Irenaeus, a luminary in the second-century church, said, "They lived lives of unrestrained indulgence" (*Against Heresies* 1.26.3). Clement of Alexandria said, "They abandon themselves to pleasure like goats...leading a life of self-indulgence" (*The Miscellanies* 2.20). Whatever the precise beliefs and behavior of this group may have been, this much is clear: Our Lord hated their actions, which led people into loose living. And we can be assured He still hates idolatry and immorality today, so we should run from any hint of them.

William Barclay summarizes it well: "The Nicolaitans were not prepared to be different; they were the most dangerous of all the heretics from a practical point of view, for, if their teaching had been successful, the world would have changed Christianity and not Christianity the world."[78] These are instructive words for us today in our churches as well. Who is changing whom?

What does it mean to be an "overcomer"?

One of the apostle John's favorite words for believers was *overcomer*. He used the word in its various forms seven times in 1 John and 17 times in Revelation. Each of the letters to the seven churches ends with a promise of reward to the one who overcomes. The issue concerning the overcomers is whether this term refers to all believers, or to a special class of Christians who are especially faithful to the Lord and have reached a higher level of the

Christian life. There are two key reasons to understand that John was referring to all believers.

First, the promises to the overcomers in Revelation 2–3 are things that, for the most part, could be said of every Christian and not just some special class of believers. For instance, in Revelation 2:11, the overcomers in Smyrna are told, "He who overcomes will not be hurt by the second death." Because the second death is hell (20:14), the promise of not being hurt by the second death has to apply to every believer, not just some who have attained a special status. Also, in Revelation 3:5, the overcomers in Sardis are told, "I will confess his name before My Father and before His angels." This promise is also true of every believer (Matthew 10:32-33).

In 1 John 5:4-5, we see a second reason to view all believers as overcomers. There, we read, "Whatever is born of God overcomes the world; and this is the victory that has overcome the world—our faith. Who is the one who overcomes the world, but he who believes that Jesus is the Son of God?" John defined an overcomer as a believer in Jesus Christ. "The term does not refer to those who have attained to a higher level of the Christian life, but identifies all Christians. The apostle John defines it that way in his first epistle...All true believers are overcomers, who have by God's grace and power overcome the damning power of the evil world system."[79]

What is the synagogue of Satan (2:9; 3:9)?

In both the letter to the church at Smyrna and the letter to the church at Philadelphia, Jesus references a group of people who are the "synagogue of Satan."

> Revelation 2:9—"I know your tribulation and your poverty (but you are rich), and the blasphemy by those

> who say they are Jews, and are not, but are a synagogue of Satan."
>
> Revelation 3:9—"Behold, I will cause those of the synagogue of Satan, who say that they are Jews and are not, but lie—I will make them come and bow down at your feet, and make them know that I have loved you."

It seems that in both Smyrna and Philadelphia, the Jewish community had allied itself with the local pagan authorities in opposition to the believers in those cities. Their cooperation with the pagan authorities in denouncing Christians probably earned them greater standing in the larger community. They had become a "synagogue of Satan" by virtue of their standing in direct opposition to God's work. This view makes sense because in the early days of the church, Jews often opposed and obstructed the spreading of the gospel and the planting of churches (Acts 13:43-45; 14:1-7; 17:13; 18:5-17; Galatians 1:13-14; 1 Thessalonians 2:14-16).

When Jesus says, "Who say they are Jews, and are not," He doesn't mean that Gentile believers have now replaced the real Jews, but simply that ethnic Jews who stand against God's work may take the label of *Jews* but that God rejects the legitimacy of that label. Buist Fanning says those who "oppose God's saving work through Christ are showing themselves to be Jewish only by physical descent, not by inward devotion and faith like that of Abraham...These are Jews outwardly and ethnically, but in their rejection of Christ they are not truly Jews inwardly, and in their opposition to the gospel they are actually allied with Satan."[80]

Some in church history have seized upon the phrase "the synagogue of Satan" to justify persecuting Jews. Of course, these statements by Jesus should never be used to defend any form of antisemitism. Jesus' main point is to reassure the churches that nothing escapes His notice. He knows what they are enduring at the hands of both Jews and Gentiles, and ultimately, they will be rescued and rewarded by their gracious Savior.

What are the "ten days" of tribulation (2:10)?

The church at Smyrna was the persecuted, suffering church. In Revelation 2:10, Jesus told them, "Do not fear what you are about to suffer. Behold, the devil is about to cast some of you into prison, so that you will be tested, and you will have tribulation for ten days. Be faithful until death, and I will give you the crown of life."

Some have interpreted the ten days symbolically as a reference to the ten main Roman persecutions that extended over the time of the emperors Nero to Diocletian. Others interpret it as referring to a short, indefinite period of persecution. This highlights the problem of interpreting time periods symbolically in the book of Revelation: If you use that approach, as some do, there is no way to be certain what a given time period means. Furthermore, in looking at the text of the passage, we do not see any good reason for taking the ten days symbolically. It is preferable to interpret the ten days of tribulation as a reference to a literal ten-day period of brief, intense trial that the believers in Smyrna were going to suffer. The trial would be intense, but God, in His grace, would limit it to ten days.

When we face trials, we can receive comfort from this passage. While we do not know in advance how long a trial will last, we can rest assured that the entire length of the trial is under God's sovereign control. I once heard a man say that his favorite words in the Bible are, "And it came to pass." That's the way it is with any trial we face, no matter how difficult it is—eventually it will come to pass, and it'll be behind us.

What is Satan's throne (2:13)?

In His letter to the church at Pergamum, Jesus said, "I know where you dwell, where Satan's throne is; and you hold fast My name, and did not deny My faith even in the days of Antipas, My witness, My faithful one, who was killed among you, where Satan dwells." Twice in this verse Jesus refers to Pergamum as the place of Satan's throne or where Satan dwells.

There are four main views as to why Pergamum was called "Satan's throne."

1. Pergamum was the seat of the worship of Asklepios, a Greek god portrayed by the image of a snake. A temple to Asklepios was located there. In the minds of believers, the tie between Asklepios and serpents would connect Pergamum with Satan.
2. The great altar of Zeus, which rose to a height of 40 feet, was located on the acropolis of Pergamum. Since Zeus was considered the king of the gods, this could have singled out Pergamum as "Satan's throne."
3. Pergamum was filled with the temples and idols of many gods: Asklepios, Zeus, Athena, Dionysius, and Demeter. This city may have been the most outwardly pagan of the ones mentioned in Revelation 2–3.
4. Emperor worship was prominent in Pergamum. It was an official center of the imperial cult.

Any of these views are possible, but I favor the second view. The presence of this impressive altar to Zeus, and its prominence in the city, made Pergamum a uniquely pagan place to such an extent that it was as if Satan had set up his headquarters there.

What is the "hidden manna" (2:17)?

In Revelation 2:17, in Jesus' message to the church at Pergamum, one of the rewards for the overcomer is that Jesus will give him "some of the hidden manna." Manna, which means "what is it," was the food from heaven that sustained the Jewish people during their long wandering in the wilderness. A pot of manna was hidden by Moses in the ark of the covenant that stood in the Holy of Holies in the tabernacle and later in the temple.

The manna here is spoken of as hidden because we can't see or taste it now. The hidden manna won't be tasted or eaten by God's people until the rewards are handed out in heaven. Some believe the manna is a reference to communion or the Lord's Supper, which will be celebrated in the coming messianic kingdom. Others maintain that it looks to God's ultimate, complete provision for His people, just as He sustained His people fully in the wilderness with manna.

While either of those views are certainly possible, the best view is that the hidden manna is simply another way of referring to Christ Himself. Jesus, after feeding the 5,000 in the wilderness, and referring to Moses and manna, spoke of Himself as "the true bread...which comes down out of heaven and gives life to the world" (John 6:32-33). Jesus said, "I am the bread of life" (John 6:35). The reward of hidden manna, then, "signifies the eschatological reward awaiting the righteous; the greatest reward is feeding on Christ himself. Those who conquer will find joys and pleasures that have been hidden up to now."[81] We will spend all eternity enjoying those pleasures that are wrapped up in knowing Jesus more intimately.

What is the "white stone, and a new name written on the stone" (2:17)?

Revelation 2:17 says, "He who has an ear, let him hear what the Spirit says to the churches. To him who overcomes, to him I will give some of the hidden manna, and I will give him a white stone, and a new name written on the stone which no one knows but he who receives it."

The meaning of the "white stone [with] a new name" on it involves a consideration of local imagery from the first century. There are three main views related to ancient customs concerning the meaning of this white stone. First, it could refer to a procedure in the legal system of that day, in which black and white stones were used to convey either a guilty or not guilty verdict. Jurors would cast either a black (for guilty) or white (for innocent) stone into an urn when they reached a verdict. In Revelation 2:17, the white stone could symbolize the believer's acquittal before God when Christ comes. The problem here is that normally, nothing was written on the stones used by the jurors.

Second, in that day, a white stone often served as an amulet or a good luck charm that was supposed to keep a person safe. These pieces "were considered doubly effective if none but the wearer knew what was written on it."[82] This proposal fits the local imagery well; however, it seems strange for our Lord to refer to a pagan practice to convey the truth of a believer's protection in Christ.

Third, it was common in that day for a ticket to the theater, a special banquet, or some other event to be issued in the form of a white stone with a person's name on it. These *tessara* stones admitted the bearer to the event. While certainty on this view is impossible, I believe that given the context, which speaks of eating the hidden manna, the reference to an admission ticket to the future messianic banquet makes the most sense. Every believer will receive his or her special ticket to the messianic feast with a new name written on it that no one knows but the individual and the Lord.

No matter which view is correct, as Charles Swindoll says, "we can understand the big picture: if you remain faithful and take a stand for truth and morality, the result will be great reward from Christ upon His return."[83]

Who is Jezebel (2:20)?

The major problem in the church at Thyatira is that the leaders were tolerating a prominent, influential woman referred to as "Jezebel," who claimed to be a prophetess. These leaders were grossly derelict in their duty to protect the flock from false teaching. Some believe Jezebel was the wife of the pastor or leader of the church because some ancient manuscripts refer to her as "your woman" or "your wife" instead of "the woman." However, this reading is doubtful.

It's highly unlikely Jezebel was her real name. Jesus assigns the symbolic name Jezebel to evoke the Old Testament imagery associated with this false prophetess. Jezebel was the wicked wife of King Ahab of the northern kingdom of Israel. She was the daughter of Ethbaal, a Phoenician king. She led her husband and the nation astray into the worship of Baal and Asherah while opposing the true prophets of God, including Elijah (1 Kings 16:31-32; 18:4; 19:1-3; 21:17-26; 2 Kings 9:7, 22).

In the church at Thyatira, this false prophetess was promoting an ungodly tolerance of sin and influencing some of the church members to commit acts of sexual immorality and eat meat sacrificed to idols. Thyatira was known for its trade guilds. A person had to be a member of a guild to maintain their livelihood. Membership in these guilds required members to participate in common meals to pagan deities, and these events were often accompanied by sexual immorality. This put believers associated with these guilds in a very difficult position because they would suffer serious economic repercussions if they lost their jobs. Jezebel solved this dilemma by catering to the culture and teaching the believers they could profess Christ and continue to be involved in the sexual immorality and pagan worship associated with the trade guilds.

This was an ancient form of moral relativism and religious syncretism. As you can imagine, this kind of teaching gained Jezebel quite a following, just as it does today with pastors and leaders who promote and celebrate sexual sin and theological ambiguity as compatible with faithfully following Christ. Yet no matter how popular and accommodating this error might be, it is condemned by Jesus in the strongest possible language.

What is the morning star (2:28)?

As with all the letters to the seven churches, the overcomers at Thyatira are promised a blessing and reward from Jesus. The second promise to the Thyatira overcomers is "and I will give him the morning star." Because Jesus is referred to later in Revelation as "the bright morning star" (Revelation 22:16), this promise is clearly related to Him in some way. The star imagery surely harkens back to Numbers 24:17-18, which points to the ultimate rule of the Davidic King.

The term *morning star* is often associated with the planet Venus, which appears brightly in the sky in the early morning hours before the day dawns. Many make a connection here to the symbol of Venus that the Roman legions carried on their banners to represent Roman invincibility. Jesus could be employing this imagery to underscore that all sovereign power belongs to Him and His followers, not Rome or any other earthly, pagan power.

The view I prefer is that the morning star is a reference to the rapture of believers to heaven to be with Christ before the dark hours of the tribulation that precede the glorious dawn of the millennial kingdom.[84]

Can the names of believers be erased from the book of life (3:5)?

I've been surprised by the number of people who have asked me if Revelation 3:5 teaches that a true believer can lose his or her salvation. How does this verse square with what other passages say about the eternal security of the believer?

In Revelation 3:5, Jesus was speaking to the church at Sardis. He said, "He who overcomes will thus be clothed in white garments; and I will not erase his name from the book of life, and I will confess his name before My Father and before His angels." The Lord promises these believers that He will never blot their names from the book of life. Yet, as John Walvoord noted, "To some this verse seems to indicate that a believer's name *could* be blotted out, which is contrary to the Bible's clear teaching of the believer's eternal security. To make the continuance of our salvation depend upon works is a gross failure to comprehend that salvation is by grace alone. If it depended upon the believer's perseverance, the name would not have been written there in the first place."[85]

This verse, rather than being a threat that a believer's name can be erased, is an ironclad promise that it will never be blotted out. The original Greek text in 3:5 is emphatic. It includes a double negative (*ou me*) that could be translated, "I will never, ever under any circumstance erase his name from the book of life." John MacArthur states, "Incredibly, although the text says just the opposite, some people assume that this verse teaches that a person's name can be erased from the book of life. They thus foolishly turn a promise into a threat."[86] Even the believers at Sardis, who were far from ideal, were promised the hope of eternal life that will never fail. Every true believer can rest in this same promise (see also Philippians 1:6).

What is the key of David (3:7)?

In Revelation 3:7, Jesus' self-description reveals that He has "the key of David." A key is a symbol of authority or ownership. Having the key to a house or car symbolizes authority over that house or car—it belongs to the possessor of the key. In the same way, the "key of David" is a symbol of Christ's authority. This looks back to Revelation 1:18, where Jesus "has the keys of death and of Hades." It also looks even farther back to Isaiah 22:22, which refers to a royal official named Eliakim, who served in the royal household of King Hezekiah. Eliakim was one of three delegates chosen to negotiate on behalf of Judah with the Assyrians. Isaiah 22:20-22 says:

> Then it will come about in that day, that I will summon My servant Eliakim the son of Hilkiah, and I will clothe him with your tunic and tie your sash securely around him. I will entrust him with your authority, and he will become a father to the inhabitants of Jerusalem and to the house of Judah. Then I will set the key of the house of David on his shoulder, when he opens no one will shut, when he shuts no one will open.

Eliakim had complete authority over the royal treasury and served in the house of David. Eliakim prefigures or foreshadows Jesus, the ultimate heir of King David. The main thrust is that Jesus is the heir to David's throne and possesses all authority over human destiny.

What is the open door (3:7)?

This question is closely related to the previous one. Jesus, who has the "key of David," goes on to tell the church at Philadelphia, "I have put before you an open door which no one can shut" (3:8). The open door is clearly related to the "key of David," but Jesus doesn't tell us what door it is He opens and shuts.

Many maintain that the open door is a reference to ministry and missionary opportunities that have been opened for this church. This view is based on the apostle Paul's use of the "wide door" open to the Gentiles (1 Corinthians 16:9; see also Acts 14:27; 2 Corinthians 2:12).

The better view, in the context, and consistent with the parallel passage in Isaiah 22:20-22, is that the open door is the door to the messianic kingdom and ultimately the New Jerusalem, which is also mentioned in the immediate context (Revelation 3:12). The reference to the "key of David" in 3:7 indicates that Jesus "controls the door to David's house which ultimately refers to the Messianic kingdom...complete authority to admit or exclude from the city of David, the new Jerusalem, was His...Like Eliakim, except in the final sense, Jesus alone has the power to admit into or exclude from His kingdom."[87]

Jesus alone can open and shut the gate to His kingdom. No one can ever change that decision.

Does Revelation 3:10 support the pretribulation rapture view?

Revelation 3:10 is a key verse in the debate over the timing of the rapture. It is used by pretribulationists as a key support for their view that believers are exempt from the seven-year time of tribulation coming upon the earth. In Revelation 3:10, Jesus makes a promise to the church at Philadelphia of deliverance from the future tribulation period. "Because you have kept the word of My perseverance, I also will keep you from the hour of testing, that hour which is about to come upon the whole world, to test those who dwell on the earth. I am coming quickly."

Notice that Jesus tells the believers He will keep them "from" the hour of testing. The Greek preposition used here (*ek*) carries the idea of "out of, or from." This is inconsistent with the posttribulationists' idea of Christ protecting believers on Earth "through" the tribulation. Also, notice that Jesus promises to keep His people from the "hour" of testing that is coming upon the whole world. The Lord promises to keep His people not just from, or out of, the testing, but from the very "time" or hour of testing. The exemption of believers is not just from the trials of the tribulation, but from the very tribulation itself. This means that the church will be immune from the hour or very time period when this testing occurs—that is, from the tribulation period itself. The most natural meaning of this promise is that believers will not be on Earth when the hour of trial takes place. This conclusion is bolstered by the next verse, where Jesus says, "I am coming quickly." The inference is that He will deliver His people from the time of worldwide testing by His coming for them. This strongly supports the pretribulationists' notion of *removal* from the time of tribulation, not the posttribulationists' idea of *protection* through it.

Dr. Charles Ryrie provides an excellent illustration that helps explain this truth in Revelation 3:10:

> As a teacher I frequently give exams. Let's suppose that I announce an exam will occur on such and such a day at the regular class time. Then suppose I say, "I want to make a promise to students whose grade average for the semester so far is *A*. The promise is: I will keep you from the exam."

> Now I could keep my promise to those *A* students this way: I would tell them to come to the exam, pass out the exam to everyone, and give the *A* students a sheet containing the answers. They would take the exam and yet in reality be kept from the exam. They would live through the time but not suffer the trial. This is post-tribulationism: protection while enduring.
>
> But if I said to the class, "I am giving an exam next week. I want to make a promise to all the *A* students. I will keep you from the hour of the exam." They would understand clearly that to be kept from the hour of the test exempts them from being present during that hour. This is pretribulationism, and this is the meaning of the promise of Revelation 3:10. And the promise came from the risen Savior who Himself is the deliverer of the wrath to come (1 Thessalonians 1:10).[88]

Revelation 3:10 is a specific, special promise from Jesus that His bride will be kept from the hour of testing or time of tribulation that is coming upon the whole world by taking the bride away entirely from the earth. This strongly supports the pretribulation view of the rapture. As Walvoord notes, "The event in view here that will deliver the true church from the tribulation is the rapture, which must occur prior to the tribulation for this promise to have its full force."[89]

Who are the "earth dwellers" in Revelation?

Beginning in Revelation 3:10, an interesting group of people are introduced as "those who dwell on the earth," or what we might call "earth dwellers." This description is found eleven times in nine verses (3:10; 6:10; 8:13; 11:10 [twice]; 13:8, 12, 14 [twice];

17:2, 8). Who are these "earth dwellers" that Revelation mentions so frequently?

The term originates in the Old Testament, as do many New Testament terms. As Thomas Ice notes, "Every global use of 'earth dwellers' in the Old Testament appears in a judgment context…It is of special significance that both 'earth dwellers' and 'world dwellers' are used multiple times in Isaiah 24–27, often called 'Isaiah's Apocalypse.'"

Ice provides an excellent overview of this group of people:

> Since one of the main purposes of the judgments of the tribulation are to "punish" (Isa. 26:21) or "test" (Rev. 3:10) the earth dwellers, it is important to know what this means…When we survey the eleven uses of "earth dwellers" in Revelation, we see an interesting composite that develops. Not only are they to be tested in order to show their true metal [sic] (3:10), they are clearly identified as those who are persecuting and killing believers during the tribulation (6:10). Many of the judgments of the tribulation are targeted for the "earth dwellers" (8:13). It is the "earth dwellers" who rejoice and send gifts to one another when the two witnesses are killed in Jerusalem during the middle of the tribulation (11:10). When the Beast (Antichrist) is introduced in Revelation 13, it is noted that "all who dwell on the earth will worship him" (13:8, 12). Thus, 100% of the "earth dwellers" receive the mark of the beast and will spend eternity in the Lake of Fire. During the tribulation, as followers of the Beast, the "earth dwellers" will be deceived by the false signs and wonders of the Beast and will erect an image of the Beast, likely in the Jewish Temple (13:14). While the target of the preaching of the gospel by an angelic messenger will be "earth dwellers"

> (14:6), not a single one of them will follow the Lamb, instead they will wander after the Beast (17:8).[90]

The Earth dwellers, then, are unsaved people who, during the tribulation, stubbornly and steadfastly continue in their rejection of God to the very end. They are those on Earth who are spiritually hardened by Satan's deception and totally given up to evil and the hatred of God and His people. The entire horizon of their lives is earthbound.

What does it mean to be a "pillar in the temple of My God" and have "the name of the city of My God" (3:12)?

The ancient city of Philadelphia was in a very earthquake-prone area. The people there frequently experienced serious earthquake shocks. The ground under their feet was constantly moving and shaking. Often, when earthquakes shook their city, all that was left standing were the pillars of buildings, especially temples. So, a promise to be a pillar in God's temple would have been especially meaningful to these believers. A pillar speaks of stability, security, and immovability. These beleaguered believers in Philadelphia had the hope of eternity in an unshakeable kingdom.

That each believer will have "the name of the city of My God" written on them confirms their right to dwell in the heavenly city, the New Jerusalem. In eternity, the fact that we are from the New Jerusalem will literally be written all over us. "The most amazing thing is not the meaning of the 'new name' but the fact that we will share it."[91]

What does it mean that Jesus is "the Amen" (3:14)?

In His letter to the lukewarm church of Laodicea, Jesus identifies Himself as "the Amen." The title "Amen" is a transliteration from a Hebrew word that means "surely, certainly," or "so be it."

The title "Amen" is an echo of what we read in Isaiah 65:16, which refers to God twice as "the God of truth" (literally, "the God of Amen"). Interestingly, the book of Revelation opens and closes with a double "Amen" related to Jesus (1:6-7; 22:20-21). Referring to Jesus as "the Amen," denotes that Jesus fulfills all the promises of God (2 Corinthians 1:20).

Unlike the Laodicean believers, and us sometimes, who live inconsistent, hypocritical, unfaithful lives, Jesus embodies consistency, trustworthiness, and certainty. He can be trusted to keep His word. We can always count on Him. He will never let us down. He is God's Amen!

What does it mean that Jesus is "the Beginning of the creation of God" in 3:14?

There are more than 30 distinct names and titles given to Jesus in Revelation. Most of them are fairly straightforward and easy to interpret, but there are a few that require some closer investigation, such as the reference to Jesus as "the Beginning of the creation of God" in Revelation 3:14. Some have mistakenly twisted this title to mean that Jesus was the first being that was created by God—that He was the beginning or initial stage of God's creative acts. This heretical view of Christ is not what this title means.

In this verse, the word "beginning" (*arche* in the original Greek text) means "origin" or "first cause." Jesus is not the first *of* creation. Rather, He is *before* all creation.[92] He is the uncreated Creator. John wrote the same truth in John 1:1-3. "In the beginning was the Word, and the Word was with God, and the Word was God. He was in the beginning with God. All things came into being through Him, and apart from Him nothing came into being that has come into being."

Thirty years earlier, Paul had written the same truth to the church at Colosse, which was a sister church to the one at Laodicea (Colossians 4:13, 16). Colossians 1:15-18 says,

> He is the image of the invisible God, the firstborn of all creation. For by Him all things were created, both in the heavens and on earth, visible and invisible, whether thrones or dominions or rulers or authorities—all things have been created through Him and for Him. He is before all things, and in Him all things hold together. He is also head of the body, the church; and He is the beginning, the firstborn from the dead, so that He Himself will come to have first place in everything.

Both Colosse and Laodicea were in the Lycus River Valley in the western part of modern Turkey. It's possible that the same Christological error that had existed at Colosse when Paul wrote in the early AD 60s was still lingering in the church of Laodicea more than 30 years later when Revelation was written. To settle the issue once and for all, Jesus emphasizes that He is the origin, the source, the originator, the creator of all things. He leaves no doubt. John Phillips said it well: "He it is who flung the stars into space, plowed out the basins of the sea reared against the skyline of the world the mighty Himalayan range. Not a blade of grass grows without His permission; not a speck of dust moves. He is the origin of the creation of God, the all-controlling One, the dynamic Christ."[93]

Remember that in Revelation 3:14-22, Jesus is addressing the wealthy, self-sufficient, complacent church at Laodicea. This self-identification had a profoundly practical impact for those steeped in self-reliance. "In their wealth and complacency, they thought of themselves as in control; Jesus is telling them that he alone controls creation; he is the very source of their wealth and power."[94] Those who are rich in the things of this world need to remember that all they possess comes from the Creator. He owns it all. This is a relevant reminder in our day as well: Jesus is the Originator of God's creation.

What is meant by "hot," "cold," and "lukewarm" in 3:15-16?

The final church Jesus addressed in Revelation 2–3 was the church at Laodicea. This is the one church that had nothing positive in its credit column and many negatives in its debit column. The church is described as self-sufficient, self-satisfied, and arrogant. The people knew the Bible but were bored by it. They understood it but didn't apply it. "Laodicea's pride is fattened on sermons; Laodicea's soul is starved for the Word of God."[95]

Jesus' indictment of the church is stinging. "I know your deeds, that you are neither cold nor hot; I wish that you were cold or hot. So because you are lukewarm, and neither hot nor cold, I will spit [vomit] you out of My mouth" (Revelation 3:15-16). Jesus' reference to different temperatures for liquids was derived from local imagery related to the water supply in the area. There were three key cities in the Lycus Valley—Colosse, Hierapolis, and Laodicea. Colosse, which was about ten miles east of Laodicea, was known for its cool, refreshing, life-giving waters. Hierapolis, which was six miles north of Laodicea, was famous for its hot springs that were sought out for their medicinal healing powers. The water in Laodicea, however, was in between—it was lukewarm. Unlike Colosse and Hierapolis, Laodicea had no water supply of its own; the water had to be piped in from the hot springs of Denizli, a city about five miles to the south. The water did not have enough time to cool in the aqueduct, so when it arrived in Laodicea, it was tepid. The stone pipe used to transport this water from Denizli to Laodicea is still visible today.

So, it's clear that Jesus was referring to the local water supply to get the attention of the Laodiceans when He spoke about their spiritual condition. He was telling them that their spiritual condition was lukewarm. All agree on this point. But what did Jesus mean when He spoke of "hot" and "cold" water? What was He communicating? What spiritual conditions do these different temperatures describe? There are two main views.

First, some maintain that "hot" (*zestos* in the original Greek text) represents a true believer in Christ with spiritual zeal and fervor—someone heated to the spiritual boiling point, an on-fire Christian. The "cold" (Greek, *psychros*) person is viewed as someone who is the total opposite of hot—that is, an unbeliever who openly rejects the gospel. The lukewarm (Greek, *chliaros*) condition is seen as the in-between hypocrite who plays like he knows Christ but is indifferent toward Him in the heart. It's the half-and-half position. "Lukewarm is a description of church people who have professed Christ hypocritically but do not have in their hearts the reality of what they pretend to be in their actions."[96] According to this view, it's better to be cold, or totally opposed to Christ, than lukewarm, or to hypocritically profess Christ but not possess Him. The lukewarm person is someone who neither genuinely accepts Christ nor openly rejects Him.

Proponents of this view suggest that the cold person who has openly, aggressively rejected the gospel is easier to win to Christ than the lukewarm professing Christian who isn't a believer at all.

> The best suggestion is that spiritual coldness even to the

> point of open hostility, is preferable to lukewarmness and repulsive indifference because it at least suggests that religion is something to be earnest about...There is more hope for the openly antagonistic than the coolly indifferent. The state of coldness is more conducive to a person's coming to Christ than a state of lukewarmness, as illustrated in the conversion of Saul of Tarsus.[97]

View #1

Hot	a fervent, zealous Christian
Cold	an openly antagonistic unbeliever
Lukewarm	a hypocrite who professes Christ but isn't saved

The second view, the one I hold, is that all three temperatures represent believers in Christ. Hot and cold both depict believers who are useful to the Lord, just as the hot water from Hierapolis and the cold water from Colosse were both useful and beneficial. Lukewarm, on the other hand, pictures a believer who is useless and unproductive. Liquids that are hot or cold are good for something. We savor hot coffee and hot tea. We enjoy cold milk and other cold, refreshing drinks. But who wants a mug of moderate coffee or tepid tea? Or who wants room-temperature soda, or a lukewarm bath? Hot and cold liquids are good, whereas lukewarm liquids are good for nothing. Laodicea "was providing neither refreshment for the spiritually weary, nor healing for the spiritually sick. It was totally ineffective."[98]

View #2

Hot and Cold	a useful, beneficial Christian
Lukewarm	a useless Christian who needs to repent

This view fits the local imagery that Jesus employs. Jesus is telling the believers at Laodicea that like their water supply, they are barren and useless to Him at the time He's writing to them, which makes Him sick. For them, the remedy is to repent and return to the Lord.

Is Revelation 3:20 a gospel invitation?

Revelation 3:20 is probably the best-known, most-often quoted, most-often memorized verse from the final book of the Bible: "Behold, I stand at the door and knock; if anyone hears My voice and opens the door, I will come in to him and will dine with him, and he with Me." This verse is beautiful in its simplicity and sincerity. It's clear to anyone reading it that it is an open invitation from Jesus for the Laodicean church—both corporately and individually—to seek His presence and open the door for Him to come in. But what is the specific invitation, and to whom is it addressed—believers or unbelievers? There are four main views of Revelation 3:20.

View #1—Salvation

Many view Revelation 3:20 as an explanation of how to become a Christian.[99] For them, the door on which Christ knocks is the heart of an unbeliever who needs to allow Christ to come in to bring reconciliation and forgiveness. The problem with this view is the context in which the Lord addresses the Laodiceans as believers. In Revelation 3:19, Jesus says, "Those whom I love, I reprove and discipline; therefore be zealous and repent." The words "love...reprove...discipline...be zealous...repent" are consistent with someone who is already a follower of Christ, not an unbeliever. If this is correct, then the very next verse could not be an offer of salvation to unbelievers. The context set in Revelation 3:19 is against this view.

View #2—Eschatological

According to this view, the door on which Jesus knocks is "the eschatological door through which Christ will enter at His second advent."[100] Christ is pictured as standing at the door and ready to return at any time, which stresses the urgency of people repenting and being ready. Support for this view is drawn from frequent uses of the door imagery to portray Christ's return (Matthew 24:33; Mark 13:29; Luke 12:36; James 5:9). Also, the mention of the "door" into Christ's kingdom in the near context of Revelation 3:7-8 bolsters this view. While this view is possible, it doesn't fit the context of Revelation 3:20 very well, where believers must open the door for Jesus to come in. Conditioning the coming of Christ on believers opening the door for Him give us far more authority over Christ's return than Scripture allows.

View #3—Corporate Fellowship

With this view, the door is the door of the church. Revelation 3:20 is directed to the church to open the door to let Jesus in. In a pathetic image, Jesus is pictured as standing outside the church, knocking at the door and seeking entrance to His own church. While this view seems credible, the invitation from Jesus seems to be extended to any person within the church who will open the door, not to the church as a whole. Jesus uses words that indicate the call is directed to individuals within the church ("anyone...him...him...he"), not the entire church.

View #4—Individual Fellowship

This position views the door as the hearts of individual believers within the church who need restored fellowship with their Lord. Christ is outside the church calling the believers within the church to repent and open the door of their heart so that He can restore fellowship with them. I believe this view is the most consistent with the context and language of Revelation 3:20.

Bible commentator Grant Osborne observes,

> Note the progression of the metaphor. Jesus arrives at the door as a visitor, identifies himself, and seeks admission. The person must respond, open the door, and allow him admittance. Fellowship results as they share a meal. Spiritually, this denotes a call to repentance and the believer's response in getting right with Christ.[101]

Charles Ryrie states this view succinctly in the note on Revelation 3:20 in the *Ryrie Study Bible*: "How incredible that Christ should be kept outside His own church! How gracious that He should still seek entrance! Christ is appealing to the worldly, compromising believers in the church to return and enjoy full fellowship with Him."

Charles Swindoll agrees that this is the interpretation of Revelation 3:20, but he also sees an application for evangelism: "Though this passage has some application for evangelism, the Lord was primarily concerned here with moving Christians from halfhearted commitment to full-blown repentance."[102]

Whatever view one takes of Revelation 3:20, the story about Holman Hunt captures the stirring appeal of this text. Hunt painted a famous picture of Christ as the Light of the World, depicting the Lord wearing a crown of thorns and standing outside the dead-bolted human heart, patiently knocking and calling for admittance. A copy of this painting now hangs in Saint Paul's Cathedral in London. When it was first displayed, critics gathered to comment on the work. One of them turned to the painter and said, "Mr. Hunt, you have painted a masterpiece, but you have made one very serious mistake. You have painted a door without a handle." "That is no mistake," replied the artist. "The handle is on the *inside*."[103]

Have you opened the door?

PART FIVE

The Consummation

(Revelation 4–22)

SECTION ONE

The Scene in Heaven

(Revelation 4–5)

Is Revelation 4:1 a reference to the rapture?

In Revelation 1:19, we are given the inspired, threefold outline of Revelation: "Therefore write the things which you have seen, and the things which are, and the things which will take place after these things." As we have already seen, "the things which you have seen" refers to Revelation 1; "the things which are" covers Revelation 2–3 (the current church age); and "the things which will take place after these things" looks to the future events of the end times that begin in Revelation 4:1 and continue to the end of the book.

In Revelation 4:1-3, we see John snatched up from the island of Patmos to heaven and transported in a kind of spiritual time machine into the future, where he receives visions concerning the end times.

> After these things I looked, and behold, a door standing open in heaven, and the first voice which I had heard, like the sound of a trumpet speaking with me, said, "Come up here, and I will show you what must take place after these things." Immediately I was in the Spirit; and behold, a throne was standing in heaven, and One sitting on the throne. And He who was sitting was like a jasper stone and a sardius in appearance; and there was a rainbow around the throne, like an emerald in appearance (Revelation 4:1-3).

The repetition of the words "after these things" (Greek, *meta tauta*) from Revelation 1:19 in 4:1 signals that the time after the present church age has been reached. For this reason, many view Revelation 4:1 as a reference to the rapture. Tim LaHaye supports this view:

> It was no coincidence that the first thing to happen after John has described the seven churches (which we have seen represent not only a message to each individual church but also to the seven periods of church history) is his being taken up into heaven. Inasmuch as John was the last remaining apostle and a member of the universal Church, his elevation to heaven is a picture of the Rapture of the Church just before the Tribulation begins. It is also noteworthy that the invitation comes from Christ Himself, who is the One who "first spoke" to John "like a trumpet" (1:10). Note how similar to this event is the promise of our Lord to His disciples near the end of His life about taking them to His Father's house (John 14:2-3)...The Rapture of the Church is not explicitly taught in Revelation 4 but definitely appears here chronologically at the end of the Church Age and before the Tribulation.[104]

Proponents of this view, who are exclusively pretribulationists, note the following similarities between the rapture of the church as described in 1 Thessalonians 4 and the relocation of John to heaven in Revelation 4:

1 Thessalonians 4	**Revelation 4**
End of the church age	End of the church age
Trumpet sounds	Voice like a trumpet
Church caught up to heaven	John caught up to heaven

It is tempting for those who hold to the pretribulation rapture view to make this connection because in the pretribulation understanding of end time events, the rapture of the church would occur at this point in the book. However, I do not believe the rapture of the church is presented either directly or indirectly in Revelation

4:1. Rather, all we see is the personal movement of John from Earth to heaven, not the movement of the church to heaven. To equate John's transfer to heaven with the rapture or make it a picture of it simply goes beyond what the text actually says.

Whether one views Revelation 4:1 as a picture of the rapture or not, I like this observation from David Jeremiah, which connects the two open doors in heaven:

> In Revelation 3 we saw a door closed and Christ was seeking entrance; now in chapter four we see an open door through which we can view the regal splendor of God. Revelation 4 leads us into a throne room, where the King is sitting.

Twice in the Book of Revelation we see an open door. The first time is in Revelation 4:1 when John sees "a door standing open in heaven," the last time is in Revelation 19:11 when he "saw heaven standing open and there before me was a white horse." The first time the door opens, somebody goes up, and the next time, somebody comes down.[105]

Will believers see God in heaven?

When I was a young boy, I remember asking a noted guest speaker at our church if he thought we would see God in heaven. He told me that we would see Jesus, who, of course, is God, but that we would not see God the Father because He is spirit. The answer seemed okay, but for some reason I was never really sure that he was correct. Something inside me said that I would someday see my heavenly Father, but I didn't have any idea if the Bible supported my impression.

What I didn't realize at that time was that all the Lord's people long to see Him. As the psalmist said, "As the deer pants for the water brooks, so my soul pants for You, O God. My soul thirsts for God, for the living God; when shall I come and appear before God?" (Psalm 42:1-2). The psalmist wanted to see God. And in the New Testament, speaking for all the disciples, Philip said to Jesus, "Show us the Father" (John 14:8).

As I grew older, I discovered some key passages that confirm we will see the manifestation of God (the Father) in heaven as well as God the Son. One of these passages is in Revelation 4.

> *Matthew 5:8*—"Blessed are the pure in heart, for they shall see God."
>
> *Revelation 4:2-3*—"Immediately I was in the Spirit; and behold, a throne was standing in heaven, and One sitting on the throne. And He who was sitting was like a jasper stone and a sardius in appearance; and there was a rainbow around the throne, like an emerald in appearance."

The One who sits on the throne in Revelation 4–5 is not Jesus, but God the Father. In Revelation 5:13, the One who sits on the throne (God the Father) is clearly distinguished from the Lamb (God the Son).

> *Revelation 22:4*—"They will see His face, and His name will be on their foreheads."

However, there are three key verses people often cite to argue that even believers in Christ will never see God in heaven:

> *Exodus 33:20*—"He said, 'You cannot see My face, for no man can see Me and live!'"
>
> *John 1:18*—"No man has seen God at any time; the only begotten God who is in the bosom of the Father, He has explained Him."

> *1 Timothy 6:15-16*—"He who is the blessed and only Sovereign, the King of kings and Lord of lords, who alone possesses immortality and dwells in unapproachable light, whom no man has seen or can see. To Him be honor and eternal dominion! Amen."

So how do we reconcile these seemingly contradictory biblical statements? We will see God, yet no man can see God and live. I believe the three verses that say that man cannot see God and live refer to man in his unperfected, unglorified condition in an earthly body. In our present state, we cannot behold the manifestation of God and survive the experience. However, in our immortal, imperishable bodies in heaven, we will be granted the inestimable privilege of seeing the localized manifestation of our heavenly Father. We will see the Father in heaven!

John MacArthur supports this view:

> I believe that in heaven we will see God Himself with our physical eyes...God will reveal the light of His glory, and through perfect eyes we will see the very face of God. God is spirit (John 4:24), and spirit is invisible; therefore, whenever God manifests Himself He does so in the form of light...Seeing Christ and the Father will eternally awe us.[106]

The fact that we will see the Father and the Son in heaven does not mean that there is more than one God. The true God is one (Deuteronomy 6:4). He is one in essence or nature, yet three in person. Another way to put it is that God is one "what" (one essence) and three "whos" (three persons—Father, Son, and Holy Spirit). We will see the manifestation of the Father in heaven as well as the face of our blessed Savior. "They will see His face, and His name will be on their foreheads" (Revelation 22:4; see also 1 Corinthians 13:12).

Who are the 24 elders?

In Revelation there are 12 references to a group called the "twenty-four elders," or "elders" (4:4, 10; 5:5, 6, 8, 11, 14; 7:11, 13; 11:16; 14:3; 19:4). There are three main views concerning their identities: (1) angelic beings; (2) all of the redeemed, including Israel (the 12 tribes) and the church (12 apostles); and (3) the church. Let's briefly survey each one.

Angelic Beings

Many believe that the elders are angelic beings, or more specifically, a special subgroup of angels who appear before God's throne in heaven, often referred to as "a council of heavenly beings who surround God's throne."[107] Several points make this view unlikely. One problem is that the term "elders" (Greek, *presbuteros*) is more easily related to humans than angels. A second problem is that the angels are distinguished from the 24 elders in Revelation 7:11. They seem to be two different groups. And third, angels could not sing the song in Revelation 5:9 that the 24 elders sing when they praise God for redeeming "us from every tribe and tongue and people and nation."[108]

The Church and Israel

Others believe the 24 elders depict the totality of God's redeemed people in heaven—Israel (the 12 tribes) + the church (the 12 apostles). The problem with this view is that Israel is not a completed group at this time. The elders are pictured as already having received their rewards (crowns); however, Old Testament saints will not be resurrected and rewarded until the second coming of Christ, which will take place after the tribulation (Daniel 12:1-3). Revelation 4 occurs before the tribulation period is unleashed on Earth in Revelation 6.

The Church

There are five main arguments for identifying the 24 elders as the glorified church or bride of Christ in heaven.

First, they are sitting on thrones. The church, or bride of Christ, is repeatedly pictured as reigning with Jesus, while angels are not (Revelation 2:26-27; 3:21; 5:10).

Second, they are clothed in white robes. Jesus promised believers in Sardis and Laodicea white garments (Revelation 3:5, 18). The church of Jesus Christ is pictured clothed in fine linen white and clean in heaven (Revelation 19:8) and when returning to Earth with Jesus (Revelation 19:14). Angels do wear white garments in Revelation 15:4, but this clothing is connected to the church much more often.

Third, they are wearing crowns. The victor's crown is promised to believers in Revelation (Revelation 2:10; 3:11, 21) but never to angels. The elders are described repeatedly in the same ways as overcomers in the churches in Revelation 2–3. This tips the scale for me that this is the group in view.

Fourth, they are called "elders." In the New Testament, "elders" are the representatives of God's people in local New Testament churches. These elders in Revelation, in the same way, are representative of the church. Significantly, angels are never called "elders" in the New Testament.

Fifth, they are 24 in number. In the Old Testament, King David divided the Levites into 24 divisions or orders, which represented the total number of priests. In the New Testament, each believer is a priest, so this is an apt way to signify a complete representation of the church.

Taking all the relevant evidence into account, I believe the 24 elders represent the completed body of Jesus Christ, which includes all believers, both Jew and Gentile, from the day of Pentecost in Acts 2 to the rapture of the church to heaven. If it is true the elders are the glorified church in heaven, then this provides another link of strong support for the pretribulation rapture view because the church is pictured as being in heaven before the tribulation begins in Revelation 6.

Who are the four creatures like a lion, calf, man, and eagle (4:7)?

When John is transported to God's throne room in heaven, in the middle of the throne and around it he sees a strange sight. He sees four living creatures. These angelic creatures combine the features of both cherubim (Ezekiel 1 and 10) and seraphim (Isaiah 6), although they are never specifically identified as either. They are simply labeled "living creatures." They are described in Revelation 4:6-7: "In the center and around the throne, [there are] four living creatures full of eyes in front and behind. The first living creature was like a lion, the second creature like a calf, the third creature had a face like that of a man, and the fourth creature was like a flying eagle." These four likenesses are drawn from the Old Testament in Ezekiel 1:5-6, 10-11. In Ezekiel, the order is different (man, lion, ox [calf], eagle).

The early church fathers viewed these four faces as related to the four Gospels; however, there was very little agreement as to which image represented which Gospel. Modern commentators who hold this view usually relate these creatures to the major emphasis in each of the four Gospels in relation to Jesus.

> Matthew: lion—Jesus is the lion of the tribe of Judah; He is king, royalty
>
> Mark: ox—the servanthood of Jesus
>
> Luke: man—the humanity of Jesus
>
> John: eagle—the deity of Jesus

This view seems too tenuous to be maintained with any reasonable degree of certainty.

Another possibility is that the face of a lion speaks of strength and majesty; the calf represents patient, humble service and labor; the man, the zenith of God's creation, pictures intelligence and reason; and the eagle, the chief among the birds, represents clear vision and speed in carrying out their divinely appointed mission, or possibly sovereignty and supremacy.[109]

While the meaning of the imagery behind these four faces is impossible to state with certainty, the best view is that the faces of these creatures, who appear continually in God's presence, represent the varied aspects of God's creation.

> Lion—wild animals
>
> Calf—domesticated animals
>
> Man—humanity
>
> Eagle—birds

These four living creatures serve as a constant picture to God and all the angels in heaven of what all creation ought to be—that is, fully submissive and devoted to God.[110]

What is the seven-sealed scroll in Revelation 5?

Revelation 4–5 forms the backdrop for all that follows. John is transported from Earth to the throne room of God in heaven. He sees many things, but the most significant scene is the transfer of a seven-sealed scroll (Greek, *biblion*) from the hand of God the Father to the hand of God the Son. The opening of this scroll in Revelation 6:1 begins the end of days.

There are many views regarding the contents of the scroll. Here are seven of the most prominent ones:[111]

1. The book of the new covenant, which has yet to be instituted with Israel in the millennial kingdom
2. A book of redemption (the Lamb's book of life)
3. The title deed to the earth
4. The events of the tribulation (a doomsday book)
5. A bill of divorce—the Lamb divorcing unfaithful Israel
6. A record of the sins of mankind
7. A testament or will

When the context and evidence are considered, the best view is that the seven-sealed scroll is a will. A will was the only document in the first-century world that was closed with seven seals. Every person in the churches John addressed would have understood this imagery. David MacLeod describes the first-century practice of executing a will or testament:

> Behind the imagery of the scroll with the seven seals is a legal practice of the Romans for plebians, who could not have formal legal wills. The testamentary disposition or will for plebians was called a *mancipatio*, from *manum capere*, meaning "to take ownership." When a man made such a document, he assembled seven people: five witnesses, an official called a *libripens* whose professional instrument was a pair of copper scales, and a family friend called a *familiae emptor* ("buyer for the family"). He would put a price on the scales and the inheritance was transferred to him. The sole guarantee that the heirs would get their inheritance was the integrity of this family friend, the *familiae emptor*. He was the executor of the estate, but he actually owned it (as interim heir) until he gave it to the heirs. All seven

> would seal the scroll. When the testator died, the *familiae emptor* would pay the debts of the estate and then give the heirs their promised inheritance.
>
> In Revelation 5 all these actions are fulfilled by Christ. He is the Testator who died for the world and bequeathed to believers their inheritance. He is Himself the Heir of the kingdom of God. In a sense He was like a *familiae emptor* who drew down the scales of divine justice with the weight of the purchase price, His own precious blood. He took the place of sinner and preserved for believers their future estate in the Father's house (Gal. 4:1-7). He appeared in open court and rendered account, paying all the debts against the estate (Rom. 3:24-25).[112]

So the scroll with the seven seals portrays the believers' inheritance, which is to rule with Christ over the world to come, or the 1,000-year kingdom on Earth that Christ establishes at His second advent (Revelation 20:4-6; see also Hebrews 2:5).

The scroll must be opened for the Son to receive His inheritance from the Father, and the seven seals are judgments. As we read onward through Revelation, we see that the seventh seal contains the seven trumpet judgments, and the seventh trumpet contains the final seven judgments, the bowls. After the scroll is completely opened, Jesus takes the throne. The kingdom is now His.

SECTION TWO

The Tribulation

(Revelation 6–18)

Why do the scenes in Revelation alternate back and forth between heaven and Earth?

One of the most interesting features in the book of Revelation is the way the reader is taken back and forth between heaven and Earth. To me, this has always been one of the most encouraging features of the book:

Scene on Earth	Revelation 1–3
Scene in heaven	Revelation 4–5
Scene on Earth	Revelation 6–7
Scene in heaven	Revelation 8:1-5
Scene on Earth	Revelation 8:6–14
Scene in heaven	Revelation 15
Scene on Earth	Revelation 16:1–20:10

Revelation 4–5 offers a breathtaking view of heaven that centers on the very throne of God. The following two chapters, 6–7, focus on earthbound events. Then, in 8:1-5, the scene switches back to heaven...and so it goes. What does this reveal to us? That the God who sits on the throne in heaven is in complete control of what transpires on Earth. The events happening on Earth—no matter how frightening and devastating—are neither haphazard nor random. They are ordered by the One seated on His throne. Heaven rules on Earth. God superintends all that takes place. This should be a supreme comfort and reassurance to us in uncertain, troubled times.

In Heaven	On Earth
The heavenly throne (4)	
The Lamb on the throne (5)	
	The first four seal judgments (6:1-8)
The fifth seal judgment (6:9-11)	
	The sixth seal judgment (6:12-17)
	The sealing of the 144,000 (7:1-8)
The great multitude (7:9-17)	
Preparations for the trumpet judgments (8:1-5)	
	The first six trumpet judgments (8:6–9:21)
	The little book (10)
	The ministry of the two witnesses (11:1-14)
The announcement of the seventh trumpet (11:15-19)	
The expulsion of Satan (12:1-12)	
	The activity of Satan (12:13-17)
	The activity of the two beasts (13)
	Judgment at the end of the Great Tribulation (14)
The announcement of the seven last judgments (15)	
	The seven bowl judgments (16)
	Babylon's destruction (17–18)
Praise for judging (19:1-10)	
	The second coming of Christ (19:11-21)
	The millennial reign of Christ (20)

Who is the rider on the white horse in 6:1-2?

Right on the heels of the heavenly scene in which the seven-sealed scroll is handed over to the Lamb, God pulls back the corner of the veil on the future and allows John to peer into the final days of this age. At the breaking of the first seal, John gets his very first glimpse of the future worldwide tribulation. And what he sees is a lone rider on a white charger, bent on conquest.

> When the Lamb broke one of the seven seals...I heard one of the four living creatures saying as with a voice of thunder, "Come." I looked, and behold, a white horse, and he who sat on it had a bow; and a crown was given unto him, and he went out conquering and to conquer (Revelation 6:1-2).

Who is this first horseman of the apocalypse? And why is his horse white?

Because we wouldn't expect a literal rider on a white horse to come riding all across the earth during the tribulation, we can conclude this is symbolic or figurative language. However, even with symbolic language in use, we can be sure this is describing something that will occur. Our job as students of the Bible is to determine what this passage is telling us.

As we examine what is present in the text, we see four things that must fit with whatever view we adopt:

1. The white color of the horse
2. The bow in the rider's hand
3. The crown on the rider's head
4. The series of victories or conquests

There are three main views regarding the identity of this first horseman. Let's look at each one, and see which best fits the language and context.

First, some believe this rider and his white horse symbolize the proclamation of the gospel. Commentator George Eldon Ladd supports this view:

> The rider is not Christ himself, but symbolizes the proclamation of the gospel of Christ in all the world. The details with which the first horseman is described do not weaken this conclusion. A bow is often used in Scripture as a symbol of divine victories...This does not necessarily mean complete and utter conquest, but it does mean that the proclamation of the gospel will win its victories. It will be preached effectively in all the world; and in spite of an evil and hostile environment characterized by human hatred, strife, and opposition, the gospel will make its way victoriously in all the world.[113]

Ladd sees this as a great encouragement to the church in the face of stern opposition by the Roman Empire. The chief problem with this view is that the four horsemen all usher in judgments. The positive preaching of the gospel is alien to this negative context. In addition, one has to ask why a bow would symbolize the preaching of the gospel. Normally, a bow portrays warfare.

Second, there are some who believe the rider on the white horse is Jesus Christ. Because Jesus appears in Revelation 19:11-21 riding a white horse, it is presumed that He is the rider here as well. It is true that the color white is often associated with Christ in Revelation (1:14; 2:17; 3:4, 5, 18; 4:4; 6:11; 7:9, 13; 14:14; 19:11, 14; 20:11). But there are two problems with this interpretation. First, there are significant contrasts between the riders in Revelation 6:2 and Revelation 19:11-19:

Rider in Revelation 6:2	Rider in Revelation 19
Bow without any arrows	Sword
Wears a *stephanos* crown	Wears many *diadem* crowns
Imitates war	Ends war
Commences the tribulation	Culminates the tribulation

Donald Grey Barnhouse shows how diametrically opposed these two riders are:

> We have only to look at the details of this prophecy to see how far removed this is from the Lord Jesus Christ of the Scriptures. The counterfeit is revealed by a detailed comparison of the two riders. The One whose name is the Word of God has on His head "many crowns." The symbol is of all royalty and majesty. The Greek word is *diadem*. The horseman of the first seal wears no diadem. The false crown is the *stephanos*. Its diamonds are paste. It is the shop girl adorned with jewelry from the ten-cent counter imitating the lady born and bred who wears the rich jewels of her inheritance. All is not gold that glitters. No amount of gaudy trappings can deceive the spiritual eye. Clothes do not make the man in spite of the proverb.[114]

A second reason to reject this view is that in Revelation 6:1, Jesus is opening the first seal. It would be strange for Jesus to open the seal and, at the same time, be one of the riders.

If the rider on the white horse is not the proclamation of the gospel, or Christ Himself, then who is he? Clearly, he must be someone who closely resembles Christ, because like Christ, he rides a white horse and wears a crown. That brings us to the third view, which is that this rider pictures the Antichrist.

For me, the most convincing evidence of this identification are the clear parallels between Matthew 24:4-14 and Revelation 6–7.

Parallels Between Matthew 24:4-14 and Revelation 6–7

Matthew 24:4-14	Revelation 6–7
False Christs (24:4–5)	The rider on the white horse (6:1-2)
Wars and rumors of wars (24:6-7a)	The rider on the red horse (6:3-4)
Famine (24:7b)	The rider on the black horse (6:5-6)
Famines and plagues (24:7b; Luke 21:11)	The rider on the pale horse (6:7-8)
Persecution and martyrdom (24:9-10)	Martyrs (6:9-11)
Terrors and great cosmic signs (Luke 21:11)	Terror (6:12-17)
Worldwide preaching of the gospel (24:14)	Ministry of the 144,000 (7:1-8)

In Matthew 24, Jesus gives the divine interpretation of the rider on the white horse. He is the final false Christ, or Antichrist. He will begin his ride at the start of the tribulation to bring peace in the midst of global upheaval and turmoil. Revelation 6:2 describes the rider on the white horse as having a bow and wearing a crown. He wears a victor's crown and has a bow—but no arrows! This indicates he will win a bloodless victory at the beginning of his career. The bow represents the threat of war, but apparently this war will never materialize because the Antichrist is able to gain victory through diplomacy and peaceful negotiations, or possibly through threats of destruction.

What does "do not damage the oil and the wine" mean (6:6)?

As the third seal is broken in Revelation 6:5-6, the jet-black horse gallops across the globe in the horrific wake of the first two horsemen. The apostle John recorded what he saw:

> When He broke the third seal, I heard the third living creature saying, "Come!" I looked, and behold, a black horse; and he who sat on it had a pair of scales in his hand. And I heard something like a voice in the center of the four living creatures saying, "A quart of wheat for a denarius, and three quarts of barley for a denarius; and do not damage the oil and the wine."

The third horse is black as midnight. Black as tar. The mere color itself signals something ominous, dark, and dreadful. But what do this horse and rider represent? Although there have been several different suggestions for the identity of this horse and rider, they clearly personify famine and hunger. The black color undoubtedly signifies the lamentation and sorrow of extreme deprivation.

Four points favor this identification of the black horse and its rider.

First, after the red horse and the outbreak of war, food shortages cannot be far behind. This is the way it has always been. Hunger is one of the wretched results of war.

Second, the identification is confirmed by the parallel with Jesus' list of end-times signs in Matthew 24:7, as we have already seen. According to Jesus, the first three birth pangs of the end times are false messiahs, war, and famine. As we have seen, this tracks parallel with the horsemen in Revelation 6:1-8.

Third, the color black often signifies the haunting specter of hunger. For instance, Lamentations 4:8-9 says, "Their appearance is blacker than soot, they are not recognized in the streets; their skin is shriveled on their bones. It is withered, it has become like wood. Better are those slain with the sword than those slain with hunger; for they pine away, being stricken for lack of the fruits of the field."

Fourth (and the clincher) is the fact that the rider holds a pair of scales in his hand. This refers to a bar with scales at both ends—or some kind of weight at one end with a pan suspended at the other.[24] In Revelation 6:6, the rider is carefully weighing food on the scales: "He who sat on it had a pair of scales in his hand." This activity reveals that food is in short supply. Consuming food in carefully weighed-out portions is a sign of famine (Ezekiel 4:16-17). The haunting phantom of famine rides forth across the earth.

With the world economy suffering hyperinflation, the kind of food people can afford will quickly degenerate. Because it will take all a person can earn in a day just to buy enough regular food for one person for one day, people will resort to lower-quality food just to put something on the table for their families.

Wheat was the main food of the ancient world. Barley was a lesser-quality grain with less nutritional value, often used to feed animals. During the famine of the end times, people will quit buying the foods they have been used to and will turn to cheaper foods. By eating food of grossly inferior quality, a family of three could eat three meals a day of barley, whereas they could only eat one meal of wheat. To put this in terms of today's market, it will take all the money a man or woman can earn in a day just to buy meat and potatoes for one person for one day *or* macaroni and cheese or beans to feed a whole family for a day. The world will be consumed by the rider on the black horse. Earth will writhe in the clutches of stabbing hunger.

Revelation 6:6 makes clear that the famine that breaks out during the first half of the tribulation will not be universal. One group will be exempt from this horror. As the masses endure runaway inflation and degenerating food quality, the wealthy will enjoy a temporary exemption from this time of judgment. Verse 6 adds, "Do not damage the oil and the wine." This means that while the basic staples for life are being decimated, the oil and wine will go untouched. And in that day, oil and wine will be in the categories of luxury than wheat and barley.[115]

During the coming tribulation, the gulf between rich and poor will grow even wider. Food will be so expensive that only the wealthy will have enough. Famine will relentlessly hammer the middle and lower classes. The vast majority of people will be wallowing in misery, but the rich will continue to bask in the comforts of their luxurious lifestyle. The wealthy will continue to flourish. They will not only have the necessities of life but will still enjoy the luxuries as well. This will make the suffering of the masses even more unbearable as they watch the privileged few indulge themselves.

In AD 92, in the face of a grain shortage, the Roman emperor Domitian ordered half of the vineyards of Asia Minor to be destroyed to make room for growing more grain. This resulted in riots in Asia Minor because wine was a major source of income in that area. In response, Domitian revoked his earlier edict and ordered that anyone who allowed their vineyards to go out of production would be prosecuted. For John's readers, this was a familiar picture of a case when grain was in shortage, but when it was illegal to harm the supply of oil and wine. Some believe that this prophecy in Revelation 6:5-6 was fulfilled in this edict of Domitian. However, I believe this will be fulfilled in the end times, during the first half of the seven-year tribulation. Domitian's edict served as an excellent contemporary illustration of Revelation 6:5-6, but not a fulfillment of it.

I don't know about you, but it seems unfair to me that the rich will be exempt from God's judgment. Will God be playing favorites? Not at all. The rich will escape this first wave of judgment, but as the tribulation moves along, they, too, will cry out in despair.

The rich will not escape God's judgment for long. Under the sixth seal judgment in Revelation 6:15-17, the wealthy will suffer the heavy hand of God's wrath.

> The kings of the earth and the great men and the commanders and the rich and the strong and every slave and free man, hid themselves in the caves and among the rocks of the mountains; and they said to the mountains and to the rocks, "Fall on us and hide us from the presence of Him who sits on the throne, and from the wrath of the Lamb; for the great day of their wrath has come; and who is able to stand?"

Eventually, during the tribulation, judgment will affect everyone. There will be no place to hide, even for the rich and famous.

What are the "wild beasts" in 6:8 that kill one-fourth of the earth?

Revelation 6:8 describes the fourth horseman, named Death, who will use four means to wreak havoc upon the earth: "Authority was given to them over a fourth of the earth, to kill with sword and with famine and with pestilence and by the wild beasts of the earth."

The first three means of devastation are clear: war, famine, and disease.

The fourth way this rider will destroy is by "the wild beasts of the earth" (6:8). The meaning of this has generated some diverse opinions. There are three main views on the identity of these wild beasts.

First, it's possible this refers to literal wild animals that will become unrestrained and ferocious during the tribulation. In the chaos of the end times they will search for prey, taking advantage of the weak and defenseless.[116] Support for this idea is found in several Old Testament verses. Leviticus 26:22 says, "I will send wild animals against you, and they will rob you of your children, destroy your cattle and make you so few in number that your roads will be deserted."

Deuteronomy 32:24 reads, "I will send wasting famine against them, consuming pestilence and deadly plague; I will send against them the fangs of wild beasts, the venom of vipers that glide in the dust." Jeremiah 15:3 says, "I will send four kinds of destroyers against them...the sword to kill and the dogs to drag away and the birds and the wild animals to devour and destroy." The problem I have with this view is that it seems implausible that crazed animals could have such a devastating impact as set forth in Revelation 6:8.

Another view is that "the wild beasts of the earth" is a reference to military and political leaders who murder and slaughter people all over the earth during the end times.[117] This view is based on the usage of the word "wild beast" (*theerion* in Greek) in Revelation. The word is found 38 times in Revelation, and in every instance, refers to the beast (the Antichrist) and his henchman, the false prophet. These two men are described in detail in Revelation 13.

While either one of the first two views are certainly possible, many excellent commentators and Bible teachers believe that the "wild beasts of the earth" refer to diseases and pandemic plagues that are transmitted from animals to humans.[118] I agree with this view because of the close connection between "pestilence" and the "wild beasts of the earth" in Revelation 6:8. At this point, Revelation 6 intersects deeply with what we see today with COVID-19 and other deadly plagues.

Adrian Rogers, a well-known pastor and teacher, said,

> What kind of animal do you think of when you think of a beast? A bear? A tiger? A rhinoceros? Beasts come in many sizes. If you look up the word in a dictionary, the definition may define a beast only as a four-footed

> mammal. Do you know what beasts carried the Black Death? Rats. These tiny four-footed mammals carried a bubonic bacterium that killed more than twenty-five million people.[119]

The devastating effect of rats is well known in history, but today the wild beasts of the earth can include bats, mosquitos, monkeys, pigs, and birds. Deadly viruses are hopping from animals to humans at an alarming rate. Our world is ripe for the pale rider. The stage could not be more perfectly set for the fourth horseman to begin his ride. The plagues from wild beasts of the earth are multiplying and intensifying.

Animal-borne plagues that jump or cross over from animals to humans are known as zoonotic diseases. A host of them have appeared throughout history, but they've mushroomed during the last few decades. Here are a few examples of zoonotic diseases.

- Bubonic plague—carried by rodents and even cats, and hopped to humans through bites from infected fleas (often rat fleas)
- Rabies—transmitted through a bite from an infected animal, usually dogs or bats
- Malaria—transmitted by mosquitos
- Dengue fever—transmitted by mosquitos
- Spanish flu—killed 50 million people worldwide, source was avian (bird) flu, an H1N1 virus
- AIDS/HIV—traced to a type of chimpanzee in Central Africa
- Lyme disease—comes from infected ticks
- Ebola—first identified in 1976, comes from infected bats
- SARS—identified in 2003, originated in bats

- MERS—identified in 2012, originated in bats and passed to camels
- Avian (bird) flu—transmitted by birds
- Swine flu—outbreak in 2009, comes from pigs

According to the Centers for Disease Control and Prevention, three out of every four new or emerging infectious diseases in people come from animals.[120] That's staggering. Seventy-five percent of all new diseases cross from animals to humans. Al Mohler notes the role animals play in so many plagues:

> Now we're talking about a coronavirus, and one of the interesting and troubling things about this kind of virus is that it appears to emerge primarily from animals, transmitted from animal to animal until some kind of mutation allows the transmission from animal to human, but the most frightening mutation takes place when the virus mutates in order to spread from human to human. Now...one of the reasons so many of these viruses start out in places like China is because there is a closer proximity between human beings and animals. Not only that, but animals and other animals. We are told that some of these viruses, these coronaviruses, exist naturally within bat populations, the bat populations then spread it to other populations. Often you hear about the role played by swine, by pigs in this process, because pigs are often the engine or the context for the mutation of the virus into a new form.[121]

An article in *Newsweek* further highlights the dramatic rise of animal diseases jumping to humans.

> This novel coronavirus is a classic example of the emergence of new microbial threats and their spread. The vast majority of the new infectious diseases that have

> presented in recent decades have come from animals... These so-called zoonotic pathogens live in animals or are carried by insects and then "jump" to humans. When they jump, they can cause new diseases that we haven't had to deal with before, like 2019-nCoV. Unfortunately, we're seeing the emergence of several new zoonotic diseases each year—any of which may become the next pandemic.[122]

New diseases are emerging at an alarming rate. Some are more deadly than others, but "on average, in one corner of the world or another, a new infectious disease has emerged every year for the past 30 years."[123] That's at least 30 new diseases that have cropped up in just the last 30 years. Novel corona virus is the newest one.

These new diseases are erupting at the same time globalism and rapid means of travel are expanding to provide the perfect vehicles to spread these plagues all over the earth with lightning speed. Coronavirus may just be the first of a new wave of pestilence that explodes across our planet. The pale horse is ready to sweep the globe, with Hades racing right behind.

The pandemics of the end times will have repercussions beyond the plagues themselves. They will further the argument of the Antichrist for a one-world leader who has the reach and power to respond to such plagues to bring them under control. The pale rider will give greater power to the rider on the white horse, enabling him to consolidate his global kingdom.

What's the relationship between the seven seals, seven trumpets, and seven bowls?

One of the ongoing issues with Revelation is how the different parts fit together chronologically. The basic issue concerning the seals, trumpets, and bowls is whether they are successive (one after the other) or simultaneous (going back over the same time period). The first view is usually referred to as the succession, progression, or chronological view, and the second view is often called the parallel, concurrent, or recapitulation view. While there are many variations of the recapitulation view, the common thread in this view is that the trumpets and bowls are parallel.

Succession View	**Simultaneous View**
seals → bowls → trumpets	seals → trumpets + bowls

There are three main reasons for concluding that these series of judgments in Revelation are successive—that is, they occur in a chronological arrangement. First, the contents of the judgments are not the same. If they are parallel or go back and are repetitious, one would expect them to be the same or at least very similar. Although there are certainly some similarities, especially between the trumpet and bowl judgments, they are not similar enough to support the parallel view. Second, Revelation 15:1 says that the seven bowl judgments are the last seven plagues "because in them the wrath of God is finished." The fact that they are the last indicates a succession or chronological progression in the judgments. Third, the judgments increase dramatically in their severity as the action advances in Revelation. This, too, indicates a chronological progression.

Another way to describe the relationship between the seals, trumpets, and bowls that supports the succession view is that they are telescopic. That is, each successive series of judgments introduces the next series. The first six seals are opened, then there's a pause between the sixth and seventh seals. When the seventh seal is opened, it unleashes the seven trumpets. Then between the sixth and seventh seals there is another pause or intermission. The seventh trumpet in Revelation 11 carries the action all the way to the second coming of Christ, so the seventh trumpet unleashes the seven bowls. Each series of judgments emerges from the previous series. This supports the succession view.

Here's a chart to help portray this telescopic view of the judgments.

Telescopic View

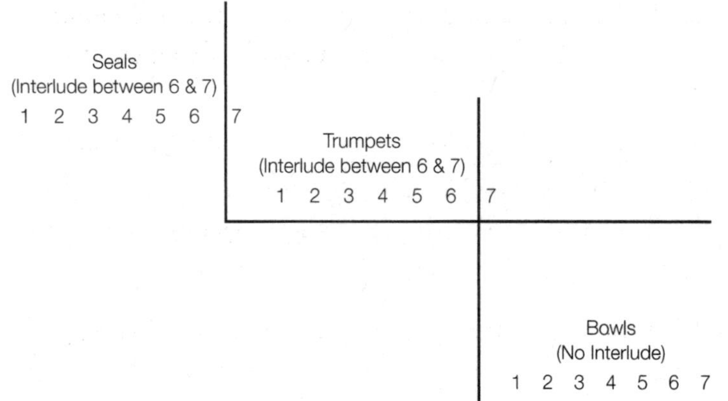

Why do some people believe the rapture occurs between the sixth and seventh seals?

The timing of the rapture of the church is a hotly debated eschatological issue. The most recent of the main views is commonly known as the pre-wrath rapture. This view was pioneered by Marvin Rosenthal, who wrote *The Pre-Wrath Rapture of the Church* (1990), and Robert Van Kampen, who wrote *The Sign* (1992). Marvin Rosenthal titled this view "prewrath rapturism."[124] Alan Hultberg is a leading proponent of this position.

According to Rosenthal, the pre-wrath view is founded on these four main pillars:

1. The Rapture of the church immediately precedes the outbreak of the Day of the Lord.
2. The Day of the Lord commences at some point within the second half of the seventieth week of Daniel, also known as the tribulation period.
3. The cosmic signs associated with the sixth seal herald the approach of the Day of the Lord.
4. The Day of the Lord begins with the opening of the seventh seal (Revelation 8:1).[125]

Hultberg states, "The prewrath position rests on two major theses: that the church will enter the last half of Daniel's seventieth week and that between the rapture of the church and the return of Christ to earth there will be a significant period of extraordinary divine wrath."[126]

Rosenthal offers this summary of his view that there is distinction between the great tribulation and the Day of the Lord:

> The Great Tribulation will be followed by cosmic disturbances, which will indicate that the Day of the Lord is about to commence. At that time God's glory will be manifested. Speaking broadly, "that day" will have two objectives. First, the Rapture of the church will occur; that will then be followed by the Lord's judgment of the wicked as He begins His physical return to the earth.[127]

To summarize, pre-wrath rapturism maintains that the rapture will transpire about three-fourths (five-and-a-half years) of the way through the tribulation. The mayhem and chaos in the first three-fourths of the tribulation is viewed as the wrath of man and the wrath of Satan, *not* the wrath of God. The outpouring of divine wrath (the Day of the Lord) is not inaugurated until the seventh seal in Revelation 8:1. Believers, therefore, will be raptured to heaven between the sixth and seventh seal judgments.

While this view has several weaknesses, I will spotlight two main problems. First, pre-wrath rapture advocates restrict the outpouring of God's wrath and the Day of the Lord to the final quarter of the seven-year tribulation. As the tribulation period progresses, there's no doubt that the frequency and intensity of God's wrath escalates like labor pains, but I believe God begins pouring out His wrath with the opening of the first seal in Revelation 6:1, not after the sixth seal.

The judgments in Revelation 6 parallel the signs of the end laid out by Jesus in Matthew 24, and Jesus describes all the judgments as birth pains, which links them all together. They're a package deal. Saying that some of them are divine judgments while others are not is at odds with the words of Jesus.

The seal judgments in Revelation 6 are opened by the Lamb (Jesus Christ), triggering the beginning of the tribulation. Jesus is in complete control. As the seals are opened, all of them are followed by the outpouring of God's wrath. The seven seals, seven trumpets, and seven bowls are all divine judgments. The trumpet judgments come out of the seventh seal (Revelation 8:1). As Paul Feinberg notes, "The entire tribulation period is a time of God's wrath, from the first seal to the last bowl."[128] "It is the Lord Jesus who breaks the seals and releases judgments on the earth. All the judgments (seals, trumpets, and bowls) come from the scroll and the One who breaks all the seals. All are demonstrations of divine wrath."[129] Limiting God's wrath to the trumpet and bowl judgments, as the pre-wrath view proposes, is not supported by the text of Scripture.

Second, there are significant issues with the pre-wrath view and the contention that the Day of the Lord begins about three-fourths of the way through the seven-year tribulation. In 1 Thessalonians 5:2-3, the apostle Paul says the Day of the Lord will come upon the world suddenly and unexpected, "like a thief in the night," like "labor pains upon a woman with child," and while unbelievers are saying, "Peace and safety!" Paul Benware highlights the challenge facing the pre-wrath view of the beginning point of the Day of the Lord:

> Such would not be the case if the Day of the Lord did not begin until approximately three-fourths of the way through the Seventieth Week, since Christ's great sign of the "Abomination of Desolation" (at the midpoint), several years of Great Tribulation, and numerous other signs and events would just have transpired. It would not seem that the coming of the Day would be sudden and unexpected as Paul taught.
>
> Paul also teaches that the unbelieving people on whom the Day suddenly breaks forth will be saying "Peace and safety" when it happened. "Peace" here points to circumstances that do not evoke a feeling of alarm; "safety" has the thought of being unshaken, secure from enemies and danger...They feel that everything is safe and secure and see not outward evidence to dispute the feeling...But it seems highly unlikely that three-fourths of the way through the Seventieth Week that people

> will be saying such things...In fact, more than one-fourth of the world's population will have recently been destroyed by famines, disease, and widespread warfare on the earth. It does not seem likely that the people of the world would be saying "Peace and safety" when more than a billion people have recently perished and incredible cosmic disturbances are taking place. But it would make sense for them to be saying "Peace and safety" if the Day of the Lord begins at the start of the Seventieth Week, well before the terrible events that take place throughout the Seventieth Week.[130]

First Thessalonians 5:2-3, and the suddenness of the outbreak of the Day of the Lord, supports a pretribulation rapture timing for the rapture and refutes pre-wrath rapturism and its view that the rapture happens at the seventh seal.

Who are the 144,000 in 7:1-8?

In the book of Revelation, the seven seals, seven trumpets, and seven bowls move the action forward. Sprinkled between these series of judgments are interludes or breaks that allow glimpses of the key players and events that are part of the unfolding drama of the ages.

The first intermission, interlude, or pause in the action in the apocalypse occurs in Revelation 7. This chapter falls between the opening of the sixth and seventh seals and describes two groups of people whose activities and ministry will begin during the time the seals are being opened. These two groups are the 144,000 and the innumerable host.

There are many views about the identity of the 144,000, and, in fact, there are groups that have tried to identify themselves as being part of the 144,000. David Jeremiah refutes two of these attempts:

> The sealed ones are not the Seventh-Day Adventists. These folks believe that the 144,000 are members of their church who are found observing the Jewish Sabbath when the Lord comes back again, and they are raptured up to glory. For this to be true, every Seventh-Day Adventist would have to be Jewish in lineage and from one of the twelve tribes.
>
> They are not the cult known as the Jehovah's Witnesses. This group used to claim that all of their members were in this number, but when the group grew to more than 144,000 members, they had to revise their teaching.[131]

There are two main views regarding the identity of the 144,000. First, many hold that they are symbolic of the church. The problem with this view is that, in the New Testament, the church is never equated with Israel. As John Walvoord says,

> The prevalent idea that the church is the true Israel is not sustained by any explicit reference in the Bible, and the word Israel is never used of Gentiles and refers only to those who are racially descendants of Israel, or Jacob. The remnant of Israel as portrayed in Revelation should not therefore be taken as meaning the church. It would be rather ridiculous to carry the typology of Israel representing the church to the extent of dividing them into twelve tribes as was done here, if it was the intent of the writer to describe the church. It is instead a clear indication of God's continued purpose for the nation Israel and their preservation through this awful time of trouble.[132]

Many who hold that the 144,000 in Revelation 7:1-8 are the church also view them as parallel to the great host of Gentiles in Revelation 7:9-18. They see these passages as describing the same group. However, a simple side-by-side comparison of the two groups reveals that they are not the same.

	Revelation 7:1-8	Revelation 7:9-18
Number	144,000	Innumerable
Nationality	Jews	Gentiles
Location	Earth	Heaven
Condition	Protected	Martyred

The second view, the one I hold, is that the 144,000 are male Jewish believers who will be saved and sealed by God for service during the tribulation. Support for this view is drawn from the clear statements of the text. As Dr. Charles Ryrie says, "The identification is no problem if the language is understood plainly."[133] There is no reason in the context to take the 144,000 as anything other than 12,000 men from each of the 12 tribes of Israel. All the other references in the New Testament to Israel refer to literal Israel or the Jewish people. Changing this consistent meaning at this late point in Scripture makes no sense.

Clearly, there will be Jews saved during the tribulation other than the 144,000. Many of them will be martyred. The 144,000 is a special group God will use to spread the gospel and that He will protect and preserve to the end of the tribulation. "These 144,000 Hebrews will serve as faithful, courageous, and diligent witnesses for Christ during the darkest period of earth's history… God will use them to fulfill the ancient Old Testament calling of the Hebrew people to be God's witnesses among the nations."[134] God never leaves Himself without a faithful witness.

Why is the tribe of Dan omitted from the list of the 12 tribes of Israel in Revelation 7?

The listing of the 12 tribes of Israel throughout the Bible is an interesting study. The lists often differ—seldom are the tribes exactly the same, and seldom do they appear in the same sequence. It seems that the biblical authors adapt the list to their specific purpose. Much of the confusion can be solved if we remember that Joseph's inheritance was split into two parts for his two sons, Ephraim and Manasseh. Sometimes Ephraim includes Manasseh, and vice versa. Also, Levi is sometimes omitted because the Levites had no tribal allotment in the land.

But this doesn't explain the absence of Dan in Revelation 7. Why is Dan missing? Many in church history have speculated that the omission rises from the fact that the Antichrist will be a Jew from the tribe of Dan. The chief problem with this view is that the Antichrist will more likely be a Gentile, as we will discuss later in conjunction with Revelation 13. Of course, from a practical perspective, John didn't include Dan in his list because he was simply recording what he heard. He was not at liberty to change anything.

John Walvoord surveys the possible reasons for the omission of Dan:

> In this list Manasseh is mentioned but Ephraim is not, and in place of Ephraim, the name of Joseph his father is given in verse 8. No explanation is made concerning this substitution. There is also no mention of the tribe of Dan, and the Bible does not tell us why Dan should be omitted. One suggestion made for this omission is that the Antichrist would come from the tribe of Dan (cf. Gen. 49:17). A more common explanation is that the tribe of Dan was one of the first to go into idolatry,

> was small in number, and probably was thereafter classified with the tribe of Naphtali, another son of Jacob born to the same mother as Dan.[135]

Swindoll wisely avoids any unnecessary speculation: "Though we may not be able to fully explain why these particular tribes were selected to make up the 144,000 sealed in Revelation 7, we can be certain that God has His reasons."[136]

Who is the great multitude in 7:9-17?

There are two great companies in Revelation 7. The first is a special group of 144,000 Jewish witnesses. The second is an innumerable host of Gentiles. Revelation 7:9-14 describes the latter group in this way:

> After these things I looked, and behold, a great multitude which no one could count, from every nation and all tribes and peoples and tongues, standing before the throne and before the Lamb, clothed in white robes, and palm branches were in their hands; and they cry out with a loud voice, saying, "Salvation to our God who sits on the throne, and to the Lamb." And all the angels were standing around the throne and around the elders and the four living creatures; and they fell on their faces before the throne and worshiped God, saying, "Amen, blessing and glory and wisdom and thanksgiving and honor and power and might, be to our God forever and ever. Amen."
>
> Then one of the elders answered, saying to me, "These who are clothed in the white robes, who are they, and where have they come from?" I said to him, "My lord,

> you know." And he said to me, "These are the ones who come out of the great tribulation, and they have washed their robes and made them white in the blood of the Lamb."

This group of believers is not the church, as some suppose. The church of Jesus Christ will be raptured to heaven before the outpouring of God's wrath on the earth (1 Thessalonians 1:10; 5:9; Revelation 3:10). The multitude in Revelation 7 is comprised of Gentiles who trust Christ after the rapture and are martyred for their faith during the great tribulation. They are tribulation saints. They are part of the final harvest of souls during the tribulation. This means there will be great revival during the great tribulation.

Why is there silence in heaven for about 30 minutes (8:1)?

The silence described in Revelation 8:1 reminds one of Habakkuk's doxology: "The Lord is in His holy temple. Let all the earth be silent before Him" (2:20). Up to this point, the mood in heaven has been that of shouting and the playing of harps. Suddenly it all changes dramatically with the opening of the seventh seal. As Bible commentator Earl Palmer says, "It is the silence of mystery and intense waiting...There is communicated in a very dramatic way in this quietness the full and awesome authority of God. Everything must wait for his kingly move."[137] Everything is on hold, pausing for what comes next. The next kingly move occurs when seven angels are given seven trumpets to sound. The response is breathless anticipation of what's coming—a holy hush in heaven before all hell breaks loose on Earth. John MacArthur says,

> After all that loudness, as the full fury of the final judgments is about to be released, silence falls on the heavenly

> scene. The implication is that when the judgment about to happen becomes visible as the seventh seal is broken and the scroll unrolled, both the redeemed and the angels are reduced to silence in anticipation of the grim reality of the destruction they see written on the scroll. The half an hour of silence is the calm before the storm. It is the silence of foreboding, of intense expectation, of awe at what God is about to do.[138]

Remember, the scroll that Jesus is opening has seven seals. When the seventh seal is opened, the inheritance will be secured. But when it's opened, the seventh seal unleashes seven more judgments. The worst is still to come. This sobering realization brings total silence to the halls of heaven. "Though thirty minutes is not ordinarily considered a long time, in this case it indicates that something tremendous is about to take place. It may be compared to the silence before the foreman of a jury reports a verdict; for a moment there is perfect silence and everyone awaits that which will follow."[139] It will be the silence before the storm.

Are the trumpet judgments symbolic or literal?

The first six trumpet judgments are outlined in Revelation 8–9:

> First Trumpet (8:7)—Bloody hail and fire: one-third of vegetation destroyed
>
> Second Trumpet (8:8-9)—Fireball from heaven: one-third of oceans polluted
>
> Third Trumpet (8:10-11)—Falling star: one-third of fresh water polluted

Fourth Trumpet (8:12)—Darkness: one-third of celestial bodies darkened

Fifth Trumpet (9:1-12)—Demonic invasion: five months of torment

Sixth Trumpet (9:13-21)—Army of 200,000,000: one-third of people killed

There is agreement among futurists that the trumpets represent judgments; however, there is disagreement about the exact nature of the judgments. The disagreement revolves around whether the language is symbolic or should be understood in a more literal sense. For those who take these visions symbolically, some would interpret the great star that falls from heaven in Revelation 8:10-11 as a person of great influence who poisons the earth with evil.[140] The sun, moon, and stars are understood as governing powers and authorities.

Then there are those who view the trumpet judgments as literal events that will happen in the end times. The first four trumpets are separated from the final three, which are designated as "woe" judgments. The first four describe real astronomical/ecological events that will pummel the earth during the tribulation. Those who interpret these judgments literally see no valid reason, based on the text, to spiritualize the judgments.

Whether we take these visions as literal or symbolic, we know this for sure: The devastation will be "so dreadful that no amount of government aid, relief efforts, or advanced preparation will be able to bring recovery."[141]

Are the trumpet judgments the result of human actions or divine judgment?

Another key interpretive issue in Revelation has to do with the source of the trumpet judgments. What is the relationship between divine sovereignty and human agency? Or to put it another way, who is doing what? Are these judgments the direct judgment of God, or are they the result of human actions, such as nuclear war, global warming, and so on?

With the seal judgments, it is clear that human agency is involved in the judgments because they represent the rise of Antichrist, war, famine, and deadly plagues (Revelation 6:1-8). All of these involve human forces operating under the hand of God's sovereign control.

But the trumpet and bowl judgments raise some questions. Many believe these judgments also result from or involve at least some human activity, especially nuclear conflagration and its fallout. Ed Hindson supports this view:

> These trumpets may be associated with nuclear or chemical warfare. The devastation they predict was unknown and unfathomable in the ancient world. These destructions are certainly beyond anything known to the people of John's day, which makes the Apocalypse all the more fascinating. There is no way John could have imagined these great catastrophes had he not seen them by divine permission in these visions. The cataclysmic destruction he pictures certainly sounds like the devastating effects of nuclear war.[142]

Yet a careful look seems to indicate the trumpet and bowl judgments are direct judgments from the hand of God, and not the result of human activity. There are two main points that support this idea. First, the trumpet and bowl judgments are eerily similar to the plagues God unleashed upon the Egyptians in Exodus. Those plagues were sent directly from God apart from any human agency. To make the judgments in Revelation the result of nuclear war or other human activity is to overlook their striking similarity to the plagues inflicted upon the Egyptians.

Second, in Revelation, the people on Earth who are experiencing the effects of these judgments understand that they are coming from God (11:13; 16:9, 11, 21). They don't blame other people, nuclear weapons, or war for their misery. Rather, they put the blame squarely on God.

What is "Wormwood" (8:11)?

The terrible third trumpet is sounded and described in Revelation 8:10-11.

> The third angel sounded, and a great star fell from heaven, burning like a torch, and it fell on a third of the rivers and on the springs of waters. The name of the star is called Wormwood; and a third of the waters became wormwood, and many men died from the waters, because they were made bitter.

The awful contamination and poisoning of the world's water supply will be caused by a burning star called "Wormwood." The plague will be so severe that many people will die. A disaster of this magnitude is difficult to imagine.

The great star that falls from heaven could be an asteroid or a meteor shower, or some form of biological or nuclear warfare if one takes a natural view of these disasters. Whatever the exact nature of this object, it has a strange name: Wormwood. The Greek word translated "Wormwood" is *apsinthos* which refers to a shrub or herb used to concoct a very bitter-tasting medicine called absinthe.

Regardless of the exact meaning of the great star called Wormwood, "None of us could imagine a third of all the rivers and lakes becoming poisonous. All the scares about polluted waters due to industrial waste in recent years seem quite pallid next to this terrible disaster."[143]

Are the trumpets in the first or second half of the tribulation?

I believe the most difficult problem that interpreters face in understanding Revelation is the chronology or sequence of events—where to place certain events in relation to the seven-year timeline of the tribulation. This is especially true when it comes to the trumpet judgments. Most futurist interpreters put the seven seal judgments in the first half of the tribulation and the seven bowl judgments in the last half just before the second coming of Christ. However, there is disagreement and debate over where to place the seven trumpet judgments. Good arguments are made by both sides. I locate the seven trumpet judgments in the second half of the tribulation for one simple reason—their severity. The fourth seal judgment kills one-fourth of Earth's population. The sixth trumpet judgment, by contrast, kills one-third of those who are left. This totals one-half of Earth's population. If the trumpets are placed in the first half of the tribulation, along with the seals, then one-half of the world's people will be dead *before* the great tribulation even begins. This seems to go against the words of Jesus in Matthew 24:21-22, where He says that the final half of the tribulation will be the worst time period in human history.

So it makes more sense to place the trumpet judgments in the second half of the tribulation. Putting the trumpets in the first half front-loads too much of the judgment into the first half of this time of trouble.

Who is the "star from heaven" who opens the bottomless pit (9:1)?

The fifth trumpet sounds in Revelation 9:1, and a bottomless pit is opened by a "star from heaven." "Then the fifth angel sounded, and I saw a star from heaven which had fallen to the earth; and the key of the bottomless pit was given to him."

The actions of this "star" and the identification of it as "him" clearly indicate that this is not a literal heavenly object but an angelic being. In Scripture, stars are often a symbol of angels (Job 38:7 and possibly Revelation 1:20, depending on one's interpretation of the stars there as humans or angels).

The main question about Revelation 9:1 is whether this is a good, elect angel or a fallen, evil angel—that is, a demonic spirit. The reason for the divergence of opinion is that the angel is described as "fallen to the earth," which leads some to conclude that this indicates he is a fallen angel or demon, or even Satan himself, who is often described as fallen from heaven (Isaiah 14:12-14; Luke 10:18; Revelation 12:7-9). It is true that Satan and demons are fallen; however, it seems that the word "fallen," in this context, is not being used in the spiritual sense but simply to denote movement from the higher level of heaven to the lower level of Earth.

Three points support the view that this is a good angel. First, why would God entrust a fallen angel with the key to his own jail cell? Second, if this is an evil angel, it would mark the only time in the book of Revelation when God uses an evil angel to carry out

His will. Third, in Revelation 20:1-3, a good angel comes to lock Satan in the shaft of the abyss or bottomless pit.[144] If a good angel locks the abyss in Revelation 20, it follows that in Revelation 9, a good angel would also unlock the abyss to set imprisoned demonic spirits free.

Of course, the key message is that God is sovereign even over the prison house of Satan and demons.

What are the "locusts" in 9:1-12?

One of the strangest texts in Revelation is the description of a swarm of locust-like creatures that rise out of the "bottomless pit" (9:1-12):

> The fifth angel sounded, and I saw a star from heaven which had fallen to the earth; and the key of the bottomless pit was given to him. He opened the bottomless pit, and smoke went up out of the pit, like the smoke of a great furnace; and the sun and the air were darkened by the smoke of the pit. Then out of the smoke came locusts upon the earth, and power was given them, as the scorpions of the earth have power. They were told not to hurt the grass of the earth, nor any green thing, nor any tree, but only the men who do not have the seal of God on their foreheads. And they were not permitted to kill anyone, but to torment for five months; and their torment was like the torment of a scorpion when it stings a man. And in those days men will seek death and will not find it; they will long to die, and death flees from them.
>
> The appearance of the locusts was like horses prepared for battle; and on their heads appeared to be crowns

> like gold, and their faces were like the faces of men. They had hair like the hair of women, and their teeth were like the teeth of lions. They had breastplates like breastplates of iron; and the sound of their wings was like the sound of chariots, of many horses rushing to battle. They have tails like scorpions, and stings; and in their tails is their power to hurt men for five months. They have as king over them, the angel of the abyss; his name in Hebrew is Abaddon, and in the Greek he has the name Apollyon. The first woe is past; behold, two woes are still coming after these things.

Several years ago, I took my family to visit Carlsbad Caverns in New Mexico. I can still feel our slow descent into the bowels of the earth and still smell the musty air of the caverns. The trip was an exciting adventure from start to finish. But the highlight was the flight of the bats from the cave at dusk, when they began their nightly exodus to feed on the insects in the surrounding area. As the thousands of bats flew out of the hole in the earth, the little light that remained at dusk was darkened by the thick clouds of bats. The scene was awesome in its beauty and uniqueness.

In a much more vivid and frightening scene, Revelation 9:2-3 describes the opening of the abyss, the release of "the smoke of a great furnace," and myriads of locust-like beings swarming out on the earth and darkening the skies. As smoke billows forth from this prison house of wickedness, these locusts will ooze from the abyss.

But what or who comes forth from this subterranean pit to block out the rays of the sun? Who are these locusts that swarm out of the abyss and darken the skies of the earth? Are they literal locusts, or are they some other creature?

The locusts in Revelation 9 have been interpreted at different times in church history to symbolize heretics, the Goths, the Mohammedans, the mendicant orders, the Jesuits, the Protestants, the Saracens, and the Turks. However, the description in Revelation 9:2-5 reveals that these locusts are demonic beings in material, visible form. They are the uncanny denizens of the abyss, locusts of a hellish species animated with infernal powers. This passage describes an unbelievable demonic invasion of the earth by Satan's war corps in the last days.

While these beings are described as locusts, they have eight other characteristics:

1. They are like horses
2. They have crowns like gold on their heads
3. They have faces like the faces of men
4. They have long hair like the hair of women
5. They have teeth like those of lions (denoting their voracity)
6. They have coverings like breastplates of iron (like heavy body armor)—this reveals that they are well protected; man is helpless against their onslaught
7. As they move, they sound like chariots or horses going to battle
8. They have tails like those of scorpions

In each case, the word "like" is used to indicate that a comparison is being made and that something other than a literal description is intended. This doesn't mean these beings are not literal; but rather, that John is describing them in the best way he can by comparing them to things that are familiar.

The following litany gives another way to list the description of these locusts from hell:

Heads: crowns like gold

Faces: like men's

Hair: like women's

Teeth: like lions'

Breastplates: like iron

Wings: like the sound of chariots, of many horses

Tails: like scorpions

Just imagine the unbelievably scary appearance of these invaders from the abyss. They are long-haired, horse-shaped, flying locusts with scorpion tails and golden crowns above human faces covered with skin like a coat of armor. They are a kind of "infernal cherubim"—a combination of horse, man, woman, lion, scorpion, and locust. Their size is not given, but they are clearly much larger than ordinary locusts.

There are six factors that support the view that these beings are demons in material form. First, as we have already seen in verse 1, their leader is a fallen angel or demon. Second, they come from the abyss, which, in the New Testament, is consistently the place where some fallen angels or demons are consigned (see, for example, Luke 8:31).

Third, they cannot be literal locusts because they attack people, not vegetation. Revelation 9:4 says, "They were told not to hurt the grass of the earth, nor any green thing, nor any tree, but only the men who do not have the seal of God on their foreheads." Literal locusts feast on vegetation, not people.

Fourth, these locusts only torture those who do not belong to God (Revelation 9:4). This is consistent with the activity of demons.

Fifth, demons apparently have the ability to appear in a variety of material forms, both human and animal. In Revelation 16:13, for example, demons appear as unclean frogs.

Sixth, the description of these beings, as given in Revelation 9:7-10, clearly goes far beyond anything from this world.

Seventh, literal locusts have no king over them. Proverbs 30:27 says, "The locusts have no king, yet all of them go out in ranks." By contrast, the locusts described in Revelation 9:11 have "the angel of the abyss" as their leader. These are demonic beings in material form led forth by their king, "the angel of the abyss." Bible teacher Charles Swindoll observes,

> Revelation 9...shows us that a time will come when the invisible warfare of today will become insignificant compared to the frontal assault of the enemy's army during the tribulation...Apparently, the abyss is also the place where certain demons have been kept in prison until judgment (Luke 8:30-31; cf. 2 Peter 2:4). Given the context of the end-time judgments, it appears that the opening of the abyss in Revelation 9 forecasts a short-term release of demons prior to their final condemnation in the lake of fire.[145]

What are the locusts of Revelation 9:1-12 who come out of the bottomless pit during the fifth trumpet judgment of the tribulation? I believe they are demons. Now, I know that these locusts originated from the bottomless pit after it was unlocked. And the only things locked in the bottomless pit (*abussos*) are demons.

In the ancient world, there was nothing more destructive than locusts. They were symbolic of destruction. The fifth trumpet judgment of the last days describes nothing less than the bowels of hell belching forth a horrid host of foul, fiendish demons to afflict unsaved people with excruciating pain and torture in the last days of the coming tribulation period.

Picture what the world would be like if the doors of the jails and penitentiaries everywhere were opened and the most vicious and violent criminals were all set free, allowing them to pour out their mayhem and infamies upon mankind. The scene in Revelation 9 is much, much worse. What will it be like when countless numbers of demons who have been chained in the abyss for thousands of years run rampant throughout the earth in visible form during the tribulation? It will be unspeakable!

Add to this the fact that in Revelation 12, Satan and his fallen host are cast down from heaven to the earth. The earth will be caught in the demonic crossfire as Satan and the fallen angels are cast from the atmospheric and divine heavens above down to the earth, and the demons from the abyss below are dredged up to the earth. The earth will literally be teeming with swarms of dreadful demonic beings. It will be an Auschwitz-type of experience for those who must endure it. The diabolical forces from both heaven and hell will be unleashed to practice their unimaginable atrocities upon mankind. Revelation 9 reveals that in the last days, the earth will be invaded by a force of "aliens" unlike anything man could ever concoct in a special-effects lab.

Who is Apollyon?

Near the end of the description of the fifth trumpet judgment, the leader of the demonic horde from the abyss is identified as Apollyon in Greek and Abaddon in Hebrew. "They have as king over them, the angel of the abyss; his name in Hebrew is Abaddon, and in Greek he has the name Apollyon" (Revelation 9:11).

"Abaddon" and "Apollyon" are synonyms that mean "destroyer" or "terminator." Some believe this is a reference to Satan, but Satan is not the king of the abyss, for he is presently free to roam about the earth (2 Corinthians 4:3-4; 1 Peter 5:8). Satan will be cast into the abyss after the second coming of Christ (Revelation 20:1-3), but he is not currently imprisoned there. For this reason, Abaddon is best identified as a powerful demon who currently resides in the abyss and is the leader of the demons confined there.

Grant Osborne makes an interesting connection between Apollyon and the first-century world in which Revelation was written:

> The name of the Greek god Apollo was taken from this term, and the locust was one of his symbols, since he was the god of pestilence and plague. Moreover, the emperor Domitian (perhaps ruler of Rome at the time

> of writing) viewed himself as Apollo incarnate. Therefore, this could be another of many references to the imperial cult. Throughout this book the Roman Empire is seen as demonic, and this would be a powerful way of getting that across. However, this is a side point even if the cryptic reference to Domitian were true. The real message is that the demonic forces are organized, powerful, terrifying, and filled with hatred and contempt for their followers.[146]

Yet we must always remember that even the king of the demons is under the sovereign control of God.

Who are the four angels bound at the River Euphrates?

When the sixth trumpet sounds, four angels bound at the Euphrates River are released to bring forth massive destruction on the earth. Revelation 9:13-14 says,

> The sixth angel sounded, and I heard a voice from the four horns of the golden altar which is before God, one saying to the sixth angel who had the trumpet, "Release the four angels who are bound at the great river Euphrates." And the four angels, who had been prepared for the hour and day and month and year, were released, so that they would kill a third of mankind.

The key question here is the nature of the four angels. Are they fallen or unfallen angels? Revelation 9 doesn't answer this question directly. Some believe they must be unfallen angels because throughout the book of Revelation, good angels are the agents of God's judgment. Nevertheless, the fact that these angelic beings are bound strongly suggests they are fallen angels. Good angels are never pictured in Scripture as bound, but only Satan and demons (Mark 3:27; Revelation 20:1-3). Additionally, these angels lead the army of 200 million described later in Revelation 9, which, as we will see in the next question, is a deadly, demonic cavalry. The connection of these angels with a demonic army, and possibly the leaders of this army, supports their identification as demonic spirits.

These demons are bound at the Euphrates River, which flowed through the ancient, evil city of Babylon, which will be resurrected, according to Revelation 17–18. The Euphrates is also mentioned in Revelation 16:12 in conjunction with the Battle of Armageddon. Its association with evil fits the demonic connection with the angels who are bound there.

The fact that these angels are "prepared for the hour and day and month and year" showcases that God sovereignly controls the action of these demons down to the very hour. They cannot act until God is ready. They are totally subservient to God's timetable. He is Lord over all!

What is the army of 200 million in 9:16?

Almost 2,000 years ago, the apostle John penned a prophecy that few, if any, in that day could ever imagine as coming to pass:

> Then the sixth angel sounded, and I heard a voice from the four horns of the golden altar which is before God, one saying to the sixth angel who had the trumpet, "Release the four angels who are bound at the great river Euphrates." And the four angels, who had been prepared for the hour and day and month and year, were released, so that they would kill a third of mankind. The number of the armies of the horsemen was two hundred million; I heard the number of them (Revelation 9:13-16).

An army of 200 million! It's been estimated that this was probably about the entire population of the world in John's day. The Roman army in the first century was composed of 25 legions, or about 125,000 soldiers, with an auxiliary army of about the same size.[147] But the army in Revelation 9:16 is a thousand times that number. And John said this immense army of 200 million will be assembled during the end times. The statement that it is prepared for "the hour and day and month and year...so that they would kill a third of mankind" means simply that the four angels and the army they lead will be especially prepared for the day of battle that follows. This also indicates that God is the one who is in sovereign control over the army and the timing of its march.

Revelation 9:15-16 describes a massive army of 200 million mounted troops who destroy one-third of all the people in the world. Prophecy teachers have debated whether this refers to a literal human army or a demonic cavalry that will be unleashed on the earth during the end times. Either view is possible.

Human Army

The possibility of Revelation 9:16 being fulfilled by a human army has been possible only in the last few decades. As far as I know, the first person to point this out in modern times was Dr. John Walvoord. In his commentary on Revelation, which was published in 1966, he pointed out in a footnote on Revelation 9:16 that China now has the capability to field an army of 200,000,000.[148]

For those who hold the human army view, the army of 200 million in Revelation 9 is viewed as parallel with the "kings from the east" in Revelation 16:12, who come into Israel from the east by crossing the dried-up Euphrates River. The main basis for relating these two passages to one another is that they both mention the Euphrates River, and they are both followed by a reference to a large army. Others who adopt this view also see a reference to the army from the east in Daniel 11:44-45.

Demonic Armada

I believe it is better to view this colossal cavalry in Revelation 9 as an armada of demonic invaders that assault the earth during the tribulation. There are three key reasons I prefer this view:

1. The fifth trumpet judgment is clearly a demonic invasion of the earth (demonic locusts), and the fifth and sixth trumpet judgments go together because they are the first two of three "woes." The linkage of these two trumpets supports interpreting the army released by the sixth trumpet as a demonic army as well.
2. This army is led by four fallen angels, just like the locusts in the fifth trumpet judgment (Revelation 9:14-15). Because the leaders are four fallen angels or demons, it makes sense the troops they are leading are also demons.
3. In the Bible, the belching fire, brimstone, and smoke from these horses are always understood as supernatural weapons and are connected with hell four times in Revelation (14:10-11; 19:20; 20:10; 21:8).

If it is correct that this is a demonic army, this means that during the tribulation, the earth will be overrun with demons who afflict men with great pain (the fifth trumpet, Revelation 9:10) and that this will be followed by another demonic outbreak that will ultimately slay one-third of the people on the earth (the sixth trumpet, 9:15, 18). But, no matter whether these 200 million horsemen are humans or demons, still, they will exact the greatest death count in the history of the world—making this a truly unparalleled prophecy.

Who is the strong angel in chapter 10? Is this a reference to Jesus?

Revelation 10:1-6 describes "another strong angel" who comes down out of heaven:

> I saw another strong angel coming down out of heaven, clothed with a cloud; and the rainbow was upon his head, and his face was like the sun, and his feet like pillars of fire; and he had in his hand a little book which was open. He placed his right foot on the sea and his left on the land; and he cried out with a loud voice, as when a lion roars; and when he had cried out, the seven peals of thunder uttered their voices. When the seven peals of thunder had spoken, I was about to write; and I heard a voice from heaven saying, "Seal up the things which the seven peals of thunder have spoken and do not write them." Then the angel whom I saw standing on the sea and on the land lifted up his right hand to heaven, and swore by Him who lives forever and ever, WHO CREATED HEAVEN AND THE THINGS IN IT, AND THE EARTH AND THE THINGS IN IT, AND THE SEA AND THE THINGS IN IT, that there will be delay no longer.

Based on this vivid, powerful description, many believe this "strong angel" is Jesus. Yet there are three clues that seem to indicate this is not Jesus, but rather, a strong angel dispatched from God's throne. First, the angel is called "another" (Greek, *allos*) angel. This word *allos* normally carries the idea of another of the same kind, as opposed to *heteros,* which is another of a different kind. This signifies at the outset that this angel is another of the same kind that just brought forth the seal judgments in Revelation 9.

Second, Jesus is never referred to in Revelation as an angel. He is given many names and titles in this book, but angel isn't one of them. It would be strange for Him to be called an angel in a book that attributes so many descriptive titles to Him. When Jesus appears in Revelation, there is no uncertainty about who He is.

Third, in 10:6, this angel "swore by Him who lives forever and ever." While God does swear by Himself in Hebrews 6:13-14, in that passage, He makes it clear that He is doing so. But here in Revelation 10, it makes more sense to view the angel as an angelic being who swears by the person of God, the great Creator.

What is the "little book" in 10:2?

The little book in Revelation 10 is often connected with the seven-sealed scroll in Revelation 5, but they don't appear to be the same. The Greek word used in each case is different. The term used in the original Greek text for the scroll in 5:1 is *biblion,* whereas the term for the book in 10:2 is *biblarion* (a small scroll), although it is called a *biblion* in 10:8.

If the little book is not the seven-sealed scroll, then what is it? The little scroll is probably the revelation from God about the remainder of the contents of Revelation in chapters 11–22. It's the rest of the prophetic message John will record. Revelation 10:11 supports this notion because John eats the little book and then prophesies again. These prophecies are the content of the little book. He eats the book, and then once he has taken it in, speaks the rest of the prophecies in Revelation.

What are the "seven peals of thunder" in 10:3-4?

In Revelation 10:3-4, the strong angel "cried out with a loud voice, as when a lion roars; and when he had cried out, the seven peals of thunder uttered their voices. When the seven peals of thunder had spoken, I was about to write; and I heard a voice from heaven saying, 'Seal up the things which the seven peals of thunder have spoken and do not write them.'" Seven peals of thunder are heard, but John is prohibited from recording what they utter.

Because the meaning of these seven peals of thunder is not stated, certainty on what they communicate is impossible. Many believe there may be a connection with the seven times God spoke in Psalm 29 and the seven peals of thunder in Revelation 10:3-4. But it seems reasonable to view the thunder as pronouncements of judgment. Bible commentator George Eldon Ladd says, "The only hint we have as to the message of the seven thunders is to be found in the fact that in all the other passages in the Revelation where thunders occur, they form a premonition of coming judgments of divine wrath (8:5; 11:19; 16:18). This fits the present context, for the angel announces that the consummation of divine judgments is about to take place."[149] So given the context, it is clear that these peals of thunder represent judgment, but we don't know the content of these judgments.

In Revelation, there are three series of judgments: seven seals, seven trumpets, and seven bowls. The fact there are seven peals of thunder reminds one of these other sevenfold judgments. It may be that these comprise another series of seven judgments that God chose not to reveal.

What does it mean for John to eat the book (10:9-10)?

In Revelation 10:9-10, the apostle John, like Ezekiel before him (Ezekiel 2:9–3:3), was commanded to eat the little book. It was sweet in his mouth, but then turned bitter in his stomach. The act of eating the book means that John is to absorb its message into his life (Psalm 19:10; Jeremiah 15:16; Ezekiel 3:1-3). While the instruction was specific to John, we should emulate him.

Wiersbe says it well: "*The directions* that the angel gave John should remind us of our responsibility to assimilate the Word of God and make it a part of the inner man. It was not enough for John to see the book or even know its contents and purpose. He had to *receive* it into his inner being."[150]

The fact that it was "sweet" and then "bitter" refers to the fact the prophecies John was giving were ultimately sweet, because they result in the coming kingdom of Christ, but they also contained a series of bitter judgments that must come forth before the kingdom could be realized. The gospel message we preach is also sweet and bitter. It is sweet to those who receive it, but bitter to those who reject it and face God's wrath.

What is the temple in Revelation 11:1-2?

Revelation 11:1-2 mentions a temple that the nations will tread underfoot for 42 months. There are three main views regarding the nature of this temple. First, the majority view among scholars is that the temple is symbolic of the church. It is true that the church is often referred to as a temple in the New Testament

(1 Corinthians 3:16; 2 Corinthians 6:16; Ephesians 2:21; 1 Peter 3:5). However, what makes this figurative view unacceptable is that the nature of the temple in this context is Jewish. The mention of the sanctuary, the altar, the court of the Gentiles, and the holy city places this text on Jewish ground.[151] As George Eldon Ladd notes, "[H]ere the temple is not represented primarily as the dwelling place of God but as the Jewish temple in Jerusalem."[152] The Jewish nature of this temple is incompatible with the New Testament church.

Also, the symbolic view fails to account for all of the details of the text. If the temple here symbolizes the church, what does the measuring of the temple mean? What is the 42 months when the temple is trampled? How do these things relate to the church? And if the temple is the church, who are the people who worship in the temple? The church, by definition, includes those who worship in it. The figurative view seems to merge the two symbols.

Second, preterists believe the temple is the second Jewish temple or the Herodian Temple. They allege that Revelation is about the destruction of Jerusalem and the Jewish temple in AD 70. The major flaw with the preterist view is that Revelation was written in AD 95, which is 25 years too late for this passage to refer to the second Jewish temple

The third view is that the temple in Revelation 11:1-2 is a literal, earthly temple that will stand in Jerusalem in the future, during the end times. This will be the third Jewish temple, which is often called the tribulation temple. There are three main points in favor of this view. First, a literal temple fits the activity of measuring the temple, altar, and worshippers and the non-measurement of the outer court in 11:2. The purpose of making these measurements was not to obtain physical dimensions, for the dimensions are never reported. The measuring appears to be a sign of divine approval or favor for the sanctuary, altar, and worshippers and divine disapproval of all the Gentile enemies who reject him.[153]

Second, support for interpreting the temple in Revelation 11:1-2 as a future, rebuilt temple is derived from the Old Testament background of the text. It is recognized by scholars of every stripe that Revelation relies heavily on the Old Testament, especially Daniel and Ezekiel. Revelation is even recognized as a "New Testament Daniel" by many scholars. Interestingly, in both Daniel and Ezekiel, a temple was mentioned that was not in existence at the time the prophet was writing. Daniel wrote his great prophecy after the destruction of the temple in 586 BC and before the temple was rebuilt in 520–516. When Daniel wrote, there was no temple standing in Jerusalem. It had been in ruins for about 50 years. However, he refers to temple sacrifices and temple desecration on several occasions: 8:11-14; 9:27; 10:31; 12:11. Daniel must have been referring to a temple that was future to his own day when he wrote. Moreover, the mention of "forty-two months" (Revelation 11:2) and "twelve hundred and sixty days" (Revelation 11:3) is an unmistakable allusion back to the second half of Daniel's seventieth week and a literal temple in Daniel 9:27. If John is the New Testament Daniel, why would we be surprised to find John also referring to a future temple that did not exist at the time he received his vision?

Who are the two witnesses?

In Revelation 11:3-14, we read about two witnesses who will prophesy for 1,260 days (or three-and-a-half years), suffer martyrdom with their bodies left exposed for three-and-a-half days, and then be resurrected and caught up to heaven.

The identity of these two witnesses is debated. Preterist interpreters spiritualize them. Hank Hanegraaff adopts this approach, saying, "In like fashion, only someone with the background music of the Old Testament coursing through their minds comprehends that the two witnesses are a metaphorical reference to Moses and Elijah and reflect Old Testament jurisprudence that mandated at least two witnesses to convict of a crime (Deuteronomy 19:15)." He continues by noting that the two witnesses "represent the entire line of Hebrew prophets testifying against apostate Israel and preside over the soon-coming judgment and destruction of Jerusalem and the second temple."[154] Others, however, firmly reject this spiritualizing of the text.

The Old Testament background for the two witnesses in Revelation 11 is Zechariah 4, which points to two literal individuals—Zerubbabel and Joshua—who led the returning remnant of Jewish people after the Babylonian captivity. The Old Testament imagery in Zechariah 4 (two olive trees on either side of a lampstand) clearly refers to two individuals, Zerubbabel (the civil leader) and Joshua (the religious leader). When this same imagery is employed in Revelation 11 in conjunction with the two witnesses, doesn't it make sense that it would also refer to two individuals? Why resort to a complicated "metaphorical reference" when the very Old Testament passage that forms the "background music" of Revelation 11 refers to two literal people? W. Graham Scroggie states the issue plainly: "The mention of these two takes us back to Zechariah 4:3, 11, 14, from which we learn that they represented two individuals—Zerubbabel and Joshua. Therefore, in this passage also, they represent two individuals."[155] Why ignore this clear Old Testament key to identifying the two witnesses and instead opt for an unnecessary metaphorical interpretation that must be imposed upon the text?

It's much better to take the temple in Revelation 11:1-2 as a literal, future temple, the 1,260 days as a literal three-and-a-half-year period of time during the future tribulation, and the two witnesses as two literal people who will serve God during this time. This maintains consistency and allows the text to speak for itself.

Just as Satan will have his two henchmen on the earth during the tribulation (the beast and the false prophet), so the Lord will have His two representatives on the earth (the two witnesses) to counteract the evil of the beast and the false prophet.

Some Bible scholars believe the two witnesses will be Moses and Elijah, who are brought forward into the end times. The textual and historical evidence for this view is compelling. Eight key factors point to this view as the proper interpretation.

First, as already noted, the Old Testament background of Zechariah 4 points to the two witnesses as two literal individuals. Zechariah presents two witnesses, Zerubbabel and Joshua, who are pictured by a lampstand and olive trees. The lampstand burned brightly, and the olive trees produced the oil that was burned in the candelabra. This picture is brought forward into Revelation 11, which reveals that these two end-time witnesses will shine in the darkness of the tribulation and will be fueled by the oil of the Holy Spirit.

Second, these two witnesses perform miracles that are identical to the ones performed by Moses and Elijah in the Old Testament. Moses and Elijah are both mentioned together in the final chapter of the Old Testament, and Malachi 4:5 says, "Behold, I am going to send you Elijah the prophet before the coming of the great and terrible day of the LORD." Moses and Elijah appeared with Jesus on the Mount of Transfiguration in an event that prefigured Christ's second coming to Earth (Matthew 17:1-5). It's consistent with the Old Testament for Elijah to make an appearance in the end-times before the return of Christ (Malachi 4:5).

Third, Revelation 11:8 argues for a literal interpretation of the two witnesses. In this verse, the text explicitly states that the city of Jerusalem is figuratively called "Sodom and Egypt." The reader is not left to his own imagination to figure out what city is represented here. It's clear in Revelation 11 that when God wants to speak figuratively or metaphorically, He has no problem indicating that He's doing so. Because Revelation 11 doesn't say that the two witnesses are to be taken metaphorically or figuratively, one would assume they are to be taken literally as two prophets, just as they are described in the text.

Fourth, the Greek word *martur* (and *martus*), translated as "witness" or "witnesses," is found five times in Revelation, and always refers to a literal person or persons. In Revelation 1:5 and 3:14 it refers to Jesus, in 2:13 it refers to Antipas, in 17:6 it refers to martyrs, and in 11:3 it refers to the two witnesses.

Fifth, the immediate context of Revelation 11 identifies the two witnesses. We need look no further than Revelation 11:10, which plainly identifies them as "these two prophets." The words "these two prophets" identify the two witnesses as two individuals who will prophesy for God during the tribulation.

Sixth, Revelation 11:9-11 describes the amazing events that will surround the death and resurrection of these two prophets. The passage says they will be killed by the beast when God lifts His hand of protection, that their bodies will be left exposed in the streets of Jerusalem for three-and-a-half days, that "peoples and tribes and tongues and nations will look at their dead bodies," that after three-and-a-half days God will bring them back to life, that their enemies will see them resurrected and caught up to heaven and will be gripped with fear, and that in conjunction with their resurrection and rapture a great earthquake will occur that will destroy 10 percent of Jerusalem and kill 7,000 people. Again, the context indicates to us that it makes better sense to see the two witnesses as two literal individuals who will fulfill these prophecies.[156]

Seventh, in the Old Testament book of Exodus, Pharaoh serves as a kind of prototype of the future beast or final Antichrist. Just as God had two witnesses, Moses and Aaron, who were the human instruments who called down the plagues on Pharaoh and Egypt, so God will use two literal witnesses in the end times to call plagues (the trumpet judgments) down on the beast and his empire.

Eighth, the early church held the view that the two witnesses are literal individuals. For example, Hippolytus, in his treatise on the Antichrist, was one of the first, if not the first, to comment on the identity of the two witnesses. Hippolytus, who was the bishop of Rome from about AD 200–235, identified the witnesses as Enoch and Elijah.[157] This is probably because neither of these men tasted physical death, and it was believed they had to return and then would die during the tribulation. Victorinus, who wrote the oldest extant Latin commentary on Revelation and died in AD 304, identified the two witnesses as individuals who will preach for three-and-a-half years followed by the Antichrist's reign. The view that the two witnesses were Enoch and Elijah transported forward into the end times was also held by Primasius, Andreas of Cappadocia, Arethas, and Adso of Montier-en-Der.[158] The only variance from this view came from Lactantius, the most important apocalyptic writer of the early fourth century, who held that the two witnesses were a single end-times prophet. However, his perspective is still consistent with the notion that a literal prophet is in view.[159]

The belief that the two witnesses were Enoch and Elijah (or Enoch and Jeremiah) was so prevalent in the early church that Le Roy Froom identified this as the view of the early church.[160] Bernard McGinn, in his work on the Antichrist, says that by the fourth century, "The standard Christian tradition, based on Apocalypse 11, had predicted two witnesses to preach before the coming of the final Antichrist."[161]

While the early church believed the two witnesses would be Enoch and Elijah, others later identified them as Moses and Elijah. Many contemporary dispensationalists, however, reject the idea that the two witnesses will be individuals from the past. They believe the witnesses will be two individuals whom God raises up during the tribulation.[162]

Whatever specific view one adopts about the precise identity of the two witnesses, the one consistent thread that appears again and again is that the two witnesses will be two literal individuals who will prophesy during the end times.

What will the two witnesses do?

All we are told about the ministry of the two witnesses is that they will prophesy for three-and-a-half years, during which time they will be divinely shielded from harm and given supernatural power to call down signs, plagues, and judgments on their evil enemies. Their sackcloth attire, which symbolizes mourning, indicates that their main ministry is that of judgment. Charles Swindoll summarizes their ministry in this way:

> Most importantly, the miraculous authority given to the two witnesses by God is similar to that of Moses, Elijah and other Old Testament prophets, demonstrating the crucial nature of their ministry during the future tribulation…We can at least say with confidence that these two figures appear to sum up the kind of miraculous and prophetic ministry that has marked other periods of biblical history. During those periods, God was making epochal changes in His plan or delivering great amounts of new revelation…Like all the prophets before them, these two end-time prophets will frustrate their enemies.[163]

Just as God used Moses and Aaron to call down the plagues on the Egyptians, it could be that God will use the two witnesses to call down the trumpet judgments in Revelation, for their time of ministry is placed during the sounding of the trumpets. If this is true, it will identify these men with the destruction that afflicts the earth and explain why people on the earth hate them so intensely.

Do the two witnesses minister during the first or second half of the tribulation?

The two witnesses will prophesy for 1,260 days, or three-and-a-half years. But during which half of the tribulation will they prophesy? This is one of the most difficult chronological issues in Revelation. There are very good arguments for both sides. Those who place the ministry of the two witnesses in the last half of the tribulation—myself included—do so for three key reasons.

First, right after the ministry of the two witnesses is described, the seventh trumpet sounds, which takes the action all the way to the second coming of Christ at the end of the tribulation. It would be strange for the two witnesses to be put in this context if their ministry occurs during the first half of the tribulation.

Second, the end-times temple is described in Revelation 11:1-2, and John said it will be trampled by the nations for 42 months (or three-and-a-half years). This period of trampling fits the second half of the tribulation, for in the very next verse, we read that the two witnesses will prophesy for 1,260 days. It makes sense for the two time periods mentioned in Revelation 11:2-3 to be the same period. If the three-and-a-half years in 11:2 takes place during the final half of the tribulation, then the three-and-a-half-year period in 11:3 is the same period.

Robert Thomas holds this view:

> It is better, therefore, to find the fulfillment of the forty-two months during the last half of the seventieth week. A principal reason for this is that the period of ill-treatment by the Gentiles fits the latter half better because of the breaking of the covenant with the Roman ruler in the middle of the week (Dan. 9:27). It also makes for a better connection with the 1,260 days

> in 11:3…So the period is a literal forty-two months just before Christ returns in power and glory.[164]

Third, the overall setting and context of Revelation 11:3-14 fits the second half of the tribulation better than the first. As John Walvoord notes,

> The fact that the witnesses pour out divine judgments upon the earth, and need divine protection lest they be killed, implies that they are in the latter half of the seven years when awful persecution will afflict the people of God. Such protection would not be necessary in the first three-and-a-half years. The punishments and judgments the witnesses inflict upon the world also seem to fit better in the great tribulation period.[165]

For these reasons, I favor the second half of the tribulation as the period of ministry for the two witnesses.

Is the seventh trumpet in 11:15 the same as the "last trumpet" in 1 Corinthians 15:52?

Midtribulationists maintain that the church will be raptured to heaven at the midpoint of the seven-year tribulation. Most of them equate the "last trumpet" in 1 Corinthians 15:52 with the seventh trumpet in Revelation 11:15, which happens to be the last trumpet in Revelation.

The best way to determine whether the two are the same trumpet is to place the characteristics of these two trumpets side by side.

	Trumpet in 1 Corinthians 15	Trumpet in Revelation 11
Subject	Church	Wicked world
Result	Catching up of the church to be with the Lord	Judgment of godless world
Character	Trumpet of God's grace	Trumpet of God's judgment
Timing	Signals the close of the life of the church on Earth—it's the last trumpet of the church age	Marks a climax in the progression of tribulation judgments—it's the last trumpet of judgment in preparation for the kingdom

These significant differences make it apparent that the trumpets in 1 Corinthians 15 and Revelation 11 are not the same.

Is the ark of the covenant in heaven?

The current location of the ark of the covenant has led to all kinds of speculation. The epic movie *Raiders of the Lost Ark* is an action-packed adventure about the search for the lost ark of the covenant. The ark was a small wooden box covered with gold that was constructed in the wilderness according to the pattern God gave in Exodus 25. It stood in the Holy of Holies in the tabernacle, and later, in Solomon's Temple. However, after the Babylonian exile, it disappears from the biblical narrative, which has led to all kinds of conjecture about its location and existence.

Based on Revelation 11, some believe the ark was transported to heaven at some point in the past. Revelation 11 begins with a vision of a temple on Earth in Jerusalem and ends with a vision of a temple in heaven. The vision of heaven continues what John saw in Revelation 4–5. In Revelation 11:19, John peered into heaven and saw a temple with the ark of the covenant inside. "The temple of God which is in heaven was opened; and the ark of His covenant appeared in His temple, and there were flashes of lightning and sounds and peals of thunder and an earthquake and a great hailstorm."

This in the only reference in the Bible to a heavenly ark of the covenant. The ark John saw in heaven is not the earthly ark transported to heaven, but the heavenly reality that the earthly ark was fashioned after. The Bible states that the temple on Earth and its furnishings was patterned after a heavenly archetype or model that was shown to Moses (Exodus 25:40; Hebrews 8:1-5). In other words, there is a temple in heaven that serves as the pattern for the earthly temple and an ark that functions as the prototype for the earthly ark of the covenant.

So, while we may not know where the earthly ark of the covenant is located today, or whether it still exists, and while the Antichrist will desecrate the earthly temple during the future tribulation, the heavenly counterparts are safe and secure in God's majestic presence.

Revelation 21:22 reveals that in the New Jerusalem, the temple will no longer be present, and I would assume that includes the ark of the covenant, as the Lord God and the Lamb will be the temple of the new city. No structure will be necessary, for God's people will be forever in the immediate presence of the Lord.

Who is the woman clothed with the sun in Revelation 12?

It's often been noted that Revelation 12 is the most symbolic chapter in the most symbolic book of the Bible. One of the key symbols in this chapter is "a woman clothed with the sun, and the moon under her feet, and on her head a crown of twelve stars; and she was with child; and she cried out, being in labor and in pain to give birth" (verses 1-2).

There are three main views of the identity of this woman. First, Roman Catholic scholars believe this refers to Mary, the mother of Jesus, because the woman here gives birth to Jesus. If that were the only part of this prophecy, the Mary view could be correct. The problem, however, is what the prophecy states in verse 6—we are told the woman will flee into the wilderness for 1,260 days. That never happened to Mary, and it never will happen.

Second, the majority view among Protestant scholars is that the woman represents the church of Jesus Christ. They make this connection because in the New Testament, the church is often pictured as a woman—the bride of Christ. But the woman here cannot be the church because the woman gives birth to Jesus. The church did not give birth to Jesus; rather, Jesus gave birth to the church. The church was born upon the death and resurrection of Christ and the sending of the Spirit.

Third, many futurists believe the woman pictures Israel in the end times. There are several important clues that support this view. Remember that the woman is "clothed with the sun, and the moon under her feet, and on her head a crown of twelve stars; and she was with child; and she cried out, being in labor and in pain to give birth." The only other place in Scripture where all these symbols are clustered together in one place is Genesis 37:9-10, where we read about a dream Joseph had.

> Now he had still another dream, and related it to his brothers, and said, "Lo, I have had still another dream; and behold, the sun and the moon and eleven stars were bowing down to me." He related it to his father and to his brothers; and his father rebuked him and said to him, "What is this dream that you have had? Shall I and your mother and your brothers actually come to bow ourselves down before you to the ground?"

The sun, moon, and 11 stars in the dream represented Joseph's father, mother, and 11 brothers. Eventually, this dream was fulfilled. These symbols clearly identify the woman as Israel, which descended from Joseph's father, Jacob. Moreover, Israel gave birth to the Messiah, which is in keeping with the imagery in Revelation 12 (Isaiah 9:6).

Therefore, the woman in Revelation 12 pictures the nation of Israel rising to prominence in the end times. What we see taking place in Israel today strikingly foreshadows this prophecy.

Who are the dragon and the "third of the stars of heaven" in Revelation 12?

Revelation 12:3-4 presents another dramatic symbol: "Another sign appeared in heaven: and behold, a great red dragon having seven heads and ten horns, and on his heads were seven diadems. And his tail swept away a third of the stars of heaven, and threw them to the earth." There are two symbols here to interpret. First, it's clear from the context that the great red dragon is Satan. Revelation 12:9 provides the key: "The great dragon was thrown down, the serpent of old who is called the devil and Satan, who deceives the whole world."

The dragon is clearly Satan, but who are the one-third of the stars of heaven that his tail swept away? In Scripture, stars are often symbolic of angels, and that appears to be the meaning here (Job

38:7; Revelation 9:1). That the stars here are angels is confirmed in the immediate context—Revelation 12:7 says, "There was war in heaven, Michael and his angels waging war with the dragon. And the dragon and his angels waged war." The event pictured here is the angelic revolt in heaven, when a third of the angels joined Satan in his rebellion against God.

What are the "two wings of the great eagle" given to the woman (12:14)?

As we have seen, the woman in Revelation 12 is the nation of Israel, who will be persecuted by Satan in the end times. According to 12:14, the woman will flee into the wilderness from the persecution of Satan through his instrument, the Antichrist, and will be given "two wings of the great eagle" to protect her. I once heard a man say that the "two wings of the great eagle" is a reference to the United States Air Force because the eagle is a symbol for the United States. He went on to say that this refers to an airlift of the fleeing Jews during the tribulation.

This kind of speculation highlights the importance of using Scripture to interpret Scripture. Revelation 12:14 echoes two Old Testament passages that describe God's protection of Israel during the Exodus, and these passages provide us the clue to interpreting this symbol.

In Exodus 19:4, God says to the Israelites, "You yourselves have seen what I did to the Egyptians, and how I bore you on eagles' wings, and brought you to Myself." And Deuteronomy 32:11 adds, "Like an eagle that stirs up its nest, that hovers over its young, He spread His wings and caught them, He carried them on His pinions." In light of these texts, it appears that the "two wings of the great eagle" refers to God's future miraculous help and protection of Israel by some supernatural means that secures her deliverance.

Is the beast of Revelation 13:1-10 an empire or an individual?

Revelation 13 presents the final beast of history in ways that fit both an empire and an emperor. This has led to some confusion over the identity of this beast.

I believe it's best to view the beast as both the empire and the emperor—the kingdom and its king. What I mean by this is that the ruler of this final empire so embodies the kingdom that he is the empire—in the same way that, in the Old Testament, we could say that Nebuchadnezzar was Babylon.

There are two main reasons for favoring this view. First, the language in Revelation 13 appears, for the most part, to be referring to an individual. The pronouns "he" and "his" are used repeatedly. In fact, the second beast, whom we read about in Revelation 13:11-18, will make an image to the first beast, "whose fatal wound was healed" (verse 12). It would be strange to construct an image of an empire that had died and come back to life. Also, the second beast, known as the false prophet, is an individual. So it makes sense that the first beast would be an individual as well.

Is the beast past or future? Could he be Nero?

Preterist interpreters (those who believe the prophecies in Revelation were fulfilled with the destruction of Jerusalem in AD 70) hold that the beast in Revelation 13:1-10 is the Roman Caesar Nero. They argue that the gematria, numerical value, of Nero's name equals 666, that he was worshipped as God, and that he persecuted God's people.

In spite of these points, there are three reasons it's doubtful that the beast in Revelation 13 was Nero. First, for the number 666 to fit the gematria value of Nero, the name and title Nero Caesar must be used (actually, Neron Caesar). This is important to note at the outset because there are many names and titles for Nero one could choose from. Choosing this specific title seems too convenient for the Nero view. How can one be sure that this is the form of the name that should be adopted? While Nero's name and title can certainly be rendered in this way, it could also be a case of adapting the facts to fit a predetermined solution. Moreover, the titles of other first-century Roman rulers also yield the sum 666. For example, the abbreviated forms of the titles of Domitian, which appeared on Roman coins, can equal 666. And coins issued in AD 72 bear a legend around the head of Vespasian, and the numerical value of the legend adds up to 666.

Second, the text of Revelation 13:17 specifically states that the numerical value 666 is "the *name* of the beast or the number of his *name*" (emphasis added). Nero Caesar was not Nero's name. It was his name with a title added. Using Nero Caesar to calculate the number of his name would be akin to someone today using the title President or Prime Minister as part of a person's name to arrive at the gematria value of his name.

G. Salmon developed three rules that have long been used by those who want to make a name equal the number 666. His rules describe what is done by those who attempt to identify Nero as the beast: "First, if the proper name by itself will not yield it, add a title; secondly, if the sum cannot be found in Greek, try Hebrew, or even Latin; thirdly, do not be too particular about the spelling… We cannot infer much from the fact that a key fits the lock if it is a lock in which almost any key will turn."[166]

Another argument against equating Nero with the beast is the fact that Irenaeus, Andreas, Victorinus, and Primasius—who were key figures in the early church who studied Revelation—never acknowledged this view. They never mentioned it. The idea of connecting Nero with the beast did not arise until at least 350 years after Revelation was written, and possibly longer. If Nero Caesar was such an obvious connection to the number 666, then why did it take at least 350 years for someone to see it? The lack of any early support for the Nero view, which is alleged to be obvious, seriously undermines the identification of Nero with 666.

The third—and strongest—argument against identifying Nero with the beast of Revelation 13 is that Nero did not carry out the activities ascribed to the beast in Revelation 13 and in other parts of Revelation. Preterists take the reference to "666" literally as the gematria value of the name Neron Caesar. They also take the 42 months in 13:5 as a literal span of time during which Nero persecuted Christians. However, they are not able to successfully point to literal fulfillments of the other prophecies mentioned in Revelation 13. This chapter states that the beast will rule the world for 42 months, that all who dwell on the earth will worship him, that he will be killed and come back to life, that all people on the earth must take his mark of 666 on their right hand or forehead, and that all must take this mark to engage in any form of commerce. These things were not literally fulfilled during the reign of Nero from AD 54–68. As Raymond Brown concludes, "too many elements in Revelation seem irreconcilable with Nero's lifetime."[167]

Rather than try to find some figure from the past and force that person into Revelation 13, it's best to follow the early church and relate this prophecy to an individual who is still future—a person who will rule the world during the great tribulation.

Will the beast be assassinated and come back to life?

Revelation 13:3-4 describes the beast's fatal wound and healing:

> I saw one of his heads as if it had been slain, and his fatal wound was healed. And the whole earth was

> amazed and followed after the beast; and they worshiped the dragon because he gave his authority to the beast; and they worshiped the beast, saying, "Who is like the beast, and who is able to wage war with him?"

There are three main views on the meaning of these words. Some believe that the death and resurrection mentioned here refer to the demise of the Roman Empire in AD 476 and its comeback in the end times. In other words, this is talking about the empire rising from the dead, not a man. The main problem with this view is how the world responds to the beast's restoration. Would the revival of the Roman Empire really cause people all over the globe to respond as described in Revelation 13:3? Note that people will be so amazed that they follow after the beast. This would be much more likely if this refers to a man rather than an empire. A revival of the Roman Empire would hardly leave the world dumbstruck and cause everyone to follow it. But if a great world leader were assassinated with a fatal wound to the head then came back to life a few days later, people would understandably respond in amazement.

The second view is that the beast in Revelation is an individual who suffers a seemingly fatal wound and only appears to be dead. For those who hold this view, the restoration is a faked or counterfeit resurrection. Proponents of this view resist the idea that the beast could actually die and come back to life because Satan has no power to restore life.

All Christians agree that only God has the power to resurrect the dead. This is a given. However, God can allow Satan to have this ability if He chooses to do so. I believe that's what will happen during the tribulation. God's permission for Satan to do this will be part of the great delusion God will send upon those who reject Him (2 Thessalonians 2:9-12).

According to Revelation 13:15, the false prophet will "give breath to the image of the beast, so that the image of the beast would even speak" (13:15). If Satan has the power to give life to a dead idol, as Revelation 13:15 states, then why is it not also possible for him (with God's permission) to resurrect a man from the dead?[168]

In addition, the Greek words used to speak of Christ's death and resurrection in Revelation are the same Greek words used to speak of the Antichrist's death and resurrection (see Revelation 2:8; 5:6; 13:3, 12). As Dr. Charles Ryrie notes, "If Christ died actually, then it appears that this ruler will also actually die. But his wound would be healed, which can only mean restoration to life."[169]

Based on the clear language of Revelation, I believe that the Antichrist will actually die and come back to life in a striking parody of the death and resurrection of Jesus Christ. This astonishing event will happen at the midpoint of the seven-year tribulation and will coincide with Satan being cast out of heaven and having but a short time left to wreak havoc on the earth (Revelation 12:12). Realizing that time is running out, Satan will make a desperate attempt to duplicate the resurrection of Christ (with God's permission) and personally seize control of the Antichrist. This will be part of the delusion that God allows during that special season of time at the end of the age. From that point on, having come back from perdition and being indwelled by Satan, the Antichrist will have the power to perform all kinds of signs, wonders, and miracles, and he will unleash his final great work of deception.

Will the Antichrist be a Jew or a Gentile?

One of the key issues involving the beast of Revelation, also known as the Antichrist, is whether he will be a Jew or a Gentile. There are three main arguments for viewing the Antichrist as a Jew.

First, if the prefix *anti* means "instead of," or in place of Christ, then many would contend this makes it more likely that he would be a Jew because the one in place of Christ must be a Jew just as

Jesus was. While this argument has some merit, the prefix *anti* can also mean "against," or opposed to Christ.

Second, many from the earliest days of church history believed the Antichrist would be a Jew from the tribe of Dan.

Third, many point to the King James Version translation of Daniel 11:37, which says, "Neither shall he regard the God of his fathers..." The entire argument rests on the phrase "the God of his fathers." Those who maintain that the Antichrist is a Jew believe that his rejection of "the God of his fathers" proves his Jewishness. However, in the original text of Daniel 11:37, the word *elohim* is often translated as "gods." If this translation is adopted, the support for a Jewish Antichrist disappears from this verse. It simply means he will reject whatever religion his forefathers held.

Support for the Jewish Antichrist theory is not impressive. In fact, to the contrary, the Bible teaches that the coming Antichrist will be a Gentile. His Gentile origin can be discerned in four key ways.

Typology

In Scripture, the only historical person who is specifically identified as a type or foreshadow of the person and work of the Antichrist is Antiochus Epiphanes—a Syrian king in the second century BC. Because the Old Testament type of the Antichrist is a Gentile, it follows that the Antichrist himself will be a Gentile too.

Symbolism

The beast or Antichrist rises out of the sea in Revelation 13:1: "I saw a beast coming up out of the sea." The word "sea," when used symbolically in the book of Revelation and the rest of Scripture, represents the Gentile nations. This is confirmed in Revelation 17:15, where "the waters...are peoples and multitudes and nations."

World Ruler

The Antichrist is presented in Scripture as the final ruler of Gentile world power. His reign is the final phase of the "times of the Gentiles" and their rule over Israel (Luke 21:24). Having a Jew as the last world ruler over Gentile power is not logical.

Antisemitism

The Antichrist will be the most virulent antisemite of all time. He will persecute the Jewish people and invade the land of Israel (Daniel 7:25; 9:27; 11:41, 45). It is problematic to have a Jew as the final great persecutor of his own people.

These points lead many to believe the Antichrist will be a Gentile.

What will the beast in Revelation 13:1-10 do?

My favorite simple outline of the description of the beast in Revelation 13:1-10 is five words in the passage that begins with the letter *w*:[170]

wonder wound worship words war

Who is the second beast or "beast coming up out of the earth" in Revelation 13:11-18?

Revelation 13 presents two beasts who will rule the world in tandem. The first beast, who will rise from the sea, is the political and military leader, while the second beast, who comes from the earth, is the religious and commercial head. This second beast is also known as the false prophet (Revelation 16:13; 19:20; 20:10).

Along with Satan, these two rulers form the unholy trinity of the end times. Satan is the false Father (the Antifather), the first beast is the counterfeit Son (the Antichrist), and the false prophet is the counterfeit Spirit (the Antispirit)

Preterists, who identify the first beast with Nero, try to relate the second beast to a man named Gessius Florus, who was the procurator or governor of Judea during Nero's reign. Yet preterists fail to provide any historical evidence that Gessius Florus ever performed great signs and wonders, that he constructed an image of Nero, that he made the image speak, that he forced the mark of the beast upon the populace as a kind of passport for commercial transactions, or that he executed those who failed to take the mark (Revelation 13:12-18). It is clear from his close association with the beast and the detailed description of his activities that the false prophet is a key religious figure who actively promotes the worship of the first beast. Josephus, the Jewish historian, discusses Gessius Florus, yet never mentions any activities by him that even remotely correspond to the prophecies of Revelation 13:11-18.[171] If Florus did perform great signs and wonders, construct an image of Nero, and give breath to a graven image, Josephus's failure to mention such stupendous feats is inexplicable.

The futurist view of the false prophet is more plausible. According to this view, the false prophet is the lieutenant or propaganda minister for the first beast. He looks like a harmless lamb, but speaks like a deadly dragon. Just as the beast out of the sea (Revelation 13:1-10) will be the Antichrist (false Christ) in the end-times' unholy trinity, the false prophet or beast out of the earth (Revelation 13:11-18) will be the Antispirit. Just as the Holy Spirit points people to Jesus Christ as the object of worship, the false prophet will point people to the Antichrist as the world's savior and messiah. J. Dwight Pentecost summarizes the person and work of the false prophet:

> He is influential in religious affairs (13:11, "two horns like a lamb"); he is motivated by Satan as the first beast

> is (13:11); he has a delegated authority (13:12 "the power of the first beast"); he promotes the worship of the first beast and compels the world to worship the first beast as God (13:12); his ministry is authenticated by signs and miracles which he does, evidently proving that he is the Elijah that was to come (13:13-14); he is successful in deceiving the unbelieving world (13:14); the worship promoted is an idolatrous worship (13:14-15); he has the power of death to compel men to worship the beast (13:15); he has authority in the economic realm to control all commerce (13:16-17); he has a mark that will establish his identity for those who live in that day (13:18).[172]

Will the second beast be a Jew or a Gentile?

The beast in Revelation 13:11-18 is described as "another beast coming up out of the earth" (13:11). Many have understood the reference to "the earth" as the land, or more specifically, the land of Israel, meaning that he will be a Jew. It is possible that the second beast will be a Jew. However, the reference here to the earth is probably better understood as a contrast to heaven. This beast, known as the false prophet, will be earthly in every sense of the word. His entire horizon will be dominated by the earth. Also, because the first beast is a Gentile, it makes sense to view his henchman as a Gentile as well.

What is the mark of the beast (666)?

Revelation 13:16-18 makes it clear the Antichrist will control the end-times global economy. He will rule over global supply and demand. A key part of this one-world economic system is the number 666, also known as the mark of the beast. What is this mysterious mark? Simply stated, the mark is a literal, visible brand, mark, or tattoo that will be placed "upon" the right hand or forehead of people during the tribulation. The mark will be given as a sign of devotion or a "pledge of allegiance" to the Antichrist and will serve as a passport for the possessor of the mark to engage in commerce.

Some believe the number 666 is symbolic of the number of man. Scripturally speaking, the number of perfection is seven, so the three consecutive sixes could be understood as an indication that the Antichrist will fall far short of the goal he desires—to usurp God Himself. John Walvoord holds this view.

> Though there may be more light cast on it at the time this prophecy is fulfilled, the passage itself declares that this number is "man's number." In the Book of Revelation, the number "7" is one of the most significant numbers indicating perfection. Accordingly, there are seven seals, seven trumpets, seven bowls of the wrath of God, seven thunders, etc. This beast claims to be God, and if that were the case, he should be 777. This passage, in effect, says, No, you are only 666. You are short of deity even though you were originally created in the image and likeness of God. Most of the speculation on the meaning of this number is without profit or theological significance.[173]

Whatever symbolism may lie behind this number, there are some who say the number 666—which will be the literal, numerical value of the Antichrist's name—will enable the tribulation saints to identify him. Those who take the mark will be taking the Antichrist's name upon them and will signal his complete ownership of them and their destiny. And more significantly, all who receive the mark will be eternally doomed (Revelation 14:9-10).

It's critical to recognize that nothing we see today is the mark of the beast. It won't appear until after the rapture has occurred, the Antichrist has been unveiled, and the seven-year tribulation has reached its midpoint. No one today should worry that he will somehow take the mark of the beast by accident. All who take it during the tribulation will do so consciously and intentionally and, in doing so, will seal their eternal fate.

Is the scene in 14:1-5 in heaven or on Earth?

The 144,000 are introduced in Revelation 7:1-8. The only other place we read about this group of 144,000 is in Revelation 14:1-5:

> I looked, and behold, the Lamb was standing on Mount Zion, and with Him one hundred and forty-four thousand, having His name and the name of His Father written on their foreheads. And I heard a voice from heaven, like the sound of many waters and like the sound of loud thunder, and the voice which I heard was like the sound of harpists playing on their harps. And they sang a new song before the throne and before the four living creatures and the elders; and no one could learn the song except the one hundred and forty-four thousand who had been purchased from the earth.

> These are the ones who have not been defiled with women, for they have kept themselves chaste. These are the ones who follow the Lamb wherever He goes. These have been purchased from among men as first fruits to God and to the Lamb. And no lie was found in their mouth; they are blameless.

The question here revolves around the location of the Lamb and the 144,000—are they in heaven or on Earth? Where is this Mount Zion on which they are all standing? Mount Zion is used in Scripture as a symbol for heaven (Hebrews 12:22), but it is also a literal location on Earth in the city of Jerusalem. The earthly location is in view here in Revelation 14 because the voice John hears comes *from* heaven (verse 2). If this scene with the 144,000 on Mount Zion were in heaven, it would be strange for John to say that the voice came *from* there.

Revelation 14:1-5 is a comforting preview of the end of the tribulation, when the Lamb will stand with the 144,000 who have been brought through the tribulation unharmed. This scene follows Revelation 13, where the beast is on the rampage against God's people. The picture of the 144,000 at the end of the tribulation shows that even though the beast will do his work, God will also do His work of protecting those He has promised to keep. Notice too that there aren't 143,998 or 143,999 men standing with Jesus. All 144,000 will have made it through the tribulation, just as God promised in 7:1-8. God keeps His Word. He will see us through to the end as well if we trust in Him (Philippians 1:6).

What is the "eternal gospel" in 14:6?

In Revelation 14:6-7, we read about an angel who flies in the sky preaching an "eternal gospel" or good news to those on Earth during the great tribulation. Today, the preaching of the good news is given to men, but during the tribulation, angels will proclaim it around the world. Revelation 14:6-7 says,

> I saw another angel flying in midheaven, having an eternal gospel to preach to those who live on the earth, and to every nation and tribe and tongue and people; and he said with a loud voice, "Fear God, and give Him glory, because the hour of His judgment has come; worship Him who made the heaven and the earth and sea and springs of waters."

We are not left to our imagination or speculation about the content of this eternal good news. When the angel speaks in Revelation 14:7, he reveals the nature of this gospel:

> It is not the eternal gospel of God's redeeming grace in Christ Jesus but, as the following verse shows, a summons to fear, honor, and worship the Creator. It is a final appeal to all men to recognize the one true God. It is an eternal gospel in that it sets forth the eternal purpose of God for man. It relates to judgment and salvation in the coming age.[174]

During the tribulation, people will be told to fear the beast and worship him. But this heavenly messenger will call people everywhere to worship, honor, and fear God alone, who has abundantly revealed Himself in nature so that people who refuse to acknowledge Him are without excuse (Romans 1:19-20).

Will hell really last for eternity (14:10-11)?

The doctrine of hell is undoubtedly the most disturbing subject in the Bible, and the most disturbing truth about hell is its duration. The idea of people being punished for their sins and misdeeds doesn't bother most people. But the notion that hell will last forever is totally repugnant to many. For this reason, there are some who have tried to soften this truth by adopting a "kinder, gentler" view of hell.

Two erroneous views regarding the fate of the lost have become popular in recent years. The first of these views is *annihilationism,* which teaches that all souls are immortal but that the wicked will lose their immortality at the final judgment and be extinguished by God. For annihilationists, the punishment for the lost is eternal extinction.

The second unbiblical view is *conditional immortality,* which teaches that human souls are not inherently immortal, and that at judgment, the wicked will pass into oblivion while the righteous are given immortality.

These two ideas are so similar that they are usually not distinguished from one other. The views are normally merged together for the sake of simplicity and termed *annihilationism.*

So how do advocates of annihilationism defend their view? First, they contend that the lost are destroyed or cease to exist either at death or at some later time determined by God. Matthew 10:28 is one of the verses they appeal to: "Do not fear those who kill the body but are unable to kill the soul; but rather, fear Him who is able to destroy both soul and body in hell."

In the original text of the New Testament, the Greek word that is translated "destroy" (*appolumi/apoleia*) most often means "to ruin, waste, or lose." In Mark 14:4, it means "to waste." In Luke 15, it's used eight times and means "lost." The coin, sheep, and son are lost, but obviously still exist.

The second argument used by annihilationists is that the *punishment* of the lost is eternal, but not the *punishing*. In other words, the fires of hell will burn forever, but the lost will not be there to endure them.

While annihilationism is certainly more appealing to the human mind than the traditional view of eternal damnation in hell, the Bible clearly teaches that punishment in hell will last forever. The Greek word *aionios,* which is translated "eternal" or "everlasting," is used 71 times in the New Testament. Fifty-one times, it is used of the happiness of the saved in heaven. It is used of both the quality and quantity of the life that believers will experience with God. The word is used another two times of the duration of God in His glory (Romans 16:26; 1 Timothy 6:16). One time it's used of the duration of the glorified bodies of believers in heaven (2 Corinthians 5:1). Several other times it is used in such a way that no one would question that it means forever. Seven times it is used of the fate of the wicked, and there should be no doubt to an objective mind that in these passages the word means "eternal, forever, or without end" (Matthew 18:8; 25:41, 46; Mark 3:29; 2 Thessalonians 1:9; Hebrews 6:2; Jude 7).

One of the clearest references in the New Testament to the eternality of punishment in hell is Revelation 14:10-11:

> He also will drink of the wine of the wrath of God, which is mixed in full strength in the cup of His anger; and he will be tormented with fire and brimstone in the presence of the holy angels and in the presence of the Lamb. And the smoke of their torment goes up forever and ever; they have no rest day and night, those who worship the beast and his image, and whoever receives the mark of his name.

In Matthew 25:46, in the space of one verse, *both* heaven and hell are described as "eternal": "These will go away into eternal punishment, but the righteous into eternal life." To limit the meaning of "eternal" for the damned, one must also be willing to limit it for the saved as well.

Mark 9:47-48 indicates that punishment and punishing in hell is eternal: "...cast into hell, where their worm does not die, and the fire is not quenched." Why would the fire in hell be eternal if no one will be there forever?

Revelation 20:10 also clearly states the eternality of punishment in hell: "The devil who deceived them was thrown into the lake of fire and brimstone, where the beast and false prophet are also; and they will be tormented day and night forever and ever." This passage makes it clear that the torment itself is eternal. The great Lutheran commentator R.C.H. Lenski said,

> The strongest expression for our "forever" is *eis tous aionan ton aionon,* "for the eons of eons"; each of vast duration, are multiplied by many more, which we imitate by "forever and ever." Human language is able to use only temporal terms to express what is altogether beyond time and timeless. The Greek takes its greatest term for time, the eon, pluralizes this, and then multiplies it by its own plural, even using articles which make the eons the definite ones.[175]

The same phrase is used multiple times to speak of the duration of God's existence (Revelation 1:18; 4:9-10; 10:6; 15:7).

The eternality of hell is sobering indeed. Knowing the terrible, everlasting judgment that awaits the lost should cause us to plead with them to be reconciled to God (2 Corinthians 5:20-21).

The real Achilles' heel of the annihilation view is the truth regarding the degrees of punishment in hell. Obviously, there would be no need for degrees of annihilation. Either you are annihilated or you aren't. May the truth of an eternal hell fill us with passion and compassion for those who are going there because they are without Christ.

Will blood literally flow as high as the horses' bridles at Armageddon (14:19-20)?

Revelation chapter 14 is a key interlude or parenthesis in the midst of all the action taking place in Revelation. There, John provides information for us about the key players and events in the book. Yet Revelation 14, unlike some of the other interludes, looks ahead. It provides a concise preview of what is to come. One of the previews describes the conflagration at Armageddon, which is presented in more detail in Revelation 16:12-16 and 19:11-21. In this advance look at Armageddon, we read this graphic description:

> The angel swung his sickle to the earth and gathered the clusters from the vine of the earth, and threw them into the great wine press of the wrath of God. And the wine press was trodden outside the city, and blood came out from the wine press, up to the horses' bridles, for a distance of two hundred miles.

All futurist interpreters would agree that this passage conveys the scope and severity of the campaign of Armageddon. The image of blood up to the horses' bridles is gory and graphic. But is this passage merely offering a symbolic description of the brutal slaughter that will take place, or is it meant to be taken literally? Some believe that the river of blood will literally flow several feet deep for 200 miles. I'm not sure how much blood that would take, but it seems to stretch the limits of credulity to believe this much blood will actually flow for that great a distance. It seems impossible to take this passage literally.

I believe the description is drawn from the imagery of the winepress that John presents. Notice that Revelation 14:20 doesn't say the blood will "flow" as deep as the horses' bridles for 200 miles, but that "blood came out from the wine press, up to the horses' bridles." This passage is comparing the spurting of the grape juice from under the bare feet of those who tread the grapes in a stone winepress with the spurting of blood from the carnage of Armageddon. The bloodletting will be so violent it will gush and squirt as high as a horse's bridle.

Nevertheless, whatever view one takes, the main point is unmistakable. Armageddon will be Armageddon.

Are the judgments in Revelation 14:14-16 and 14:17-20 the same?

In Revelation 14:14-16, the judgment of God is pictured as a grain harvest, while in Revelation 14:17-20, there's a grape harvest. The first judgment involves Christ pictured as the Son of Man. This is an allusion to Daniel 7:13, which points to Christ's second coming in judgment. The judgment in 14:17-20 is carried out by an angel and looks to the events of Armageddon. There are three main views of the relationship between these two judgments.

First, some believe these scenes are two aspects of God's judgment. They view the grain harvest as the harvest of saints from the earth (Matthew 13:24-30), and the harvest of grapes as the harvest of sinners. However, the scenes in Revelation 14 are previews of events that will appear later in Revelation, and there is no specific harvest of saints in the final chapters of Revelation.

Second, others believe that both judgments involve sinners, but the first judgment in 14:14-16 is general in nature while the following one in 14:17-20 is the final, climactic judgment at the end of the tribulation. The problem with this view is that both judgments picture the end of the age.

The third view, which I hold to, is that these two passages picture the same judgment at the end of the tribulation from two different angles. The wheat harvest is presented with brevity, which "dramatizes the suddenness of the judgment."[176] The grape harvest depicts its severity. These two complementary descriptions of God's judgment leave little to the imagination.

What is the song of Moses in 15:1-3?

Revelation 15 is the calm before the storm. It sets the stage for the final series of judgments, or the bowl judgments. In this chapter a heavenly choir, consisting of tribulation martyrs, sings "the song of Moses" (verse 3). What is this song? There are two main songs of Moses in the Old Testament that could fit the context of Revelation 15, and they appear in Deuteronomy 32 and Exodus 15. The question is, which one is in view here?

While either one could be in view, I favor Exodus 15 as the song of Moses in this context for two reasons:

1. Deuteronomy 32 deals with God's punishment of Israel for unfaithfulness, while Exodus 15 focuses on God's punishment of the wicked and the deliverance of His people.
2. The similarity in Revelation 16 between the seven bowl judgments and the plagues of Egypt points to the Exodus setting. The entire scene is reminiscent of what took place in Exodus.

This song will echo through the chambers of heaven as the final series of God's judgments are about to be unleashed.

When will the bowl judgments be poured out?

One of the main issues connected with the book of Revelation revolves around the chronology or flow of the book. I see the judgments in Revelation as chronological and sequential. I believe the seven seal judgments (Revelation 6–8) will be opened during the first half of the tribulation and the seven trumpet judgments (Revelation 8–9; 11:15) will be unleashed during the second half of the tribulation. The seven bowl judgments (Revelation 16) will be poured out on the earth in the final days of the tribulation.

Four points support this timing. First, the bowls are poured out right before God's final judgment on Babylon (Revelation 17–18) and the second coming of Christ (Revelation 19). This placement in the flow of the book indicates they immediately precede these events.

Second, with the seven seals, there is a break between the sixth and seventh seals (Revelation 7). The seven trumpets also contain a break or intermission between the sixth and seventh trumpets (Revelation 10:1–11:14). The seven bowls have no break. This supports the view that they are poured out in rapid succession at the very end of the tribulation.

Third, in the prelude to the bowl judgments, Revelation 15:1 says, "I saw another sign in heaven, great and marvelous, seven angels who had seven plagues, which are the last, because in them the wrath of God is finished." In Revelation 16:17, when the seventh bowl is poured out, we read this: "The seventh angel poured out his bowl upon the air, and a loud voice came out of the temple from the throne, saying, 'It is done.'" From these statements, it's clear that these judgments are the last of God's plagues, which means they must be near the climax of the tribulation.

Fourth, the severity of the bowl judgments necessitates their opening right before Jesus returns to Earth. With Earth's ecology in total ruin due to water turned to blood, darkness, and

100-pound hailstones pummeling the planet, humanity could not survive if these conditions persisted for any extended period. The bowls will be the final blow before Jesus returns to end humanity's rebellion and establish His righteous rule over the earth.

What does *Armageddon* mean? Is it a real place (16:12)?

Armageddon has become a popular word in our culture today to describe any terrible, devastating event. The word *Armageddon* appears only one time in the Bible, in Revelation 16:16: "They gathered them together to the place which in Hebrew is called Har-Magedon."

The term "Har-Magedon" literally means "Mount Megiddo." It refers to an actual place in northern Israel called Megiddo, which sits on a raised area overlooking a huge valley known as the Valley of Armageddon, the Valley of Jezreel, or the Plain of Esdraelon. This valley is about 10 miles wide and 35 miles long. Napoleon is reported to have said it would make for an ideal battlefield.[177] It is in this place that the armies of the nations will gather for the final war of this age.

What will happen during Armageddon?

Armageddon is often referred to as a battle, but it is more accurate to call it a war or campaign because it will stretch over a distance of 200 miles and involve several stages or phases. John calls it "the *war* of the great day of God, the Almighty" (16:14, emphasis added).

Several key military movements are part of this campaign. While we cannot be absolutely certain regarding all the details of this chronology, here are some of the key stages of the struggle: Various armies will muster at Armageddon in the north of Israel (Revelation 16:12-16); Jerusalem will be attacked (Zechariah 12:1-3); Jesus will return to the Mount of Olives, and while He is coming, the armies gathered against Him will be slain by the breath of His mouth (Zechariah 14:1-4; 2 Thessalonians 2:8; Revelation 19:11-21); Jesus will travel to Edom in southern Jordan evidently to deliver the Jewish remnant who fled there from the Antichrist (Isaiah 34:1-7; 63:1-3).

Armageddon will be the final military campaign of this age. After Jesus defeats the armies of Antichrist and the rebellious nations gathered with him, the kingdom of God will come to the earth.

Who are the kings of the East (16:12)?

Revelation 16 describes the coming campaign of Armageddon. The armies of the world will be gathered to Israel for this final, suicidal war. Among the specific participants in this horde of nations are "the kings from the east" (16:12). So that this army can make its way to Israel, God will supernaturally dry up the Euphrates River. Many relate this invading force to the army of 200,000,000 in Revelation 9:13-19 because both contexts mention the Euphrates River. Those who make this connection usually identify this army with China because that country can now field an army of this magnitude. But for reasons stated earlier, I view the army in Revelation 9 as a demonic one, not a human one.

While it is always tempting to speculate about the identity of the various end-time players that Scripture doesn't specifically identify, all John tells us here is that the kings of the East will bring a human army that comes from east of the Euphrates. It's best to leave it at that. What we do know is that whoever these nations are, they will pour into Israel at the appointed time to the appointed place, just as God said.

Why will the kings of the earth gather at Armageddon?

It seems clear from Revelation 16 and 19 that at the end of the tribulation the armies of the world will gather in the Middle East to come against Israel in a final great death struggle. That they *will* gather is clear. And *where* they will gather is clear—they will come to Armageddon in northern Israel, and their struggle will spill over throughout the land. And *what* will happen to them is also clear—Christ will return from heaven to destroy them by the word of His mouth.

The key unanswered question is this: *Why* will they gather? The text never provides an explicit answer. Several options have been presented. Some believe they will gather to fight against the Antichrist. After enduring years of disasters, the world will tire of the Antichrist's rule. By this time, the world environment will have been ruined by the trumpet judgments, and more than half of the world's population will have died. The world economy will have unraveled and been replaced by a one-world economy ruled by the Antichrist and the false prophet. These are hardly positive talking points for a world ruler intent on staying in power.

While this view makes sense in light of what will be happening at the end of the tribulation, the problem is that the nations of the world will have been gathered to Armageddon by demonic spirits "coming out of the mouth of the dragon and out of the mouth of the beast and out of the mouth of the false prophet" (Revelation 16:13). It seems strange that demonic spirits from the unholy trinity of the end times would gather the armies of the world to fight against their own kingdom.

So why do the demons gather the armies to Israel? It makes

more sense that they are brought together for a final, all-out assault on Israel and the Jewish people. Satan's age-long vendetta against the Jews will reach its climax. In this last-ditch effort, Satan will gather the armies in an attempt to wipe out any final vestige of the Jewish race. Revelation 12 describes Satan's attempt to kill Jesus when He was born and his onslaught against the Jews during the end times. Satan is the source of all antisemitism because he knows that God has promised to send Jesus, the Messiah, to rule and reign from Jerusalem and sit on David's throne to rule over David's kingdom. If Satan can eliminate the Jews, then he can thwart God's promise from becoming fulfilled.

According to Revelation 14:19-20, the events of Armageddon will cover the entire land of Israel. Then Christ will return to Jerusalem to defeat the enemies and deliver the Jewish people (Zechariah 12:1-14; 14:1-15). Taking all these facts into account, it seems likely that the armies are gathered to Armageddon by demonic spirits in an all-out attempt to forever get rid of the Jewish people.

What is Babylon in Revelation 17–18?

Many people would probably be surprised to know that the most prominent subject in Revelation, based on the number of verses devoted to it, is Babylon. Revelation has 404 verses, and 44 of those verses (about 11 percent) deal with Babylon.

Babylon first surfaces in Genesis 10–11, just after the flood, as the place of man's first post-deluge organized rebellion against God. It was apparently the first city built after the flood. It was founded and ruled over by the world's first dictator, a man named Nimrod. It was also the location of the famous Tower of Babel.

From its inception, Babylon was both a literal city and the wicked false religious system that emanated from it. It's pictured as mankind's city, and it is the second-most-mentioned city in the Bible, appearing about 290 times. Jerusalem holds the title of most mentioned (about 800 times).

Most of the Bible's references to Babylon concern the Neo-Babylonian Empire that ruled the ancient world from 605–539 BC. King Nebuchadnezzar was the dominant leader of this empire, and he invaded Judah three times (605, 597, and 586 BC).

The Old Testament prophets repeatedly warned the people of Judah to repent or else God would send the Babylonians as an instrument of His discipline. After the final incursion in 586 BC, when the Babylonians destroyed the Solomonic temple, the message of the prophets turned from one of judgment on Judah to one of hope for the future. Part of this message of comfort and hope was that God would eventually repay Babylon for her sin. This message was intended to encourage God's people. Indeed, we read detailed descriptions of the destruction of Babylon in three key Old Testament passages: Isaiah 13; Isaiah 46–47; and Jeremiah 50–51.

The Babylon Prophecies

Isaiah 13:4-5 says, "Hear the noise on the mountains! Listen, as the vast armies march! It is the noise and shouting of many nations. The Lord of Heaven's Armies have called this army together. They come from distant countries, from beyond the farthest horizons. They are the Lord's weapons to carry out his anger. With them he will destroy the whole land" (TLB). Isaiah continues in 13:10-13:

> The stars of heaven and their constellations will not flash forth their light; the sun will be dark when it rises and the moon will not shed its light. Thus I will punish the world for its evil and the wicked for their iniquity; I will also put an end to the arrogance of the proud and abase the haughtiness of the ruthless. I will make mortal man scarcer than pure gold and mankind than the gold of Ophir. Therefore I will make the heavens tremble, and

> the earth will be shaken from its place at the fury of the LORD of hosts in the day of His burning anger.

In this chapter, written by Isaiah in about 700 BC, it appears that the prophet is peering down the corridors of time to the far destruction of Babylon in the end times. The reason for this conclusion is that nothing even close to this description has ever happened to Babylon in the past. Jesus even quoted Isaiah 13:10 in Matthew 24:29 when He described the stellar signs that will accompany His second coming to Earth. This places the fulfillment of the Babylon prophecy in the end times.

The prophet also seems to refer to the far view—that is, the destruction of Babylon in relation to the second coming of Christ in Isaiah 13:20-22, which says,

> Babylon will never be inhabited again. It will remain empty for generation after generation. Nomads will refuse to camp there, and shepherds will not bed down their sheep. Desert animals will move into the ruined city, and the houses will be haunted by howling creatures. Owls will live among the ruins, and wild goats will go there to dance. Hyenas will howl in its fortresses, and jackals will make dens in its luxurious palaces. Babylon's days are numbered; its time of destruction will soon arrive.

Isaiah 13:19 even says that when Babylon is finally destroyed, it will be like what happened to Sodom and Gomorrah: "Babylon, the most glorious of kingdoms, the flower of Chaldean pride, will be devastated like Sodom and Gomorrah when God destroyed them." The prophet Jeremiah says the same:

> Behold, she will be the least of the nations, a wilderness, a parched land and a desert. Because of the indignation of the LORD she will not be inhabited, but she will be completely desolate...Come to her from the farthest

> border; open up her barns, pile her up like heaps and utterly destroy her, let nothing be left to her...Therefore the desert creatures will live there along with the jackals; the ostriches also will live in it, and it will never again be inhabited or dwelt in from generation to generation. "As when God overthrew Sodom and Gomorrah with its neighbors," declares the LORD, "No man will live there, nor will any son of man reside in it" (Jeremiah 50:12-13, 26, 39-40).

It is apparent from both Scripture and history that these verses have not yet been literally fulfilled. The city of Babylon has never been destroyed suddenly and cataclysmically like Isaiah 13 describes. Babylon continued to flourish after the Medes conquered it under the leadership of Cyrus. When the Persians under King Cyrus conquered Babylon in 539 BC, the city wasn't destroyed. Rather, it went into a long and steady decline. The city continued in one form or another until as late as AD 1000, and even then it did not experience a sudden, cataclysmic termination such as is anticipated in this prophecy.

So what does this tell us? Babylon has never been literally destroyed as prophesied by Isaiah and Jeremiah, which means their prophecies have yet to be fulfilled. Instead, the city died a centuries-long, drawn out, agonizing death. Even today, numerous small villages dot the area in and around the ancient city. In fact, during the time of the US military's presence in Iraq, Camp Babylon was inhabited in the location of the ages-old city.

Commenting on Isaiah 13:20-22, prophecy expert John Walvoord said,

> As far as the historic fulfillment is concerned, it is obvious from both Scripture and history that these verses have not been literally fulfilled. The city of Babylon continued to flourish after the Medes conquered it, and though its glory dwindled, especially after the control

> of the Medes and Persians ended in 323 B.C., the city continued in some form or substance until A.D. 1000 and did not experience a sudden termination such as is anticipated in this prophecy.[178]

Because the city of Babylon has never known sudden and complete destruction in its long and storied history, and because the Bible is God's Word and must be literally fulfilled, we must conclude that Isaiah and Jeremiah's prophecies point to a future event. And there's only one time in man's history when all this will occur: at the end of the future tribulation period in conjunction with the second coming of Jesus Christ.

Isaiah 14 seems to further confirm that the city's ultimate destruction is related to the second advent of Christ and the final Day of the Lord. The timing of the destruction of Babylon is related to the period of final restoration for the Jewish people (Isaiah 14:1-3). When Babylon is destroyed, Israel is viewed as being restored to her land and forgiven of all her sins. This was hardly true of ancient Babylon; thus, its total demise is still future.

The final key Old Testament prophecy about Babylon is found in Zechariah 5:5-10. There, we see an indication that Babylon will be rebuilt in the end times. In Zechariah 5, the prophet Zechariah sees a vision of a basket or ephah that is full of wickedness, which is personified as a woman. Note that the ephah is a symbol of commerce, and Babylon is described in Revelation 18 as a great commercial city. Also note that Babylon is also personified as a woman in Revelation 17–18. A heavy lid is put on the basket to keep the evil in check. God doesn't want the wickedness to get out. As Zechariah sees the basket being carried away, he asks where the basket is being taken. An angel replies, "To the land of Babylonia, where they will build a temple for the basket. And when the temple is ready, they will set the basket there on its pedestal" (NLT).

When Zechariah wrote those words, the Babylonian empire had already been conquered by the Medo-Persians about 25 years earlier. And there is no event after Zechariah's prophecy that could be seen as the legitimate fulfillment of this prophecy. So what does this mean? It means that Zechariah's prophecy is still future even today. It means that someday, when the necessary preparations have been made, wickedness will once again be concentrated in the land of Babylon. It will rear its ugly head in the place of its origin—Babylon.

The city has never been completely destroyed, as indicated in the prophecies in Isaiah 13 and Jeremiah 50–51. These texts predict utter desolation like that which took place in Sodom and Gomorrah—no brick from the city will ever be used again, no one will ever live there. And the city will never be rebuilt, and the Jewish people will be fully restored to their land and forgiven by God. For Isaiah and Jeremiah's prophecies to be literally fulfilled, Babylon must be rebuilt to all its former glory and then destroyed once and for all at the end of the time of great horror. To discover Babylon's final destiny, we must turn to the end of the story in the book of Revelation.

Back to Babylon

Amazingly, as noted earlier, the book of Revelation has 404 verses, and 44 of these verses deal with Babylon (Revelation 17–18). When you add in Revelation 14:8 and 16:19, which also speak of Babylon's future, the total number of verses dealing with Babylon goes up to 46. That's 11 percent of the entire book of Revelation devoted to one subject—Babylon.

Think about that for a moment. In the final book of the Bible—God's great apocalypse or unveiling of the future—more than one out of every ten verses concerns Babylon. Clearly, Babylon holds a central place in God's final plan for the ages. But what does Revelation have to say about this great city?

Down through church history, most Bible interpreters have thought that in Revelation 17–18, Babylon was some kind of code word for some other entity, like the city of Rome, the Roman

Empire, Roman Catholicism, Jerusalem, apostate Christianity, the United States, New York City, or Great Britain. However, I believe that just like Israel always refers to Israel in the Bible, so also Babylon always refers to Babylon. In Scripture, Babylon always means literal Babylon, with one possible exception: Many scholars believe that in 1 Peter 5:13, Babylon is used symbolically as a code word for Rome. But that appears to be the lone exception to the rule.

That being the case, and because the Old Testament prophets form the backdrop for Revelation, it would be strange for Babylon to mean literal Babylon every time it's found in the Old Testament, yet for the meaning to suddenly change in the final book of the Bible, which draws so heavily from the ancient Scriptures.

Henry Morris supports a literal understanding of Babylon. "It must be stressed again that *Revelation* means 'unveiling,' not 'veiling.' In the absence of any statement in the context to the contrary, therefore, we must assume that the term Babylon applies to the real city of Babylon, although it also may extend far beyond that to the whole system centered at Babylon as well."[179]

Babylon is clearly identified in Revelation 17:5 as the source or mother of all false religion—"the mother of harlots and of the abominations of the earth." What biblical city is the genesis or fountainhead of all false religion? Only one—Babylon.

In Revelation 17–18, the city of man is symbolized by a seductive harlot riding on the back of the Antichrist, who is depicted as riding a wild beast. This connection between Babylon and the beast, or the Antichrist, indicates that the two will be closely allied. Babylon in the end times, like Babylon in the beginning, will be both a false religious system and a literal city on the Euphrates River that will serve as an economic, commercial capital for Antichrist. It will be both a city and a system.

More specifically, Revelation 17 seems to focus on the religious aspect of Babylon, while Revelation 18 focuses on the city's political and economic characteristics. The false religious system of Revelation 17 is probably a kind of religious amalgamation or world church that will pull together people of various religious backgrounds into one great ecclesiastical alliance after the disappearance of the true church at the rapture. And this world church will evidently have its center in the rebuilt city of Babylon.

Revelation 18, which describes the political and economic system based in Babylon under the rule of the Antichrist, prophesies the final destruction of the city of Babylon just before the second coming of Jesus Christ. Babylon, the pinnacle of human materialism and sensuality, will fall. The final act of God before His Son returns to Earth will be the destruction of Babylon, man's city.

Then, a few chapters later, in Revelation 21–22, God introduces the heavenly city, the New Jerusalem. The contrast is clear. Man's city, Babylon, is a corrupt harlot; God's city, the New Jerusalem, is a clean bride. Man's city is eliminated; God's city is enshrined. Man's city is removed from the earth; God's heavenly city will come to the earth. The call for God's people is to live for that which is above, that which will last, as we await our Lord's coming.

What do the seven heads (seven kings) in 17:9 represent?

Revelation 17:9-12 describes the seven heads on the beast as seven kings:

> Here is the mind which has wisdom. The seven heads are seven mountains on which the woman sits, and they are seven kings; five have fallen, one is, the other has not yet come; and when he comes, he must remain a little while. The beast which was and is not, is himself also an eighth and is one of the seven, and he goes to destruction. The ten horns which you saw are ten kings who have not yet received a kingdom, but they receive authority as kings with the beast for one hour.

There are three main views regarding the identity of the seven kings.

Symbolic

The first view is that the seven heads and seven kings are symbolic of a complete set of Roman rulers, or possibly world kingdoms, regardless of how many there actually were. The number seven is regarded as an apocalyptic symbol indicating completeness.[180] While all agree that Revelation contains highly symbolic language, the chief problem with interpreting this text in a symbolic manner, as well as in the rest of Revelation, is that the symbol has no concrete, meaningful referent. If all the text means is that the Roman rule is complete, why is the vision so detailed and particular in noting that "five have fallen, one is, the other has not yet come; and when he comes, he must remain a little while. The beast which was and is not, is himself also an eighth and is one of the seven, and he goes to destruction" (Revelation 17:10-11)? Also, if seven is the number of completion, why is the beast referred to as "an eighth"? As you can see, attempting to interpret the text symbolically fails to do justice to the intricate details of the text.

Furthermore, in Daniel, the Old Testament counterpart to Revelation, symbols have real, historical referents. When Daniel interpreted Nebuchadnezzar's dream about a great statue, he said to the king, "You are the head of gold" (Daniel 2:38). In Daniel 7:17, an angelic interpreter identified the four beasts earlier in Daniel 7 as "four kings who will arise from the earth." In Daniel 8:20-21, the ram and goat are identified as the "kings of Media and Persia" and "the king of Greece." Even more significantly, in Revelation itself symbols have identifiable, specific referents: the seven stars are seven literal messengers (1:20), the seven lampstands are seven literal, historical churches (1:20), the Lamb is Jesus (5:5-7), the golden bowls of incense are the prayers of the saints (5:8), and the dragon is the devil (12:9). To make the seven kings in Revelation 17:9-11 symbolic in some general way of the full set of Roman rulers fails to fully account for the way symbols are used elsewhere in Scripture and within the Apocalypse itself.

Successive Roman Emperors

This view is adopted by preterists. They identify the seven kings as seven individual Roman emperors who rule in succession. The reference to the seven mountains on which the woman sits is viewed as an unmistakable reference to the city of Rome, which sits on seven hills, which are named Palatine, Aventine, Caelian, Esquiline, Viminal, Quirinal, and Capitoline.

Here is a list of the 12 Roman emperors (and the lengths of their reigns) from Julius Caesar to Domitian:

1. Julius Caesar (49–44 BC)
2. Augustus (27 BC–AD 14)
3. Tiberius (AD 14–37)
4. Caligula (37–41)
5. Claudius (41–54)
6. Nero (54–68)
7. Galba (June 68–January 69)
8. Otho (January–April 69)
9. Vitellius (April–December 69)
10. Vespasian (69–79)
11. Titus (79–81)
12. Domitian (81–96)

Preterists point to Nero, the sixth king, as the one who was reigning when John wrote Revelation. There are some problems with this.

First, there are many different schemes for counting the seven kings in Revelation 17:9-11. David Aune lists nine alternate ways of counting the Roman emperors.[181] G.K. Beale provides five different schemes of enumerating the emperors.[182] J. Massyngberde Ford lists four viable constructions.[183] The reason for these different schemes is that there are many ways to count the Roman emperors, depending upon several factors.[184]

1. With what emperor should one begin counting—Caesar Augustus, Julius Caesar, or even Caligula? The evidence is far from conclusive. Several ancient sources support beginning sequentially with Julius Caesar (Josephus, *Antiquities* 18.2.2; 18.6.10; 19.1.11; *Sibylline Oracles* 5.12–15; *4 Ezra* 12:15; and Seutonius, who begins his *Lives of the Caesars* with Julius). Against this starting point is the fact that Julius Caesar was not part of New Testament history. Other ancient sources commence with Augustus as the first emperor (Virgil, *Aeneid* 6.789–97; Tacitus, *Annals* 1.1).[185] In support of Augustus as the first king, the Roman Empire was officially established under his rule, and he was the first to be proclaimed emperor.[186]
2. Are all the emperors to be counted, or only those deified by an act of the Senate?
3. Should the brief reigns of Galba, Otho, and Vitellius, all of whom ruled during the 18 months between Nero's death and Vespasian's capture of Rome (December 21, 69), be excluded from the count?

Unfortunately for preterists, one must be absolutely correct when answering all three of these questions in order to arrive at the proper solution. And each of these decisions is purely arbitrary.[187] As Robert Mounce concludes, "However people try to calculate the seven kings as Roman emperors, they encounter difficulties that cast considerable doubt on the entire approach."[188] Gentry and other preterist interpreters, in order to support their view of the date of Revelation, have to begin with Julius Caesar to arrive at Nero as the sixth king. But, as already noted, the counting can begin with Julius Caesar, Augustus, or even Caligula.[189] Beginning with Caligula makes Domitian the sixth king. We must also remember that there was a 13-year gap between the death of Julius Caesar and the beginning of Augustus's reign.[190]

Successive Kingdoms

The best solution understands the seven kings primarily as representing seven successive Gentile world powers or kingdoms.[191] This interpretation is supported by the parallels between Revelation 17:9-12 and Daniel 7:17, 23, where kings and kingdoms are interchangeable, thus revealing that a king can stand for the kingdom that he rules.

Adopting this interpretation, the eight kingdoms are the eight Gentile world powers that encompass the sweep of history: Egypt, Assyria, Neo-Babylon, Persia, Greece, Rome, the reunited Roman Empire in a ten-king form, and the future kingdom of the beast or final world ruler that emerges out of the reunited Roman Empire.[192]

This view has antiquity on its side. It can be traced all the way back to Andreas of Caesarea, who lived in the sixth and seventh centuries. He interpreted the seven kings in Revelation 7:9-10 as representing seven successive kingdoms, each of which was associated with a specific king: (1) Assyria (Ninus), (2) Media (Arbakus), (3) Babylon (Nebuchadnezzar), (4) Persia (Cyrus), (5) Macedonia (Alexander), (6) the old Roman Empire (Romulus), and (7) the new Roman Empire (Constantine), followed by (8) the kingdom of the Antichrist.[193] Andreas's blending of the kingdom and the main king who ruled the kingdom is attractive and makes sense because in Revelation, the beast appears to be both a kingdom and the satanically empowered individual who embodies that kingdom.

There are minor variations of the successive kingdom scheme, but almost all include Egypt, Assyria, Neo-Babylon, Medo-Persia, Greece, historical Rome, Rome II or the reunited Roman

Empire, and then the final world empire under Antichrist. Under all the variations, the first five empires or kingdoms are said to have already fallen and Rome is the sixth kingdom, the kingdom described as "one is" in Revelation 17:10.

This is the best view for two key reasons. First, the seven heads are seven mountains (Revelation 17:10), and "mountains" often symbolize kingdoms or empires in the Old Testament and in Jewish writings (Psalms 30:7; 68:15-16; Isaiah 2:2; 41:15; Jeremiah 51:25; Ezekiel 35:3; Daniel 2:35; Habakkuk 3:6, 10; Zechariah 4:7).[194]

Second, the successive kingdoms approach fits the Old Testament imagery of the beast and its heads as drawn from Daniel 7. The imagery of the seven-headed beast in Revelation 13 and 17 clearly alludes to Daniel 7, where there are four beasts with a total of seven heads. The reference to the beast like a leopard, bear, and lion in Revelation 13:2 is an allusion to Daniel 7, as are the ten horns of the beast in Revelation 13:1; 17:3, 7, 12. In Daniel 7, the four beasts that come up out of the sea and the seven heads on these beasts symbolize four great kingdoms. The parallel between the beast kingdoms and seven heads in Daniel 7:3-7 and the beast and seven heads in Revelation 17:9-11 is unmistakable.

Beasts in Daniel 7:1-7	**Corresponding Empire**
Lion (one head)	Babylon
Bear (one head)	Medo-Persia
Leopard (four heads)	Greece
Terrible beast (one head)	Rome
Total of seven heads	

Moreover, Daniel 7:17 and 7:23 state that the four beasts are four kings, although they in fact represent four kingdoms or empires: Babylon, Medo-Persia, Greece, and Rome. In Daniel 7, kings represent kingdoms. Because Revelation 17:9-11 draws its imagery from Daniel 7 and the beasts/kings there are successive kingdoms, it makes sense that the same principle of interpretation should be applied in Revelation 17:9-11, and the kings in this text should likewise be interpreted as successive kingdoms.

Therefore, under this interpretation, the eight kingdoms in Revelation 17:9-11 represent these kingdoms and the kings that embody them:

1. Egypt (Pharaohs)
2. Assyria (Assyrians kings)
3. Neo-Babylon (Nebuchadnezzar)
4. Medo-Persia (Cyrus)
5. Greece (Alexander the Great)
6. Rome (Caesars)
7. Reunited Roman Empire (ten kings)
8. Final Gentile world kingdom (Antichrist)

While no interpretation of the kings in Revelation 17:9-11 is without difficulty, the successive kingdoms view avoids the nebulous nature of the symbolic view, is consistent with the Old Testament imagery from Daniel 7, and provides a consistent interpretation of all eight kings. For these reasons, this is the preferred view.

SECTION THREE

The Second Coming of Christ

(Revelation 19)

Can people in heaven see what's happening on Earth?

This is a question that every believer has probably asked at one time or another. We are curious about what we will know and be able to see when we get to heaven, and whether our loved ones in heaven can look down and observe what we're doing on Earth.

The Bible never answers this question conclusively, but it does give some hints that people in heaven can see some of what is transpiring on Earth. One passage that supports this conclusion is Revelation 19:1-6, where the multitude in heaven is aware of the destruction of Babylon the Great on Earth in Revelation 17–18 and sings the "Hallelujah Chorus." This is the only occurrence of the word "hallelujah" in the New Testament, and it occurs four times in these six verses.

> After these things I heard something like a loud voice of a great multitude in heaven, saying, "Hallelujah! Salvation, glory, and power belong to our God, because His judgments are true and righteous; for He has judged the great harlot who was corrupting the earth with her immorality, and He has avenged the blood of His bond-servants on her." And a second time they said, "Hallelujah! Her smoke rises forever and ever." And the twenty-four elders and the four living creatures fell down and worshiped God who sits on the throne, saying, "Amen. Hallelujah!" And a voice came from the throne, saying, "Give praise to our God, all you His bond-servants, you who fear Him, the small and the great." Then I heard something like the voice of a great multitude and like the sound of many waters and like

> the sound of mighty peals of thunder, saying, "Hallelujah! For the Lord our God, the Almighty, reigns."

The response of the multitude in heaven clearly indicates that they are aware of what has happened on Earth to Babylon.

There are three other texts that support the notion that those in heaven have some knowledge of what's happening on Earth. First, Samuel the prophet, after his death, appeared to king Saul and was aware of at least some of the events relating to Saul and his kingdom (1 Samuel 28:16-18). Second, the rejoicing in heaven over the salvation of a sinner on Earth seems to include believers already in heaven as well as angels (Luke 15:7, 10). Third, the martyrs in heaven in Revelation 6:9-10 are aware that their persecutors are still alive on Earth.

Whether our knowledge of events on Earth is limited by God or whether we will know everything that transpires is not specifically stated. Some people often question why God would allow those in heaven to look down and see all the sin, sorrow, and misery in this world. They say this might take a lot of the happiness out of heaven. What can be stated scripturally is that those who are in heaven know at least some of what is happening on the earth and follow these events with intense interest.

However, it is also safe to say that once we get to heaven, we may not be as interested in watching the events on Earth as we might think. In Revelation 4–5, the church in heaven is pictured by the 24 elders who are preoccupied with falling down and worshipping the Lord.

While believers in heaven certainly know at least some of the main events that are occurring on Earth, it is clear from Revelation that when we get to heaven, we will primarily be consumed with worshipping the Lamb on the throne, not watching events on Earth.

What and when are the marriage and marriage supper of the Lamb?

The marriage and marriage supper of the Lamb are mentioned in Revelation 19:7-9:

> "Let us rejoice and be glad and give the glory to Him, for the marriage of the Lamb has come and His bride has made herself ready." It was given to her to clothe herself in fine linen, bright and clean; for the fine linen is the righteous acts of the saints. Then he said to me, "Write, 'Blessed are those who are invited to the marriage supper of the Lamb.'" And he said to me, "These are true words of God."

The marriage of the Lamb will take place in heaven while the tribulation is raging on Earth.

The marriage experience of believers and Christ parallels the four stages of a wedding in ancient Jewish culture:

1. The *selection* of the bride by the father—this was fulfilled when God the Father chose the church to be His Son's bride (Ephesians 1:4).
2. The *betrothal* of the bride and groom—betrothal is similar to what we know as the engagement period today, but the betrothal was much more formal and binding. This is fulfilled when a person trusts Christ as his or her Savior. Those who know the Lord are in the betrothal phase now (2 Corinthians 11:2-3).
3. The *presentation* (marriage) of the bride and groom. The couple was officially joined as husband and wife when the bridegroom came to the bride's house and she was presented to him by her father. The coming of the

bridegroom for His bride is pictured in Matthew 25:1-13. For those of us who are believers, this presentation will occur when Christ comes for His bride at the rapture and takes us up to the Father's house to be presented to Him (John 14:1-3; Ephesians 5:27).

4. The *marriage supper* or feast. In ancient Israel, the marriage celebration was a lengthy party given by the bridegroom's family and attended by many guests. Revelation 19 states that Christ's bride, arrayed in white linen, will return with Him to the earth at His second coming. The marriage supper of the Lamb and His bride will occur on the earth during the millennial reign of Christ. Jesus frequently compared His millennial reign to a wedding feast (Matthew 8:11; 22:1-14; 25:1-13; Luke 14:16-24). Many guests, including resurrected Old Testament saints and tribulation saints, will be invited to the messianic banquet (Matthew 8:11).

The presence of the bride of Christ in heaven with Jesus before He returns to Earth is strong evidence that the church must be raptured or caught up to heaven prior to that time. This is consistent with a pretribulation timing for the rapture. Like a bride-to-be waiting for her wedding day, we who are believers should be looking forward to the day when our Bridegroom comes to take us to heaven. We should be faithful and prepared as we await His coming.

When Jesus comes, will He really ride on a white horse?

Revelation 19:11-19 pictures the glorious return of the King of kings to the earth. When He comes, He will do so on a white stallion. In addition, those who return with Christ from heaven will also ride on white horses (19:14). Are these horses real, heavenly creatures, or are they just symbolic of Christ's victory?

In favor of the nonliteral view is the fact that Revelation 19 contains quite a bit of language that we don't expect to be literally fulfilled. For instance, Jesus is pictured with a sharp sword coming out of His mouth "so that with it He may strike down the nations" (19:15). The sword, a common biblical symbol for God's Word, clearly symbolizes the spoken word of Jesus, which He will employ to slay His enemies (2 Thessalonians 2:8; Hebrews 4:12). Military victors in ancient times rode white horses as a symbol of their conquest. The white horse in Revelation 19 could be understood as a striking symbol of the overwhelming victory Jesus will achieve. Unlike ancient conquerors, who rode a white horse *after* their victory, Jesus will ride a white horse *in anticipation* of victory. His success is certain.

While the symbolic interpretation is a viable option, the literal view also has good support. There are other examples in Scripture of supernatural steeds. For example, horses of fire swept Elijah up to heaven in 2 Kings 2:11. Horses and chariots of fire protected Elisha at Dothan (2 Kings 6:13-17). And even Satan has a demonic cavalry consisting of ferocious creatures (Revelation 9:16-19). It is not inconceivable, then, that God has some special heavenly horses that will carry Christ and His people back to Earth when the Lord returns.

My preference is to merge these two views. I see no reason, in light of biblical precedent, to reject the idea of literal heavenly horses. But the imagery of Christ on a white horse would have clearly been understood by the original audience as a symbol of military victory. Either way, the message of Revelation 19 is evident: Jesus will crush His enemies. His victory is guaranteed.

Who are the armies in heaven who will return with Jesus?

When the rider on a white horse descends from heaven to the earth, He will not come alone. Revelation 19:14 says, "The armies which are in heaven, clothed in fine linen, white and clean, were following Him on white horses."

Many maintain that this is an angelic army based on numerous scriptural texts that associate angels with the second coming of Jesus (Matthew 13:41; 16:27; 24:30-31; Mark 8:38; Luke 9:26; 2 Thessalonians 1:7). While it is true that angels will accompany Jesus when He returns in glory and will play a significant role in this event, three factors support the conclusion that the personnel in the army in Revelation 19:14 includes redeemed humans.

First, their clothing is "fine linen, white and clean" which is parallel to the bride's clothing a few verses earlier in Revelation 19:8. Second, Revelation 17:14 states that "the Lamb will overcome them because He is Lord of lords and King of kings, and those who are with Him are the called and chosen and faithful." The identification of those who come with Jesus as "the called and chosen and faithful" fits a human army much better than an angelic one. Third, believers are promised they will rule with a rod of iron (Revelation 2:27) just as Jesus does in Revelation 19:15.

Again, let me emphasize that identifying this army as human rather than angelic in no way diminishes the role angels will play in Christ's return. Angels will be part of the entourage that escorts the King to planet Earth, but here in Revelation 19:14, the focus is on redeemed people who will return with Jesus to judge the world.

Will the armies of heaven join in the fight against Jesus' enemies?

Having identified the army in Revelation 19:14 as human, the question arises: What role will we play? Will we engage the Antichrist and his armies and assist Jesus in the extermination of the rebel forces? Revelation 19 gives no indication that the human army plays any active role in Armageddon and the destruction of the armies of the Antichrist. Second Thessalonians 2:8 says, "Then that lawless one will be revealed whom the Lord will slay with the breath of His mouth and bring to an end by the appearance of His coming." The breath of Jesus' mouth is symbolized in Revelation 19:15 by a sword that protrudes from His mouth. "From His mouth comes a sharp sword, so that with it He may strike down the nations." Jesus will do all the fighting by means of the withering power of His spoken word. Robert Thomas concurs: "This heavenly army, unlike their leader, has no swords or spears. They take no part in the action. They wear no armor because, being immortal, they are immune to injury. They are noncombatant supporters of the Messiah as He wages the war single-handedly."[195]

Jesus will slay the armies of Antichrist with the sword that protrudes from His mouth, which signifies His Word. As my beloved professor at Dallas Theological Seminary, Dr. Pentecost, used to say, "There won't really be a battle. All Jesus will have to say is 'Drop dead,' and it will all be over."

Is the rapture the same event as the second coming?

The relationship between the rapture and the second coming is one of the most debated issues in eschatology. Are the rapture and the second coming part of a single event, or are they separated by several years of time? There are five major perspectives regarding the timing of the rapture, and the two most common are the pretribulation view and the posttribulation view.

Pretribulationists believe the rapture will occur before the seven-year tribulation, a span of time also known as the seventieth week of Daniel 9:27. They say believers who are alive on the earth at the time of the rapture will be caught up to meet the Lord in the air, and the bodies of departed saints will be resurrected and rejoined with their perfected spirits.

Posttribulationists maintain that the rapture and the second coming happen just a few minutes apart. They believe living saints will be caught up to meet Jesus as He comes from heaven at the second coming, will do a quick U-turn, and return with Jesus to Earth.

There are several strong arguments in favor of the pretribulation view, and four of them come from the book of Revelation. I have already mentioned two of them. Revelation 3:10, which I discussed on pages 99-101, supports the pretribulation rapture view. Also, if the 24 elders in heaven in Revelation 4 represent the church, as many believe, this bolsters the pretribulation position because the elders are already in heaven before the tribulation commences in Revelation 6.

The other two pretribulation rapture arguments in the book of Revelation are arguments from silence. I realize that one must be careful with arguments from silence, but I believe you will see that in both cases, the silence is truly significant.

The Missing Church in Revelation 4–18

The first argument is simple. The word translated "church" (Greek, *ekklesia*) occurs 20 times in Revelation. It appears 19 times in Revelation 1–3 and doesn't show up again until Revelation 22:16. Why the sudden absence of any mention of the church on Earth? This silence supports the pretribulation view that the church will be raptured before the tribulation and therefore will be absent from the earth during the tribulation.

The Missing Rapture in Revelation 19

Revelation 19:11-21 is the classic New Testament text on the second coming of Christ. Yet it makes no mention of believers being caught up to meet Christ as He returns. In fact, to the contrary, it mentions a group of people coming down with Christ from heaven (19:14)—people who have already been rewarded, which supports the view that they were raptured to heaven at some earlier point. This is consistent with the pretribulation view.

With regard to the absence of any mention of the rapture in Revelation 19, John Walvoord observed:

> When all the evidence is put together, one must conclude that in the most comprehensive and detailed account to be found anywhere in the Bible of the second coming of Christ, there is no resurrection or translation mentioned as an event occurring in the second coming itself. The posttribulational Rapture, which should have been a prominent feature of the Book of Revelation if it were indeed part of the great climax of the second coming of Christ, is totally missing in the narrative. If details like the casting of the beast and the false prophet into the lake of fire are mentioned and the specific resurrection of the tribulation saints is described, how much more the Rapture and translation of the church as a whole should have been

> included if, as a matter of fact, it is part of this great event. Revelation 19–20 constitutes the major problem of posttribulationists. They have no scriptural proof for a posttribulational Rapture in the very passages that ought to include it.[196]

If the rapture occurs in conjunction with the second coming of Christ, as posttribulationists contend, then why isn't the rapture mentioned in Revelation 19? The absence of the rapture in Revelation 19 is inexplicable if it happens at the same time as the second coming.

Thus, Revelation supports the concept of the rapture taking place before the seven-year tribulation begins.

SECTION FOUR

The Millennium, Final Revolt, and Great White Throne

(Revelation 20)

What is the millennium?

A little girl once heard a sermon on the millennium. When she got home, she asked her father, "Dad, what's the millennium?" He responded, "It's just like a centennial, only it has more legs." Some people are just as confused as that father about the meaning of the millennium.

The word *millennium* is made up of two Latin words: *mille* ("thousand") and *annum* ("years")—so the term simply means "one thousand years." This word appears six times in Revelation 20:1-7, which talks about the length of Christ's reign over His kingdom on Earth.

What are the different views of the millennium?

Historically, there have been three major views regarding the millennial kingdom—they are called the premillennial, amillennial, and postmillennial views. All of them agree that Jesus Christ is King and that He rules over His kingdom. That much is settled. The differences have to do with the nature and timing of the kingdom.

Premillennialism was the view of the church for the first 300 years of church history. In the early church, when Greek was the dominant language, this view was known as *chiliasm* because the Greek word for 1,000 is *chilias*. When Latin became more prevalent, the word *millennium* replaced *chiliasm*. Premillennialists believe the kingdom of Christ will be a literal 1,000-year kingdom on the earth, and that it is future. It will follow the second coming of Christ, which means that the coming of Christ is, according to this view, "pre" or before the millennium.

Amillennialism ascended in the church through the influence of Saint Augustine in the early fifth century and continued as the dominant view until the nineteenth century. Amillennialists maintain that the kingdom is not a literal 1,000 years in duration. They believe the number 1,000 is symbolic of a long period of time. They also contend that the kingdom is present now. For amillennialists, the kingdom commenced at the first coming of Christ and will culminate at His second advent. They believe that Satan is presently bound. For them, the present kingdom is spiritual in nature—they say Christ rules and reigns in the hearts of His people on Earth and over the redeemed in heaven.

Postmillennialism was developed in the sixteenth century by a Unitarian minister named Daniel Whitby. It is similar to amillennialism in that postmillennialists view the kingdom as present during the current age and as a long period of time rather than a literal 1,000 years. The key distinction is that postmillennialists believe the world will eventually become better and better as it is Christianized through the preaching of the gospel. Proponents of this view believe that this era will crescendo into a golden age and that Christ will come back after ("post") the millennium.

The following charts should help portray the differences between these three views.

The Timeline of Premillennialism

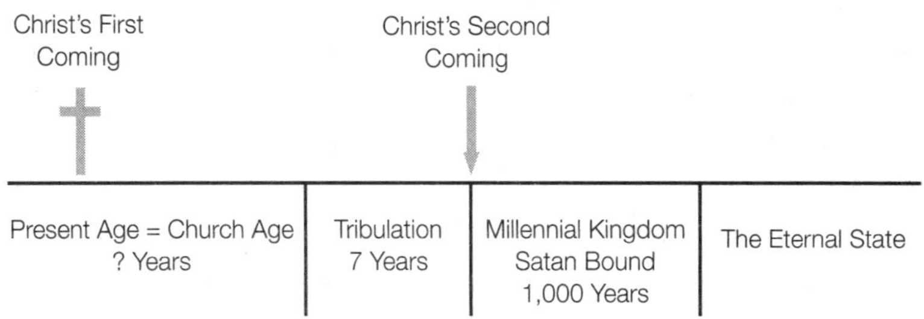

The Timeline of Amillennialism

The Timeline of Postmillennialism

Which view of the millennium best represents scriptural teaching?

I believe that the premillennial view is the view that best represents the teaching of Scripture. While there are many points in favor of this view, five stand out as most significant, and they have to do with church history, the chronology of the passage, the confinement of Satan, the immediate context, and the consummation of history.

Church History

Premillennialism was the view of the early church. It was called chiliasm based on the Greek word for 1,000. This was the view held by Papias (AD 60–130), who knew the apostle John and studied under him. Other early church figures who taught of a literal 1,000-year reign of Christ on Earth were Irenaeus, Apollinarius, Tertullian, Victorinus, Lactantius, and Justin Martyr (AD 100–165).

Speaking of the millennial view of the early church fathers, the noted nineteenth-century church historian Philip Schaff wrote:

> The most striking point in the eschatology of the ante-Nicene age [AD 100–325] is the prominent chiliasm, or millenarianism, that is the belief of a visible reign of Christ in glory on earth with the risen saints for a thousand years, before the general resurrection and judgment. It was indeed not the doctrine of the church embodied in any creed or form of devotion, but a widely current opinion of distinguished teachers, such as Barnabas, Papias, Justin Martyr, Irenaeus, Tertullian, Methodius, and Lactantius.[197]

In his *Dialogue with Trypho*, Justin Martyr said, "I and every other completely orthodox Christian feel certain that there will be a resurrection of the flesh, followed by 1,000 years in the rebuilt, embellished, and enlarged city of Jerusalem, as was announced by the prophets Ezekiel, Isaiah, and others." This clearly indicates that in the second century, premillennialism was the dominant view. It held sway until the rise of amillennialism under Tyconius and Augustine in the fifth century. The fact that premillenialism was the dominant, overwhelmingly held view of the early church doesn't prove that it's correct, but it does lend strong support from those who lived closest to the writing of Revelation.

Chronology of the Passage

A second point in favor of the premillennial position is the chronological flow and sequence of the text in Revelation 19–22. Repeatedly, John stated the words "and I saw" as he described various events unfolding in order. The flow of the passage seems sequential:

- second coming of Christ (19:11-21)
- millennium/Satan bound (20:1-6)
- Satan released/final battle of Gog and Magog (20:7-10)
- Great White Throne Judgment (20:11-15)
- eternal state (21–22)

Amillennialists and postmillennialists look to Revelation 20:1-6 and believe that the millennium was inaugurated at the first coming of Christ. They contend that after the description of the second coming in Revelation 19 the scene moves back to a description of events that occurred in conjunction with the first coming of Christ. The difficulty with that position is simply that it must be read into the text; it doesn't rise naturally from it.

In the progressive sequence of events in Revelation, the millennium, as presented in Revelation 20:1-6, immediately follows the description of the second coming of Christ in 19:11-21. I see no reason, in the text itself, to break the sequential flow of events from the second coming all the way to the eternal state in Revelation 21–22. In Revelation, the second coming of Christ is premillennial.

Confinement of Satan

The third point in support of premillennialism, which is found in Revelation 20:1-6, is the imprisonment of Satan for 1,000 years. Amillennialists and postmillennialists argue that the spiritual kingdom is present now and that Satan is currently bound so that he cannot deceive the nations. They often equate the binding of Satan in Revelation 20:1-3 with the bindings mentioned in Matthew 12:29 and Mark 3:27, and with the disarming that's described in Colossians 2:15.

This, however, is inconsistent with the way Satan is presented in the New Testament. He is portrayed as…

- the ruler of this world (John 12:31; 14:30)
- the god of this world (2 Corinthians 4:4)
- an angel of light (2 Corinthians 11:14)
- the prince of the power of the air (Ephesians 2:2)
- a roaring lion, seeking someone to devour (1 Peter 5:8)

The New Testament further states that Satan schemes against us (2 Corinthians 2:11; Ephesians 6:11), hinders us (1 Thessalonians 2:18), accuses us (Revelation 12:10), and blinds the minds of the lost (2 Corinthians 4:4).

Amillennialists counter this by saying that Satan's power to deceive the nations is restricted today. Kim Riddlebarger, an amillennial scholar, states:

> The amillennial interpretation of the binding of Satan is simply this. With the first advent of Jesus Christ and the coming of his kingdom, Satan was, in some sense, bound from the beginning of our Lord's messianic

> ministry...The binding of Satan simply means that Satan cannot deceive the nations until he is released at the end of the millennium...The imagery that Satan is presently bound means that he cannot deceive God's people *en masse* nor can he attack the covenant community with relative impunity as he did before the coming of the Messiah.[198]

The problem is that Riddlebarger's claim is not supported by Scripture. The qualifications he makes have to be read into Revelation 20:1-3. Satan is *not* bound today the way Revelation 20:1-3 describes. The binding of Satan is clearly set forth in Revelation 20:1-3 by a series of forceful actions:

- "laid hold of "
- "bound"
- "threw him into the abyss"
- the abyss is said to be "shut" and "sealed"

This description leaves little doubt that this binding of Satan is total. "There is no indication that Satan has freedom to exercise any power during that period of time."[199] As Michael Svigel notes, "Had the vision been intended simply to portray particular limitations placed on Satan's activities, this imagery appears far too strong...This emphatic description makes the standard explanation of this 'binding of Satan' by amillennialists quite implausible."[200]

Moreover, it's not just that Satan is bound that supports premillennialism but the place he is bound. Satan is bound for 1,000 years in the abyss or bottomless pit. In the first century, the Greek word *abussos* "already carried with it not a mere limitation of activity in the world but total banishment from the present world—the spiritual equivalent of solitary confinement."[201] Remember, in Revelation 9, hordes of demons are released from the abyss to afflict people on Earth during the tribulation. The imagery of their being released "indicates that prior to their release, they were unable to exercise any power in the world."[202] In the same way, when Satan is bound in the abyss for 1,000 years, he will be unable to exercise any influence in the world.

Because nothing like what is described in Revelation 20:1-3 happened at the first coming of Christ, the binding of Satan in the abyss for 1,000 years must be future, and therefore supports the premillennial position.

Context

Fourth, the context of Revelation 20:1-6 strongly supports a literal 1,000-year reign. The time frame "thousand years" is mentioned six times in Revelation 20:1-7. The frequent repetition of this phrase alone argues for its literalness. Why state a symbolic number six times? Also, the number 1,000, which is a specific number, is used in the same context where John speaks of "a short time," or a nonspecific time period (Revelation 20:3). If 1,000 is merely symbolic of a long period of time and not to be taken literally, why didn't John just say "a long time" given the fact that, in the very same context, he used the phrase "a short time"?

Consummation of History

A fifth point in favor of premillennialism is the fact that it supplies a fitting consummation to history. Think about it: Without a millennium, without Christ's reign on Earth, God's purpose for this Earth will never be fulfilled. Amillennialists and postmillennialists believe the kingdom is now, and that after the second coming, this present heaven and Earth will pass away and the new heaven and new earth will be created, ushering in the eternal state. These views, however, leave some unfinished business—some loose ends that are not brought together. God's original purpose for this Earth is to bring all things under the dominion of man and to submit all things to Himself through man (Genesis 1:26-27). Apart from the reign of Christ on Earth, God's purpose for this Earth will never be fully realized. As J. Dwight Pentecost says, "God's purpose for the earth would be unrealized and the problem generated by Satan's rebellion would never be resolved. Thus, the physical, literal reign of Christ on the earth is a theological and biblical necessity—unless Satan is victorious over God."[203] The millennium will bring creation full circle as God brings to pass with the second Adam, Jesus Christ, what the first Adam failed to do. As James Montgomery Boice says, "To my mind, however, the best and ultimate reason why there must be a literal millennium is that only in a literal millennium do we have a meaningful culmination of world history."[204] I agree. The millennium will put the capstone on God's purpose for this world.

Based on these five points, I believe the premillennial view best represents what Scripture states about the last days.

What is meant by "came to life" and "the first resurrection" in 20:4-6?

Revelation 20:4 refers to people who "came to life," and this is referred to in 20:5 as "the first resurrection." There are two main views of what is meant by "came to life" and "the first resurrection." Amillennialists believe that the descriptions refer to the *spiritual* conversion or salvation of lost people. The resurrection is viewed as a spiritual resurrection that occurs throughout this current age, which they view as the millennium. Premillennialists, on the other hand, believe the resurrection refers to the *physical* resurrection of believers at the end of the age. That raises the question: Do these phrases refer to physical life in the future, or spiritual life in the present? Three points favor the premillennial view of physical resurrection in the future.

First, the verb "made alive" (Greek, *ezesen*) is used 12 times in

Revelation and refers to physical life 11 of the 12 times. The lone exception is Revelation 3:1, where it refers to the believer's spiritual life. Also, as Harold Hoehner says, "this verb is used again in the next verse where the rest of the dead do not come to life until the 1,000 years are completed. Both uses of the term must be taken in the same way."[205]

Second, the word "resurrection" (Greek, *anastasis*) appears 42 times in the New Testament and refers to physical resurrection 41 times. Why alter the meaning here? Everything in this text points to the resurrection of the body and nothing indicates the regeneration of the soul. Because Revelation 20:4-6 refers to the physical resurrection that will occur at the end of the age, this supports the premillennial view.

Where will believers be during the millennium, and what will they do?

When Jesus Christ returns to the earth at His second coming, according to Jude 14 and Revelation 19:14, He will bring His saints with Him. This, of course, means that church-age believers must have been caught up to heaven some time before that. After Jesus defeats the armies of the Antichrist at Armageddon and judges the nations, He will establish His 1,000-year kingdom on the earth.

Many have wondered what God's people will do during the millennium. While we will certainly worship and serve our Lord during that time, Scripture also emphasizes that we will rule with Christ as well. The Bible says that all believers from every age will reign with the Lord for 1,000 years. Let's look at some Scripture passages that highlight what glorified believers will do during the millennial kingdom:

Daniel 7:18, 22, 27—"In the end, the holy people of the Most High will be given the kingdom, and they will rule forever and ever...Then the time arrived for the holy people to take over the kingdom...Then the sovereignty, power, and greatness of all the kingdoms under heaven will be given to the holy people of the Most High. His kingdom will last forever, and all rulers will serve and obey him" (NLT).

1 Corinthians 6:2-3—"Don't you realize that someday we believers will judge the world? And since you are going to judge the world, can't you decide even these little things among yourselves? Don't you realize that we will judge angels? So you should surely be able to resolve ordinary disputes in this life" (NLT).

Revelation 2:26-28—"To all who are victorious, who obey me to the very end, to them I will give authority over all the nations. They will rule the nations with an iron rod and smash them like clay pots. They will have the same authority I received from my Father, and I will also give them the morning star!" (NLT).

Revelation 20:4, 6—"They all came to life again, and they reigned with Christ for a thousand years...but they will be priests of God and of Christ and will reign with him a thousand years" (NLT).

This is just a brief overview of what is coming. We who are believers will rule the nations with Christ for 1,000 years on the earth.

During this present age, we are being tested by God to determine our future position of authority and responsibility in the kingdom. According to Luke 19:11-26, we will be given rulership in the kingdom over people and angels based on what we did with the treasures and talents God entrusted us with here on the earth. Some will become governors over ten cities; some will become rulers over five cities. We will all reign on the earth with Christ, but the extent and responsibility of that reign is being determined right now in your life and mine.

Who is "Gog and Magog" in 20:8?

At the end of the 1,000-year reign of Christ, Satan will be released from his long sentence in the abyss. Upon his release, it will be clear that his long incarceration did not change his character. And it will also be evident that man's long hiatus from Satan's presence won't have changed man's nature either. The devil will immediately organize a worldwide rebellion against Christ, and tragically, he will find millions of willing rebels.

Revelation 20:8 refers to this insurrection as "Gog and Magog." The only other time this title is used in Scripture is in Ezekiel 38–39. So, the question naturally arises: What connection is there between these two events? Many commentators believe they are describing the same event.

But upon careful comparison, it seems more likely that the two passages are describing two separate events.

	Ezekiel 38–39	**Revelation 20:8**
Participants	Specific nations	All nations
Timing	Before the millennium	After the millennium

If these are two distinct events, separated by more than 1,000 years, then why is the same title used for both? The best explanation is that John uses the phrase as a kind of shorthand way to describe what will happen. In Revelation 20 he's saying, "It's going to be Gog and Magog all over again." If this is true, then John may be using the phrase much the same way that people today use the term *Waterloo* (the scene of Napoleon's major defeat in 1815) to describe a crushing defeat.

Others explain John's use of "Gog and Magog" as using the same title from Ezekiel 38–39 to describe phase two of the same kind of war. Again, we do the same thing: We identify Super Bowl XX and Super Bowl XL. The teams may be different and the locations may vary, but it's the same event. Everyone knows what is meant by the Super Bowl. Likewise, we speak of World War I and World War II. In the same way, I believe the Bible speaks of Gog and Magog I and Gog and Magog II. When John uses the words "Gog and Magog," everyone familiar with the Old Testament knows he is describing an all-out war against God and His people, in which the invaders are decimated.

Either of these explanations makes sense in the contexts of Ezekiel and Revelation.

Why will God release Satan at the end of the 1,000 years?

After Satan is bound in the abyss for 1,000 years, God will unchain him and allow him to be unleashed on the earth for one final stand, one last gasp. That much is clear, but the nagging question is...why? Why would God release Satan from the abyss at the end of the 1,000 years?

While we don't know all the reasons God will allow Satan a brief reprieve from his life sentence, I believe that doing this will prove once and for all, beyond any doubt, that man's heart is black as midnight and that only the grace of God can save us. Revelation 20:7-10 says that when Satan is released, he will gather a vast multitude of people who are willing to battle against the Lord. This will be the final rebellion. These people who were born and raised during the millennium, living under the righteous reign of the King of kings with Edenic conditions restored, will turn on Him the first time they get an opportunity. This sounds unbelievable, but it's true. Man will quickly fall prey to the archdeceiver.

Charles Swindoll describes those who will join the evil insurrection:

> So, those enlisting in Satan's army will likely be *geographically remote,* from among those cities and regions farthest from the center of Messiah's kingdom in Jerusalem. They also will be *generationally removed* from their original ancestors who had survived the onslaught of the Beast, the memory of which will sound to those distant descendants like mere fables. Finally, the rebels will be *spiritually distant,* perhaps conforming to the outward expectations of worship and civil duty, but inwardly harboring decades of cynicism, selfishness, and rebellion.[206]

J. Vernon McGee provides valuable insight on the possible reason for God's release of Satan at the end of the 1,000 years:

> When the late Dr. Chafer (founder of Dallas Theological Seminary) was once asked why God loosed Satan after he once had him bound, he replied, "If you will tell why God let him loose in the first place, I will tell you why God lets him loose the second time." Apparently Satan is released at the end of the Millennium to reveal that the ideal conditions of the kingdom under the personal reign of Christ do not change the human heart. This reveals the enormity of the enmity of man against God. Scripture is accurate when it describes the heart as "desperately wicked" and incurably so. Man is totally depraved. The loosing of Satan at the end of the 1,000 years proves it.[207]

Henry Morris adds:

> One of the most amazing commentaries on the fallen human nature to be found in all the Word of God is right here in this passage. After one thousand years of a perfect environment, with an abundance of material possessions and spiritual instruction for everyone, no crime, no war, no external temptation to sin, with the personal presence of all the resurrected saints and even Christ Himself, and with Satan and all his demons bound in the abyss, there are still a multitude of unsaved men and women on earth who are ready to rebel against the Lord the first time they get a chance.[208]

The release of Satan from the abyss and the final revolt will show that even under the most ideal circumstances imaginable, man is still totally depraved and in desperate need of a new heart—a heart regenerated by the Spirit of God.

What is the Great White Throne Judgment in 20:11-15?

The Bible presents several different judgments. Many make the mistake of lumping them all together, which creates unnecessary confusion. Here are the seven future judgments mentioned in Scripture:

> Judgment of church-age believers in heaven (1 Corinthians 5:12)
>
> Judgment of Gentile survivors of the tribulation (Matthew 25:31-46)
>
> Judgment of Jewish survivors of the tribulation (Ezekiel 20:34-38; Matthew 25:1-30)

Judgment of Old Testament saints after the second coming (Daniel 12:1-3)

Judgment of tribulation saints after the second coming (Revelation 20:4-6)

Judgment of Satan and demons (Revelation 20:10)

Judgment of unbelievers (Revelation 20:11-15)

The final judgment in God's program is the Great White Throne Judgment. After the 1,000-year reign of Christ and before the eternal state, God will bring human history to its consummation by judging all the lost men and women of all the ages. At the judgment described in Revelation 20:11-15, all the unbelievers of all time will be resurrected and brought before the Lord they rejected. And Jesus will be the judge (John 5:22). There will be no place to hide from this date with destiny. Dr. Charles Ryrie provides a succinct description of this judgment.

> This judgment will not separate believers from unbelievers, for all who will experience it will have made the choice during their lifetimes to reject God. The Book of Life which will be opened at the Great White Throne judgment will not contain the name of anyone who will be in that judgment. The book of works which will also be opened will prove that all who are being judged deserve eternal condemnation (and may be used to determine degrees of punishment). It is not that all their works were evil, but all were dead works, done by spiritually dead people. It is as if the Judge will say, "I will show you by the record of your own deeds that you deserve condemnation." So everyone who will appear in this judgment will be cast into the lake of fire forever.[209]

SECTION FIVE

The New Heaven, New Earth, and New Jerusalem

(Revelation 21–22)

Will this present heaven and Earth be destroyed or just renovated?

All Christians agree that after Jesus comes there will be a final resurrection, final judgment, and a new heaven and new earth. The new heaven and new earth are described in Revelation 21:1: "I saw a new heaven and a new earth; for the first heaven and the first earth passed away, and there is no longer any sea."

One issue that is unclear about the coming new world order is the nature of the new heaven and new earth. Will it be the current Earth and universe simply remodeled and renovated, or will the present order be destroyed and replaced by a brand-new heaven and Earth?

Randy Alcorn, author of the book *Heaven*, advocates the renovation view:

> Romans 8:19-23 inseparably links the destinies of mankind and earth. As such, the earth will be raised to new life in the same way our bodies will be raised to new life...The perfection of creation once lost will be fully regained, and then some...It will be as if an artist wiped away the old paint, stained and cracking, and started a new and better painting, but using the same images on the same canvas...The cleansing with fire will be more thorough than the Flood in that it will permanently eliminate sin. But just as God's judgment by water didn't make the earth permanently uninhabitable, neither will God's judgment by fire.[210]

While it's possible God could renovate or restore the earth, there are several Bible passages that support the complete destruction of the present heaven and Earth and their replacement by a new heaven and new earth.

> *Psalm 102:25-26*—"Of old You founded the earth, and the heavens are the work of Your hands. Even they will perish, but You endure; and all of them will wear out like a garment; like clothing You will change them and they will be changed."
>
> *Isaiah 34:4*—"All the host of heaven will wear away, and the sky will be rolled up like a scroll; all their hosts will also wither away as a leaf withers from the vine, or as one withers from the fig tree."
>
> *Isaiah 51:6*—"Lift up your eyes to the sky, then look to the earth beneath; for the sky will vanish like smoke, and the earth will wear out like a garment and its inhabitants will die in like manner; but My salvation will be forever, and My righteousness will not wane."
>
> *Matthew 24:35*—"Heaven and earth will pass away."
>
> *2 Peter 3:10, 12*—"The day of the Lord will come like a thief, in which the heavens will pass away with a roar and the elements will be destroyed with intense heat, and the earth and its works will be burned up...looking for and hastening the coming of the day of God, because of which the heavens will be destroyed by burning, and the elements will melt with intense heat!"
>
> *Revelation 20:11*—"I saw a great white throne and Him who sat upon it, from whose presence earth and heaven fled away, and no place was found for them."
>
> *Revelation 21:1*—"I saw a new heaven and a new earth; for the first heaven and the first earth passed away, and there is no longer any sea."

It's difficult to reconcile these passages with the notion of a remodel job for the present creation. Every one of them uses the language of destruction and re-creation.

In addition to the clear statements in these verses, there's an additional textual point in favor of the destruction/re-creation view. The term "pass away" (Greek, *apeelthan*) in Revelation 21:1 is the same word used in Revelation 21:4, which says, "He will wipe away every tear from their eyes; and there will no longer be any mourning, or crying, or pain; the first things have passed away." The meaning of the words "pass away," as used in Revelation 21:4, is unambiguous. No one would argue that the tears, mourning, crying, or pain are only renovated, restored, or remodeled. Everyone would agree that they are destroyed or eliminated forever. They are gone. Because the same Greek word is used just three verses apart, it's safe to assume that it carries the same meaning in verse 1 that it does in verse 4. This meaning supports the idea that the present heaven and Earth will be destroyed and completely removed to make way for a new heaven and new earth.

What's the relationship between the new heaven and new earth and the New Jerusalem?

Revelation 21–22 describes three key features of the eternal state: the new heaven, the new earth, and the New Jerusalem. The new heaven and new earth are a new planet and new universe for God's people to inhabit and explore for eternity. But what is the relationship of the New Jerusalem, the heavenly city, to the new earth?

Some believe that the New Jerusalem will be suspended above the new earth—that it will hover about the new earth like a giant satellite city. This may be the location of the city during the millennium, but it appears to come down to the earth after the millennium is ended. While it's impossible to be certain, it seems that the New Jerusalem will descend to the new earth, settle on it, and serve as the capital city for the eternal state. In Revelation 21:2, 14 we read, "I saw the holy city, new Jerusalem, coming down out of heaven from God, made ready as a bride adorned for her husband…And the wall of the city had twelve foundation stones, and on them were the twelve names of the twelve apostles of the Lamb." The fact that the city comes down out of heaven and has foundation stones supports the notion that it will sit on the new earth as the capital city of the new heaven and new earth.

What is the size and shape of the New Jerusalem?

It's interesting to observe that the Bible begins in a garden (Genesis 2) and ends in a city (Revelation 21–22). It's also debated whether the garden in Genesis 2 was real and whether the city in Revelation 21–22 is real. I believe they are both real and literal.

The New Jerusalem is pictured as a great Edenic city—many of the features found in the garden in Genesis 2 reappear in the city of God. And it's a massive city—Revelation 21 clearly states that the New Jerusalem will be 1,500 miles high, wide, and deep. These measurements could describe either a perfect cube or a pyramid—both are possible, and one can find excellent Bible commentators who hold to one view or the other. I myself favor the cube configuration.

The city will be roughly the size of a continent—Randy Alcorn provides an excellent description:

> A metropolis of this size in the middle of the United States would stretch from Canada to Mexico and from the Appalachian Mountains to the Californian border…
>
> The ground level of the city will be nearly two million square miles. This is forty times bigger than England

> and fifteen thousand times bigger than London. It's ten times as big as France or Germany and far larger than India. But remember, that's just the ground floor.
>
> Given the dimensions of a 1,400-mile cube, if the city consisted of different levels...and if each level were a generous twelve feet high, the city could have over 600,000 stories. If they were on different levels, billions of people could occupy New Jerusalem, with many square miles per person...
>
> The cube shape of New Jerusalem reminds us of the cube shape of the Most Holy Place in the Temple (1 Kings 6:20), the three dimensions perhaps suggestive of the three persons of the Trinity. God will live in the city, and it is his presence that will be its greatest feature.[211]

What is meant by "the kings of the earth will bring their glory" into the heavenly city (21:24-26)?

Revelation 21:24-26 says, "The nations will walk by its light, and the kings of the earth will bring their glory into it. In the daytime (for there will be no night there) its gates will never be closed; and they will bring the glory and the honor of the nations into it."

According to this passage, it appears that in the eternal state, there will be people living outside the holy city. Who are these "kings of the earth," and where will they come from? Some believe this looks back to the millennial reign of Christ, when people will be living outside the heavenly city on the earth. The problem with this view is that John is no longer discussing the millennium, but has moved on to the New Jerusalem. Making this refer to the millennium doesn't fit the context.

A second view is that these are people in unresurrected bodies who will live for eternity on the new earth, outside the heavenly city. Robert Thomas, who holds this view, says,

> "[T]he nations" are composed of saved people who survive the millennial kingdom without dying and without joining Satan's rebellion and who undergo some sort of transformation that suits them for life in the eternal state. They will be like Adam and Eve in the Garden of Eden prior to the Fall. They will be unresurrected human beings who will inhabit the new earth, Paradise restored (22:1-5), throughout eternity. These will be the ones over whom God's resurrected saints will reign (22:5). Nations, peoples, and men on earth must continue in the flesh as Adam and Eve did before the Fall. What conditions prevail outside the New Jerusalem in parts of the new earth from which the nations and kings come to the city is not a matter of revelation.[212]

This view is fascinating and does help explain who believers will reign over for eternity, but for some, this raises more questions than it answers. If there will be people living in unresurrected bodies on the new earth for all eternity, why doesn't the Bible tell us more about this? Why is this mentioned in such a veiled way (if at all)? One would think if this were the case, God would provide us with more information.

The best answer is that this is simply referring to Gentiles who have been saved by God's grace and who bring whatever glory they had on Earth to heaven and give it all to the Lord. Any glory that anyone possessed here on Earth will dissolve and be swallowed up in the eternal worship of God. Walvoord says it well: "That the kings of the earth bring their glory and honor into the city means that those among the saved who have honored positions on earth will ascribe the glory and honor that once were theirs to the Lord and God."[213]

This simply means that all glory in heaven will be given to the one great triune God.

Will people in heaven need to be healed (22:2)?

Revelation 22:2 refers to the leaves of the tree of life in the New Jerusalem, which are "for the healing of the nations." This statement has confused many people because Scripture is clear that there won't be any illness or injury in heaven that will require healing.

In the original Greek text of the New Testament, the word translated "healing" is *therapeian,* from which the English words *therapy* or *therapeutic* are derived. This seems to refer to the health-giving effect of these leaves that "promote the enjoyment of life in the New Jerusalem and are not for correcting ills that do not exist."[214] In other words, the leaves of the tree of life "can be likened to supernatural vitamins, since vitamins are not taken to treat illness, but to promote general health. Life in heaven will be fully energized, rich, and exciting."[215]

The text does not specifically say that God's people will eat the leaves of the tree, but this seems to be implied. The fruit of the tree of life will forever sustain and energize God's people both physically and spiritually.

Are the gold, gems, and measurements of heaven literal or symbolic?

Questions abound about the description of the new heaven, new earth, and New Jerusalem in Revelation 21–22. And among the most frequent questions are how literally we should take the descriptions about the streets of gold, the gates that are giant pearls, and a city that's a 1,500-mile cube. Are these to be understood literally, or should we look for deeper, symbolic meanings? Or, as some say, is John simply using familiar imagery to describe what we could never otherwise understand?

I am among those who believe the descriptions in Revelation 21–22 are literal. There is nothing in the text that signals any other meaning is intended. John is describing the literal new heaven, new earth, and New Jerusalem, and what they will be like. John MacArthur expresses the literal view very well:

> Human language is inadequate to fully describe the unimaginable magnificence of the believers' indescribable eternal home. Unwilling to take the language of Scripture at face value, many seek for some hidden meaning behind John's description. But if the words do not mean what they say, who has the authority to say what they mean? Abandoning the literal meaning of the text leads only to baseless, groundless, futile speculation. The truth about the heavenly city is more than is described, but not less and not different from what is described. It is a material creation, yet so unique as to be unimaginable to us. The words of John provide all the detail we have been given by God to excite our hope.[216]

There is no reason in the text—nor is there any solid reason otherwise—to abandon the literal meaning of the very specific details that are presented concerning our eternal home. It will be a visual and sensory smorgasbord that will astound us forever.

Why is John told not to seal up the words of the book of Revelation (22:10)?

As Revelation nears its end, John is commanded, "Do not seal up the words of the prophecy of this book, for the time is near" (Revelation 22:10). Sealing up a book can carry the idea of keeping it secure or secret as in the book of Daniel, where Daniel was told to "seal up" his visions to keep them safe until the time of the end (Daniel 8:26; 12:4, 9). Revelation 22:10 is the opposite. John is commanded to make his book as accessible and widely known as possible in his own day and all subsequent generations up until the time his prophecies are consummated at the end of the age. The words "for the time is near" indicate that the events of Revelation are imminent—that is, they can break in at any time. For that reason, the content of Revelation must be open and accessible to warn and give hope to every generation.

What does it mean that those who do wrong are still to do wrong (22:11)?

In Revelation 22:11 we read one of the more perplexing, unexpected statements in the book:

"Let the one who does wrong, still do wrong; and the one who is filthy, still be filthy; and let the one who is righteous, still practice righteousness; and the one who is holy, still keep himself holy." At first blush, this verse sounds like it's condoning or at least permitting filthy, vile behavior. But the context of the next verse, Revelation 22:12, reveals that these words must be understood in light of Christ's coming. "Behold, I am coming quickly, and My reward is with Me, to render to every man according to what he has done."

Understood in the context, Revelation 22:11 is simply saying that when Jesus comes, a person's behavior and character will become permanent and unchangeable. Christ's return will happen so suddenly that there will be no opportunity for people to change. Leon Morris observes: "He probably means that the Lord's coming will be so swift that there will be no time for change. As they are at that moment, so the Lord will find them…The Lord's return is sure and soon…John is saying that there will be no opportunity for a last-minute repentance. The Lord will come too quickly for that. But now there is time. Let people repent while they can."[217]

When Jesus comes, your destiny will be sealed forever.

What does the warning about adding to or taking away from Revelation mean (22:18-20)?

The book of Revelation opens with a blessing in 1:3 and closes with a curse from Jesus Himself to any who would add to or subtract from what is written in the apocalypse:

> I testify to everyone who hears the words of the prophecy of this book: if anyone adds to them, God will add to him the plagues which are written in this book; and if anyone takes away from the words of the book of this prophecy, God will take away his part from the tree of life and from the holy city, which are written in this

> book. He who testifies to these things says, "Yes, I am coming quickly." Amen. Come, Lord Jesus.

Most commentators agree this warning is similar to that which appears in Deuteronomy 4:2, which says, "You shall not add to the word which I am commanding you, nor take away from it, that you may keep the commandments of the LORD your God which I command you." Deuteronomy 12:32 also warns against any tampering with God's Word: "Whatever I command you, you shall be careful to do; you shall not add to nor take away from it."

Some maintain that the focus in Revelation 22:18-20 is a "warning against false teachers who distort the meaning of the prophecies by adding their own teaching to it or removing the meaning that God intended."[218]

That idea may be included, but at a minimum, this warning would prohibit any intentional adding to or subtracting from the book of Revelation itself. That much is obvious. However, because Revelation is the final book of the New Testament canon, I believe this warning extends to all of Scripture. This is God's final seal upon His Word. Bible commentator John Phillips says,

> By application this warning takes in the entire canon of Scripture. God will not have His Word tampered with. Eve, when she encountered the serpent, added to what God said and subtracted from what God said. Her sin opened the door for all that followed of curse, of banishment from the tree of life, of peril and eternal doom. God's wrath abides on those who tamper with His Word, cutting out the parts that offend them and adding their own ideas thereto.
>
> The initial scope of the warning has to do with the Apocalypse. God guards this book that so many have scorned; He guards it with a terrible warning. Thus the Apocalypse opens with a blessing for those who read it, hear it, and keep it. It ends with a curse for those who

> tamper with it. The closing word that guards the Apocalypse is set as a sentinel to all of Scripture, for God places this book at the end of all the rest.[219]

This means that the inspired canon of Scripture was closed at the end of the first century when Revelation was finished. Therefore, any false prophet, counterfeit, or charlatan who adds alleged new revelation to it will face divine vengeance. This is a sober warning to all the cults that add to God's Word and to all the critics who take away from God's Word by denying the inspiration of Scripture and cutting out the supernatural events within it.

There's an ironic twist here in God's judgment upon those who add to or subtract from His Word: "Those who add to Scripture will have the plagues added to them; those who take away from Scripture will have the blessings of heaven taken away from them."[220]

May the Lord help us to guard His Word and be careful to do what it says. May the Lord strengthen us to never subtract from its authority and power in our lives.

How can I be sure I'm going to heaven?

There are many last words recorded in the Bible—the last words of Moses (Deuteronomy 33), Jesus on the cross, Jesus before His ascension (Acts 1:8), Paul (2 Timothy), Peter (2 Peter), and more. The most important of all are the last words of Jesus Christ to those on this Earth. We find them in Revelation 22, where Jesus states His Last Invitation:

> "I, Jesus, have sent My angel to testify to you these things for the churches. I am the root and the descendant of David, the bright morning star." The Spirit and the bride say, "Come." And let the one who hears

> say, "Come." And let the one who is thirsty come; let the one who wishes take the water of life without cost (verses 16-17).

Why do people come to Christ? Because they're thirsty. They are dying of spiritual thirst—a thirst that nothing can quench. The strongest physical desire we know as humans is thirst. Likewise, the strongest spiritual desire we know is the thirst to find something that will quench our parched souls. People try to slake their thirst with all kinds of things—work, multiple marriages and relationships, success, money, the good life. But they are still parched, dry, and empty. Only Jesus can give the true water of life.

The gospel of Jesus Christ is so simple. There are no restrictions on who can come. It's the one who is thirsty. It's the one who wishes. There is only one condition—take freely of the water of salvation. You don't bring your good works or merit. All you have to do is recognize your need, admit your thirst, and come to Him for salvation.

Revelation 22 includes the Last Invitation (verses 16-17), the Last Warning (verses 18-20), and the Last Word (verses 20-21).[221] This last word has to do with grace. It's comforting to know that in a book filled with judgment and wrath, the last word is a word of grace: "The grace of our Lord Jesus Christ be with all. Amen" (verse 21).

The Old Testament ends with a curse (Malachi 4:6), and the New Testament ends with grace. God gives us what we don't deserve. Why not come to Christ now and drink from the fountain of His amazing grace? Take the free gift of eternal life and be saved from the penalty of your sins.

Come!

When you do that, you will be able to join the chorus of God's people and say, "Amen. Come, Lord Jesus" (Revelation 22:20).

Recommended Further Reading on Revelation

Fanning, Buist M. *Revelation*. Exegetical Commentary on the New Testament, gen. ed. Clinton E. Arnold. Grand Rapids, MI: Zondervan Academic, 2020.

Heitzig, Skip. *You Can Understand the Book of Revelation*. Eugene, OR: Harvest House, 2011.

Hindson, Ed. *Approaching Armageddon: The World Prepares for War with God*. Eugene, OR: Harvest House, 1997.

Jeremiah, David. *Escape the Coming Night: An Electrifying Tour of the World as It Races Toward Its Final Days*. Dallas, TX: Word, 1990.

Kinley, Jeff. *God's Grand Finale*. Eugene, OR: Harvest House, 2023.

LaHaye, Tim. *Revelation Unveiled*. Grand Rapids, MI: Zondervan, 1999.

MacArthur, John. *Revelation 1–11*. Chicago, IL: Moody, 1999.

MacArthur, John. *Revelation 12–22*. Chicago, IL: Moody, 2000.

Morgan, Robert J. *The 50 Final Events in World History*. Nashville, TN: W Publishing, 2022.

Morris, Henry M. *The Revelation Record*. Wheaton, IL: Tyndale, 1983.

Osborne, Grant R. *Revelation*. Baker Exegetical Commentary on the New Testament, ed. Moises Silva. Grand Rapids, MI: Baker Academic, 2002.

Patterson, Paige. *Revelation*. The New American Commentary, gen. ed. E. Ray Clendenen, vol. 39. Nashville, TN: B&H Publishing, 2012.

Phillips, John. *Exploring Revelation*. Neptune, NJ: Loizeaux Brothers, 1991.

Rogers, Adrian. *Unveiling the End Times in Our Time*. Nashville, TN: B&H Publishing, 2004.

Ryrie, Charles Caldwell. *Revelation*. Everyman's Bible Commentary. Chicago, IL: Moody, 1968.

Stedman, Ray C. *God's Final Word: Understanding Revelation*. Grand Rapids, MI: Discovery House, 1991.

Swindoll, Charles R. *Insights on Revelation*. Grand Rapids, MI: Zondervan, 2011.

Thomas, Robert L. *Revelation 1–7: An Exegetical Commentary*. Chicago, IL: Moody, 1992.

Thomas, Robert L. *Revelation 8–22: An Exegetical Commentary*. Chicago, IL: Moody, 1995.

Walvoord, John F. *Revelation*, rev. ed. Chicago, IL: Moody, 2011.

Notes

1. Donald Grey Barnhouse, *Revelation: An Expository Commentary* (Grand Rapids, MI: Zondervan, 1971), 13.
2. Charles Caldwell Ryrie, *Revelation* (Chicago, IL: Moody, 1968), 10-11.
3. R.C. Sproul, *The Last Days According to Jesus* (Grand Rapids, MI: Baker, 1998), 228.
4. Sproul, *The Last Days According to Jesus*, 24.
5. Steve Gregg, ed. *Revelation: Four Views* (Nashville, TN: Thomas Nelson, 1997), 43.
6. Gregg, ed. *Revelation: Four Views*, 44.
7. J. Daniel Hays, J. Scott Duvall, and C. Marvin Pate, *Dictionary of Biblical Prophecy and End Times* (Grand Rapids, MI: Zondervan, 2007), 172.
8. Ed Hindson, *Approaching Armageddon* (Eugene, OR: Harvest House, 1997), 28.
9. Grant R. Osborne, *Revelation*, Baker Exegetical Commentary of the New Testament, ed. Moises Silva (Grand Rapids, MI: Baker Academic, 2002), 21.
10. Arnold G. Fruchtenbaum, *The Footsteps of the Messiah*, rev. ed. (Tustin, CA: Ariel Ministries, 2003), 10-11.
11. Paul Benware, *Understanding End Times Prophecy: A Comprehensive Approach* (Chicago, IL: Moody Press, 1995), 21-22.
12. Fruchtenbaum, *The Footsteps of the Messiah*, 11-12.
13. For a more complete list, see J.B. Smith, *A Revelation of Jesus Christ: A Commentary on the Book of Revelation* (Scottsdale, PA: Herald Press, 1961), 18.
14. Smith, *A Revelation of Jesus Christ*, 19.
15. Steve P. Sullivan, "Premillennialism and an Exegesis of Revelation 20," 37-38, www.pre-trib.org/data/pdf/Sullivan-PremillennialismAndA.pdf.
16. John F. Walvoord, *Revelation*, rev. ed. (Chicago, IL: Moody Press, 2011), 29-30.
17. Sullivan, "Premillennialism and an Exegesis of Revelation 20," 39-40.
18. Buist Fanning holds that the human author of Revelation is "A prophet 'John,' different from the other two, who was active among the churches of Asia

Minor in the first century and known to them but unknown to us except for this book" (Buist M. Fanning, *Revelation* [Grand Rapids, MI: Zondervan, 2020], 25). Fanning concludes "it was written not by the apostle but by another church leader, a prophet known to the churches of Asia Minor, also named John and influenced by the apostle" (Fanning, *Revelation*, 28).

19. For an excellent discussion of the issues of authorship of Revelation, see Osborne, *Revelation*, 2-5; and Robert L. Thomas, *Revelation 1–7* (Chicago, IL: Moody, 1992), 2-19.
20. Osborne, *Revelation*, 4.
21. Osborne, *Revelation*, 5.
22. Thomas, *Revelation 1–7*, 9-10.
23. Kenneth L. Gentry, Jr. "The Days of Vengeance: A Review Article," *The Council of Chalcedon* (June 1987): 11. I would strengthen Gentry's point by adding that if it could be proved that Revelation was written one year after AD 67, then preterism would go up in smoke.
24. Sproul, *The Last Days According to Jesus*, 140.
25. Philip Schaff strongly supported the reliability and trustworthiness of Irenaeus. Schaff, *History of the Christian Chuch*, 2:750-51. Milligan lists four considerations that add weight to Irenaeus' testimony: (1) his nearness to the apostolic age, (2) he was a disciple and friend of Polycarp, (3) his mention of the date of Revelation is in conjunction with a section of Revelation that he approached with utmost seriousness (Revelation 13:16-18), and (4) the confidence of Eusebius in the statement made by him. William Milligan, *Discussions on the Apocalypse* (London: MacMillan, 1893), 78-79.
26. Irenaeus, *Against Heresies* 5.30.3. The Greek version of Irenaeus's statement is preserved in two places in Eusebius's *Ecclesiastical History* 3.18.3; 5.8.6.
27. Colin J. Hemer, *The Letters to the Seven Churches of Asia in Their Local Setting*, The Biblical Resource Series, eds. Astrid B. Beck and David Noel Freedman (Sheffield, UK: Sheffield Academic Press, 1986; reprint, Grand Rapids, MI: Eerdmans, 2001), 3, 5.
28. This chart is from Charles R. Swindoll, *Insights on Revelation* (Grand Rapids, MI: Zondervan, 2011), 17.
29. Hindson, *Approaching Armageddon*, 22-23.
30. Osborne, *Revelation*, 81.
31. Thomas, *Revelation 1–7*, 52.
32. Thomas Ice, "Preterist 'Time Texts,'" 102-105; John F. Walvoord, *Revelation*, rev. ed. (Chicago, IL: Moody Press, 2011), 37-38.
33. John F. Walvoord, *Revelation*, 37-38. Both Ice and Walvoord interpret "soon" as primarily indicative of the manner (suddenness or swiftness) of the

events in Revelation once they begin. Ice, "Preterist 'Time Texts,'" 102-8; Walvoord, *Revelation*, 37-38. However, they both interpret "near" or "at hand" as primarily indicative of imminency or nearness from the standpoint of prophetic revelation.

34. Walter Bauer, William F. Arndt, and F. Wilbur Gingrich (BDAG), *A Greek-English Lexicon of the New Testament and other Early Christian Literature* (Chicago, IL: University of Chicago, 1968), 993.

35. Thomas, *Revelation 1–7*, 55.

36. BDAG, *A Greek-English Lexicon*, 271.

37. Alan F. Johnson, "Revelation," in *The Expositor's Bible Commentary*, ed. Frank E. Gaebelein, vol. 12 (Grand Rapids, MI: Zondervan, 1981), 416; Ben Witherington III, *Revelation*, New Cambridge Bible Commentary, ed. Ben Witherington III (Cambridge: Cambridge University Press, 2003), 66.

38. Philip Edgcumbe Hughes, *The Book of Revelation: A Commentary* (Grand Rapids, MI: Eerdmans, 1990), 16.

39. Thomas, *Revelation 1–7*, 55-56. Morris, *Revelation*, 47.

40. G.K. Beale, "Eschatology," in *Dictionary of the Later New Testament and Its Development*, eds. Ralph P. Martin and Peter H. Davids (Downers Grove, IL: InterVarsity, 1997), 331.

41. W. Hall Harris notes that the phrase "last hour" can refer to a period of time, since Jesus used it to refer to the entire period just prior to His crucifixion until His return to the Father (John 2:4; 7:30; 8:20; 12:23; 12:27; 13:1; 17:1). Harris refers this time to the final stage of history between the two advents of Christ. W. Hall Harris III, *1, 2, 3 John: Comfort and Counsel for a Church in Crisis* (Dallas, TX: Biblical Studies Press, 2003), 104-5.

42. D. Edmond Hiebert, *The Epistles of John: An Expositional Commentary* (Greenville, SC: Bob Jones University Press, 1991), 107-8. Marshall supports this same idea. He says that John used the reference to the "last hour" to stress the imminency of the *parousia* and the urgency of being ready for the Lord's coming at any time. I. Howard Marshall, *The Epistles of John*, New International Commentary on the New Testament, ed. F.F. Bruce (Grand Rapids, MI: Eerdmans, 1978), 148-51.

43. William R. Newell, *The Book of the Revelation* (Chicago, IL: Moody, 1935), 362.

44. Thomas, *Revelation 1–7*, 56.

45. J.A. Seiss, *The Apocalypse: Lectures on the Book of Revelation* (New York: Charles C. Cook, 1900; reprint, Grand Rapids, MI: Zondervan, 1966), 23; Hughes, *Revelation*, 237, 241.

46. Vern S. Poythress, *Returning King* (Phillipsburg, NJ: P&R Publishing, 2020), 35.

47. Robert H. Mounce, *The Book of Revelation*, rev. ed., New International Commentary on the New Testament, ed. Gordon D. Fee (Grand Rapids, MI: Eerdmans, 1998), 41; cf. Osborne, *Revelation*, 55, 59; Hughes, *Revelation*, 241; Thomas, "Dating Revelation," 198.

48. Johnson, "Revelation," 416-17.

49. Swindoll, *Insights on Revelation*, 14; see also George Eldon Ladd, *A Commentary on the Revelation of St. John* (Grand Rapids, MI: Eerdmans, 1972), 22.

50. Adrian Rogers, *Unveiling the End Times in Our Time* (Nashville, TN: B&H Publishing, 2004), 8.

51. Gordon D. Fee, *Revelation*, New Covenant Commentary Series, eds. Michael F. Bird and Craig Keener (Eugene, OR: Cascade Books, 2011), 6.

52. Fee, *Revelation*, 6.

53. Fee, *Revelation*.

54. Tim LaHaye, *Revelation Unveiled* (Grand Rapids, MI: Zondervan, 1999), 32.

55. John F. Walvoord, *Matthew: Thy Kingdom Come* (Chicago, IL: Moody, 1974), 190.

56. Thomas, *Revelation 1–7*, 90.

57. John MacArthur, *Revelation 1–11* (Chicago, IL: Moody, 1999), 41.

58. Michael Holmes, ed., *The Apostolic Fathers*, 2d ed., trans. J.B. Lightfoot and J.R. Harmer (Grand Rapids, MI: Baker, 1989), 146-47.

59. Thomas, *Revelation 1–7*, 91.

60. Ray C. Stedman, *God's Final Word: Understanding Revelation* (Grand Rapids, MI: Discovery House, 1991), 21.

61. Robert Dean, "The Meaning of Angels in Revelation 2 and 3," www.pre-trib.org/articles/view/meaning-of-angels-in-revelation-2-and-3. Dean does an excellent job of summarizing all the views and giving a fair, thorough evaluation of the strengths and weaknesses of each position.

62. Thomas, *Revelation 1–7*, 117.

63. Thomas, *Revelation 1–7*, 34.

64. See at http://www.soniclight.com/constable/notes/pdf/revelation.pdf.

65. Thomas, *Revelation 1–7*, 93.

66. Thomas, *Revelation 1–7*, 93-4.

67. Thomas, *Revelation 1–7*, 93.

68. Richard Mayhue, *What Would Jesus Say About Your Church?* (Ross-shire, UK: Christian Focus, 1995), 28.

69. Paul W. Powell, *The Last Word: The Lord's Last Message to His Church* (Tyler, TX: 2004).

70. See at http://www.soniclight.com/constable/notes/pdf/revelation.pdf.

71. See at http://www.soniclight.com/constable/notes/pdf/revelation.pdf.

72. Robert Thomas provides an excellent, thorough discussion of this issue. Thomas, *Revelation 1–7*, 505-15.

73. William Lee, "The Revelation of St. John," in *The Holy Bible*, ed. F.C. Cook, vol. 4 (London: John Murray, 1881), 513-14.

74. Wayne Stiles, quoted in Charles R. Swindoll, *The Church Awakening* (New York: FaithWords, 2010), 227.

75. Walvoord, *Revelation*, 58.

76. Thomas, *Revelation 1–7*, 148.

77. Osborne, *Revelation*, 120-21.

78. William Barclay, *The Revelation of John*, rev. ed., vol. 1 (Philadelphia, PA: Westminster, 1976), 68.

79. MacArthur, *Revelation 1–11*, 64-65.

80. Fanning, *Revelation*, 128, 174.

81. Thomas R. Schreiner, *Revelation*, Baker Exegetical Commentary on the New Testament, eds. Robert W. Yarbrough and Joshua W. Jipp (Grand Rapids, MI: Baker Academic, 2023), 153.

82. Thomas, *Revelation 1–7* (Chicago, IL: Moody, 1992), 200.

83. Swindoll, *Insights on Revelation*, 55.

84. Walvoord, *Revelation, 77.*

85. Walvoord, *Revelation*, 80.

86. MacArthur, *Revelation 1–11*, 115.

87. Thomas, *Revelation 1–7*, 275.

88. Charles C. Ryrie, *Come Quickly, Lord Jesus* (Eugene, OR: Harvest House, 1996), 137-38.

89. Walvoord, *Revelation*, 84.

90. Thomas Ice, "The Earth-Dwellers of Revelation," www.pre-trib.org/articles/view/earth-dwellers-of-revelation.

91. Osborne, *Revelation*, 199.

92. Walvoord, *Revelation*, 88.

93. John Phillips, *Exploring Revelation* (Neptune, NJ: Loizeaux Brothers, 1991), 73.

94. Osborne, *Revelation*, 205.

95. Barnhouse, *Revelation*, 82.

96. Thomas, *Revelation 1–7*, 308.

97. Thomas, *Revelation 1–7*, 306.

98. Robert H. Mounce, *The Book of Revelation*, The New International Commentary on the New Testament, gen. ed. F.F. Bruce (Grand Rapids, MI: Wm. B. Eerdmans, 1977), 125.

99. Several well-known commentators hold this view. LaHaye, *Revelation Unveiled*, 89-91; David Jeremiah, *Escape the Coming Night* (Dallas, TX: Word, 1997), 81; Stedman, *God's Final Word*, 107. Stedman calls Revelation 3:20 "the most moving and powerful explanation in the Bible of how to become a Christian" (107).

100. Thomas, *Revelation 1–7*, 323. Thomas's view is a kind of hybrid position. He sees Revelation 3:20 as "an opportunity for those who have not yet experienced conversion to Christ to do so and thereby to make ready for His return" (323).

101. Osborne, *Revelation*, 213.

102. Swindoll, *Insights on Revelation*, 82.

103. Phillips, *Exploring Revelation*, 76-77.

104. LaHaye, *Revelation Unveiled*, 99-100.

105. Jeremiah, *Escape the Coming Night*, 101-2.

106. John MacArthur, *Heaven* (Chicago, IL: Moody, 1988), 90.

107. Fanning, *Revelation*, 200-01.

108. Many modern translations of Revelation 5:9 omit the word "us" or substitute "people" or "men." However, the Greek pronoun for "us" occurs in the oldest manuscripts and the majority of manuscripts.

109. Jeff Kinley, *God's Grand Finale* (Eugene, OR: Harvest Prophecy, 2023), 91; Walvoord, *Revelation*, 109-10.

110. Fanning, *Revelation*, 203.

111. David J. MacLeod, "The Lion Who Is a Lamb," *Bibliotheca Sacra* 164 (July-September 2007), 325-28.

112. MacLeod, "The Lion Who Is a Lamb," 329-30.

113. George Eldon Ladd, *A Commentary on the Revelation of John* (Grand Rapids, MI: Eerdmans, 1972), 99.

114. Barnhouse, *Revelation*, 122.

115. Morris, *Revelation*, 116; Thomas, *Revelation 1–7*, 432–4.

116. Thomas, *Revelation 1–7*, 439.

117. Henry M. Morris, *The Revelation Record* (Wheaton, IL: Tyndale House, 1983), 118.

118. MacArthur, *Revelation 1–11*, 184; Jeremiah, *Escape the Coming Night*, 120-21. Grant Osborne seems to view the wild beasts of the earth as the birds that will feed on the carrion described further in Revelation 19:17-18, 21. Osborne, *Revelation*, 283.

119. Adrian Rogers, *Unveiling the End Times in Our Time* (Nashville, TN: B&H Publishing, 2004), 90.

120. "About Zoonotic Diseases," *CDC*, https://www.cdc.gov/onehealth/basics/zoonotic-diseases.html.

121. Albert Mohler, "Coronavirus Spreads in China as Government Quarantines 25 Million People: Echoes of Plagues Past, Present, and Future," *The Briefing*, January 24, 2020, https://albertmohler.com/2020/01/24/briefing-1-24-20.

122. Margaret Hamburg and Mark Smolinski, "The Coronavirus Outbreak Is A Wake-up Call Showing How Unprepared We Are To Deal With Biological Threats," *Newsweek*, February 3, 2020, https://www.newsweek.com/coronavirus-outbreak-wake-call-showing-how-unprepared-we-are-deal-biological-threats-1485316.

123. Ed Yong, "The Next Plague Is Coming. Is America Ready?," *The Atlantic*, July/August 2018, https://www.theatlantic.com/magazine/archive/2018/07/when-the-next-plague-hits/561734/.

124. Marvin Rosenthal, *The Pre-Wrath Rapture of the Church* (Nashville, TN: Thomas Nelson, 1990), 59.

125. Rosenthal, *The Pre-Wrath Rapture of the Church*, 60.

126. Alan Hultberg, *Three Views on the Rapture: Pretribulation, Prewrath, and Posttribulation* (Grand Rapids, MI: Zondervan, 2010), 109. Hultberg locates the rapture in Matthew 24:31, the same place as posttribulationsts, which is confusing. He interprets Matthew 24:30-31 as an extended *parousia*; however, he admits that this passage never mentions the rapture (115).

127. Rosenthal, *The Pre-Wrath Rapture of the Church*, 112-13.

128. Paul Feinberg, *The Rapture: Pre-, Mid-, or Post-Tribulational* (Grand Rapids, MI: Zondervan, 1984), 223.

129. Benware, *Understanding End Times Prophecy*, 220.

130. Benware, 234-35.

131. Jeremiah, *Escape the Coming Night*, 135.

132. Walvoord, *Revelation*, 141.

133. Ryrie, *Revelation*, 51.

134. Swindoll, *Insights on Revelation*, 119.

135. Walvoord, *Revelation*, 140.

136. Swindoll, *Insights on Revelation*, 119.

137. Earl Palmer, *1, 2, 3 John, Revelation*, The Communicator's Commentary, gen. ed. Lloyd J. Ogilvie (Waco, TX: Word, 1982), 185.

138. MacArthur, *Revelation 1–11*, 237-8.

139. Walvoord, *Revelation*, 149.

140. H.A. Ironside, *Lectures on the Book of Revelation* (Neptune, NJ: Loizeaux Brothers, 1930), 151.

141. Swindoll, *Insights on Revelation*, 130.

142. Hindson, *Approaching Armageddon*, 142.

143. Osborne, *Revelation*, 355.

144. Osborne, *Revelation*, 362.

145. Swindoll, *Insights on Revelation,* 133-34.

146. Osborne, *Revelation*, 374.

147. Osborne, *Revelation*, 381.

148. Walvoord, *Revelation*, 166, n. 13.

149. Ladd, *A Commentary on the Revelation of John*, 143.

150. Warren W. Wiersbe, *The Bible Exposition Commentary*, New Testament, vol. 2 (Wheaton, IL: Victor Books, 1989), 598 (emphasis in original).

151. Thomas, *Revelation 8–22*, 81; cf. J.A. Seiss, *Apocalypse*, 236.

152. Ladd, *A Commentary on the Revelation of St. John*, 152.

153. Thomas, *Revelation 8–22*, 80-81.

154. Hank Hanegraaff, *The Apocalypse Code* (Nashville, TN: Thomas Nelson, 2007), 131.

155. W. Graham Scroggie, *The Great Unveiling: An Analytical Study of Revelation* (Grand Rapids, MI: Zondervan, 1979), 66.

156. Revelation 11:5 says, "If anyone desires to harm them, fire proceeds out of their mouth and devours their enemies." Hanegraaff uses this to justify his metaphorical interpretation of the two witnesses. He says "the two witnesses will not literally turn their mouths into blow torches on the streets of Jerusalem" (*The Apocalypse Code*, 133). The imagery of something proceeding out of someone's mouth is interpreted for us in Revelation 1:16 and 19:15, 21. These verses say that the resurrected, glorified Lord Jesus appears with a sharp two-edged sword coming out of His mouth. Of course, we know that Jesus doesn't have a literal sword coming out of His mouth. This is an obvious symbol for the Word of God that He speaks (see Hebrews 4:12). Yet Hanegraaff would not say that because this symbol is used that Jesus is not a literal person.

Likewise, he shouldn't say that just because this figurative imagery is used of the two witnesses that they aren't literal persons. The fire out of their mouths is symbolic of the fiery plagues they call forth on the earth during the tribulation. Again, the key to interpreting Revelation is often found within the book itself, and consistency is very important.

157. Hippolytus, *Antichrist* 43. According to Bernard McGinn, Hippolytus is also the first to state explicitly that the Antichrist will rebuild the temple in Jerusalem (*Commentary on Daniel* 4.49). Bernard McGinn, *Antichrist: Two Thousand Years of the Human Fascination with Evil* (San Francisco, CA: Harper, 1994), 297 n. 22.

158. Le Roy Edwin Froom, *The Prophetic Faith of Our Fathers*, vol. 1 (Washington, DC: Review and Herald, 1950).

159. McGinn, *Antichrist*, 67.

160. Froom, *The Prophetic Faith of Our Fathers*, 1:461.

161. McGinn, *Antichrist*, 67.

162. J. Dwight Pentecost, *Things to Come: A Study in Biblical Eschatology* (Grand Rapids, MI: Zondervan, 1958), 308. Pentecost provides an excellent discussion of the various views concerning the two witnesses (304-8).

163. Charles R. Swindoll, *Insights on Revelation* (Grand Rapids, MI: Zondervan, 2011), 158-59.

164. Thomas, *Revelation 8–22*, 85.

165. Walvoord, *Revelation*, 181.

166. G. Salmon, *An Historical Introduction to the Study of the Books of the New Testament*, 9th ed. (London: John Murray, 1904), 230-31.

167. Raymond Brown, *Introduction*, 805.

168. Wiersbe, *The Bible Exposition Commentary*, 605.

169. Ryrie, *Revelation*, 83.

170. Wiersbe, *The Bible Exposition Commentary*, 605.

171. Josephus *Antiquities* 20.11.1.

172. Pentecost, *Things to Come*, 336-37.

173. John F. Walvoord. *The Prophecy Knowledge Handbook* (Wheaton, IL: SP Publications, 1990), 587.

174. Mounce, *The Book of Revelation*, 72-73.

175. Quoted by Larry Dixon, *The Other Side of the Good News* (Wheaton, IL: BridgePoint, 1992), 93.

176. Thomas, *Revelation 8–22*, 221.

177. Eric H. Cline, *The Battles of Armageddon* (Ann Arbor, MI: University of Michigan, 2002), 142.

178. John F. Walvoord, *The Nations in Prophecy* (Grand Rapids, MI: Zondervan, 1967), 63-64.

179. Morris, *The Revelation Record*, 323.

180. Isbon T. Beckwith, *The Apocalypse of John* (New York: Macmillan, 1919; repr., Grand Rapids, MI: Baker, 1979), 704-8; Mounce, *Revelation*, 317; Witherington, *Revelation*, 223; G.R. Beasley-Murray, "Book of Revelation," in *Dictionary of the Later New Testament & Its Development*, eds. Ralph P. Martin and Peter H. Davids (Downers Grove, IL: InterVarsity, 1997), 256-57; Osborne, *Revelation*, 620; David E. Aune, *Revelation 17–22*, Word Biblical Commentary, ed. Ralph P. Martin, vol. 52C (Dallas, TX: Word, 1998), 948.

181. Aune, *Revelation 17–22*, 947-48.

182. Beale, *Revelation*, 874.

183. J. Massyngberde Ford, *Revelation*, Anchor Bible, eds. William Foxwell Albright and David Noel Freedman, vol. 38 (Garden City, NY: Doubleday, 1975), 289.

184. J. Ramsey Michaels, *Interpreting the Book of Revelation* (Guides to New Testament Exegesis), ed. Scot McKnight (Grand Rapids, MI: Baker, 1992), 44-45; Adela Yarbro Collins, "Dating the Apocalypse of John," *BR* 26 (1981): 35-36; Beale, *Revelation*, 872-73; Robinson, *Redating*, 242-43.

185. Kenneth Gentry argues that Tacitus never denies the role of Julius as the first king of the empire. However, Tacitus begins his annals with the reign of Augustus, not Julius, and it is clear that he views Augustus as the first Roman king (*Before Jerusalem*, 154). See Aune, *Revelation 17–22*, 947, n.c.

186. Donald Guthrie, *New Testament Introduction* (Downers Grove, IL: InterVarsity, 1970), 958.

187. Thomas, *Revelation 8–22*, 297.

188. Mounce, *Revelation*, 316-17; Witherington, *Revelation*, 223; G.R. Beasley-Murray, *Revelation*, 256.

189. Collins views beginning the count with Caligula as a credible theory because he was "the first emperor to come into conflict with the Jews and the first to encourage the ruler cult" ("Dating the Apocalypse," 36). Beale notes that Caligula was the first Roman emperor to come to power after the death and resurrection of Christ (*Revelation*, 874).

190. Thomas, "Dating Revelation," 195.

191. Thomas, *Revelation 8–22*, 297; Seiss, *Apocalypse*, 391-94; Ladd, *Revelation*, 227-29; William Hendriksen, *More Than Conquerors* (Grand Rapids, MI: Baker, 1939), 170-71; Walvoord, *Revelation*, 250-54; Henry Alford, *The Greek Testament: With a Critically Revised Text: A Digest of Various Readings: Marginal*

References to Verbal and Idiomatic Usage: Prolegomena: And a Critical and Exegetical Commentary, vol. 4 (Cambridge, UK: Deighton, Bell, and Co., 1866), 710-11; E.W. Hengstenberg, *The Revelation of St. John*, trans. Patrick Fairbairn, vol. 2 (Edinburgh: T & T Clark, 1852), 200-4.

192. Thomas, *Revelation 8–22*, 296-300; Seiss, *Apocalypse*, 392-93; Alford, *Greek Testament*, 710; Hengstenberg, *Revelation*, 2:200-4. Beale prefers the successive kingdoms view to the Roman emperor view but raises several issues with it (*Revelation*, 874-75). He objects that the empires in Daniel 7 are different from those in Revelation. This objection is only partially correct. Six of the eight kingdoms are the same in both texts (1) Babylon, (2) Medo-Persia, (3) Greece, (4) Rome, (5) the reunited Roman empire under ten kings, and (6) the empire of Antichrist, or the little horn. The only two that are different are Egypt and Assyria. It could be argued that God omitted these nations in the revelation to Daniel because the focus was on what would happen from Daniel's day forward. Beale's second main objection is that this theory does not account for the major world empires between the time of the Roman Empire and the end times. However, if one views Revelation through the lens of Daniel 9:24-27 and sees a gap of time between the sixty-ninth and seventieth weeks, this objection disappears. See Harold W. Hoehner, *Chronological Aspects of the Life of Christ* (Grand Rapids, MI: Zondervan, 1977), 115-39; Thomas Ice, "The 70 Weeks of Daniel" in *The End Times Controversy*, eds. Tim LaHaye and Thomas Ice (Eugene, OR: Harvest House, 2003), 307-53.

193. Andreas, *PG* 106:379-83.

194. The seven mountains' imagery should not be interpreted as a reference to the city of Rome. Most commentators see a reference to Rome in the mention of the seven mountains because Rome was widely known as the city on seven hills. However, in the context, there is no need to guess about the meaning of the seven mountains or import a meaning from outside the text. Revelation 17:10 says plainly that the seven mountains are "seven kings." The text requires a strict political identification of the seven mountains with seven kings rather than a geographical location.

195. Thomas, *Revelation 8–22*, 387.

196. John F. Walvoord, *The Rapture Question*, rev. ed. (Grand Rapids, MI: Zondervan, 1979), 268.

197. Philip Schaff, *History of the Christian Church: Ante-Nicene Christianity* (Edinburgh: T & T Clark, 1884), 614. Charles Hill has authored a book that challenges the long-held view that premillennialism (known in the early church as the chiliastic view, after the Greek word for one thousand). Charles E. Hill, *Regnum Caelorum: Patterns of Millennial Thought in Early Christianity*, 2d ed. (Grand Rapids, MI: Eerdmans, 2001). In my view, Hill's work is primarily based on arguments from silence and theological conclusions not directly related to the view of the early church on a literal millennium. For an

excellent critique of Hill's work, see, Craig A. Blaising, "Early Christian Millennialism and the Intermediate State," *Bibliotheca Sacra* 177 (April 2020).

198. Kim Riddlebarger, *A Case for Amillennialism: Understanding the End Times* (Grand Rapids, MI: Baker, 2003), 210-11.
199. Harold W. Hoehner, "Evidence from Revelation 20," in *A Case for Premillennialism: A New Consensus*, gen. eds. Donald K. Campbell and Jeffrey L. Townsend (Chicago, IL: Moody, 1992), 250.
200. Michael J. Svigel, *The Fathers on the Future* (Peabody, MA: Hendrickson, 2024), 131.
201. Svigel, *The Fathers on the Future*, 133-34.
202. Svigel, *The Fathers on the Future*, 134.
203. J. Dwight Pentecost, *Thy Kingdom Come: Tracing God's Kingdom Program and Covenant Promises Throughout History* (Wheaton, IL: Victor Books, 1990), 316.
204. James Montgomery Boice, *The Last and Future World* (Grand Rapids, MI: Zondervan, 1977), 27.
205. Hoehner, "Evidence from Revelation 20," 253.
206. Swindoll, *Insights on Revelation*, 263 (emphasis in original).
207. J. Vernon McGee, *Reveling Through Revelation* (Pasadena, CA: Thru the Bible, 1974), 74-75.
208. Morris, *The Revelation Record*, 419-20.
209. Charles C. Ryrie, *Basic Theology* (Wheaton, IL: Victor, 1986), 515.
210. Randy Alcorn, *Heaven* (Wheaton, IL: Tyndale, 2004), 147-48.
211. Alcorn, *Heaven*, 242-43.
212. Thomas, *Revelation 8–22*, 478.
213. Walvoord, *Revelation*, 339.
214. Walvoord, *Revelation*, 342.
215. MacArthur, *Revelation 12–22*, 287.
216. MacArthur, *Revelation 12–22*, 280.
217. Leon Morris, *Revelation*, 252.
218. Osborne, *Revelation*, 795.
219. Phillips, *Exploring Revelation*, 264.
220. MacArthur, *Revelation 12–22*, 310.
221. Phillips, *Exploring Revelation*, 262-64.

To learn more about our Harvest Prophecy resources, please visit:

www.HarvestProphecyHQ.com

HARVEST PROPHECY
AN IMPRINT OF HARVEST HOUSE PUBLISHERS